EDUTECH

Computer-Aided Design Meets Computer-Aided Learning

IFIP – The International Federation for Information Processing

IFIP was founded in 1960 under the auspices of UNESCO, following the First World Computer Congress held in Paris the previous year. An umbrella organization for societies working in information processing, IFIP's aim is two-fold: to support information processing within its member countries and to encourage technology transfer to developing nations. As its mission statement clearly states,

> *IFIP's mission is to be the leading, truly international, apolitical organization which encourages and assists in the development, exploitation and application of information technology for the benefit of all people.*

IFIP is a non-profit making organization, run almost solely by 2500 volunteers. It operates through a number of technical committees, which organize events and publications. IFIP's events range from an international congress to local seminars, but the most important are:

- The IFIP World Computer Congress, held every second year;
- Open conferences;
- Working conferences.

The flagship event is the IFIP World Computer Congress, at which both invited and contributed papers are presented. Contributed papers are rigorously refereed and the rejection rate is high.

As with the Congress, participation in the open conferences is open to all and papers may be invited or submitted. Again, submitted papers are stringently refereed.

The working conferences are structured differently. They are usually run by a working group and attendance is small and by invitation only. Their purpose is to create an atmosphere conducive to innovation and development. Refereeing is less rigorous and papers are subjected to extensive group discussion.

Publications arising from IFIP events vary. The papers presented at the IFIP World Computer Congress and at open conferences are published as conference proceedings, while the results of the working conferences are often published as collections of selected and edited papers.

Any national society whose primary activity is in information may apply to become a full member of IFIP, although full membership is restricted to one society per country. Full members are entitled to vote at the annual General Assembly, National societies preferring a less committed involvement may apply for associate or corresponding membership. Associate members enjoy the same benefits as full members, but without voting rights. Corresponding members are not represented in IFIP bodies. Affiliated membership is open to non-national societies, and individual and honorary membership schemes are also offered.

EDUTECH

Computer-Aided Design Meets Computer-Aided Learning

IFIP 18th World Computer Congress
TC10 / WG10.5 EduTech Workshop
22–27 August 2004
Toulouse, France

Edited by

Carlos Delgado Kloos
Abelardo Pardo
Universidad Carlos III de Madrid, Spain

Springer Science+Business Media, LLC

Electronic Services <http://www.wkap.nl>

Library of Congress Cataloging-in-Publication Data

A C.I.P. Catalogue record for this book is available from the Library of Congress.

EDUTECH: Computer-Aided Design Meets Computer-Aided Learning
Edited by Carlos Delgado Kloos and Abelardo Pardo

DOI 10.1007/978-1-4020-8162-0

Printed on acid-free paper.

www.springer.com/mycopy

Contents

Contributing Authors vii
Preface ix
Foreword xi
Acknowledgments xv

INVITED CONTRIBUTIONS

1. Open Source Approaches to Eductional Technology Innovation 3
2. Towards Ambient Schooling 7
3. Can Learning Objects Be Reused – and How? 19

E-LEARNING STANDARDS

4. Towards an Enhanced Learning Design Language 27
5. A Type-Based Taxonomy of Items in Assessments 39

USE OF STANDARDS IN A TECHNICAL SETTING

6. Implications of Learning Technology Standardization in Electronic Design 51
7. Review of Standards and Standardisation Activities 55
8. Requirements for Computer-Aided Learning from the Point of View of Electronic Design 63
9. Learning Technology Standardization in Europe 69

E-LEARNING IN SYSTEM DESIGN

10. Optimiller: An Interactive Environment that Helps Students in the Understanding, Design and Optimization of Miller Electronic Oscillator Circuits for QCM Sensors ... 77

11. Educational Tools for Industrial Communication Networks Design ... 89

12. Remote System of Design and Test of DC-DC Converters ... 99

MOBILE E-LEARNING

13. An Open Abstract Framework for Modeling Interoperability of Mobile Learning Services ... 113

DEVELOPMENT OF E-LEARNING TOOLS

14. Virtual Community in the Classroom: An Innovating Tool for Elearning ... 123

15. The E-Learning Grid: Peer-to-Peer Approach ... 133

16. An Intelligent Virtual Environment for Distance Learning ... 143

17. Development and Implementation of a Biometric Verification System for E-learning Platforms ... 155

18. A Testing Methodology for an Open Software E-learning Platform ... 165

E-LEARNING EXPERIENCE

19. Learning Objects Definition and Use in <e-aula> ... 177

20. E-learning Engineering: Recommendations for Consumer-Driven Blended Learning ... 187

IMPACT OF TECHNOLOGY ON E-LEARNING

21. Impact of Technology on Learning Paradigms and Teaching Practices ... 199

22. E-learning Issues for Advanced Technical Topics ... 201

23. Telecad Course Online and Evaluation Procedure ... 207

24. Weblabs: A Virtual Laboratory for Collaborative E-learning ... 215

25. Building the E-learning Environment ... 223

Contributing Authors

Alexandrov, Nia 133
Alexandrov, Vassil 133
Anido Rifón, Luis 27, 51
Argones-Rúa, Enrique 155
Bhana Ismail 133
Brendel, R. 77
Bruschi, F. 123
Caeiro Rodríguez, Manuel 27
Cavalli, Ana 165
Corno, Fulvio 199, 201
Da Bormida, Giorgio 113
Dahn, Ingo 113
Delgado Kloos, C. 39
Di Girolamo, Marco 113
Dominguez, M. A. 89
Doval, J. 99
Duval, Erik 19
Ebey, Tina 199, 223
Eguizabal, L. 99
Essa, Alfred 3
Fariña, J. 77
Faverio, P. 123
Fernández-Manjón, Baltasar 177
Gabriel, Roland 187
Gabrielli, C. 77
Gachev, George 215

García-Mateo, Carmen 155
Gersch, Martin 187
González, M. J. 77
González-Agulla, Elisardo 155
Grabowska, Anna 199, 207
Hernandez, H. 89
Hodges, R. 123
Johnson, David 133
Lago, A. 99
Lindner, Rolf 55
Llamas Nistal, Martín 27
Maag, Stéphane 165
Machado, F. 89
Manero, Borja 177
Marcos, J. 99
Mari, L. 123
Mariño, P. 89
Márquez-Flórez, Óscar W. 155
Moneva, Liliana 215
Muñoz Merino, P. 39
Murelli, Elena 113
Nikolova, Iliana 199, 215
Nogueira, A. 99
Papagiannaki, Sofia 165
Pardo, A. 39
Peñalver, C. 99
Pérez Pérez, N. 39
Perrot, H. 77
Poza, F. 89
Reis, Ricardo 63
Restelli, D. 123
Rodríguez-Pardo, L. 77
Sancho, Pilar 177
Santos Osório, Fernando 143
Sciuto, D. 123
Sendova, Evgenia 199, 215
Trojahn dos Santos, Cássia 143
Urbain, Olivier 223
Van Assche, Frans 7, 69
Verigakis, Georgios 165
Weber, Peter 187
Zaïdi, Fatiha 165

Preface

Computation and communication technologies underpin work and development in many different areas. Among them, Computer-Aided Design of electronic systems and eLearning technologies are two areas, which are different, but share in fact many concerns. The design of CAD and eLearning systems already touches on a number of parallels, such as system interoperability, user interfaces, standardisation, XML-based formats, reusability aspects (of content or designs), intellectual property rights, etc.

Furthermore, the teaching of Design Automation tools and methods is particularly amenable to a distant or blended learning setting, and implies the interconnection of typical CAD tools, such as simulators or synthesis tools, with eLearning tools. There are many other aspects in which synergy can be found, when using eLearning technology for teaching and learning technology.

These proceedings correspond to the EduTech2004 workshop that has been organized in Toulouse, 26-27 August 2004 in the context of the World Computer Congress 2004. The workshop has been sponsored by IFIP WG 10.5 Design and Engineering of Electronic Systems in cooperation with IFIP WG 3.6 Distance Education, explores the interrelationship between these two subjects, where Computer-Aided Design meets Computer-Aided Learning.

The topics of interest that were announced in the Call for Papers were:

- Educational technology for technical courses
- Frameworks for teaching microelectronics and technical subjects
- Impact of technology on learning paradigms and teaching practices
- Classroom technology

- Laboratory innovations
- Virtual laboratories
- Simulation infrastructure for eLearning
- Virtual reality in education
- System interoperability
- Cooperative learning
- Blended learning
- Web-based applications
- Mobile eLearning
- eLearning standards
- Open source initiatives
- Experimental experiences

The result of the call for papers and the subsequent reviewing process and invitation of keynote speakers and panellists are these proceedings. They include papers related to eLearning in the area of electronic CAD, but they also include contributions, which tackle general issues of eLearning that are applicable to this and to many other areas. Examples of these are hot issues such as reusability, standards, open source tools or mobility.

Carlos Delgado Kloos, Abelardo Pardo
Universidad Carlos III de Madrid
Leganés, May 2004

Foreword

European education policy and E-Learning

The European Council at Lisbon, March 2000, is a watershed for European policy making. The strong and inspiring objective of "making of Europe the most advanced knowledge-based economy in the world, with more and better jobs and more social cohesion" has had an unprecedented impact in the European scene; it has caught the imagination and it has become a basic reference for political and social leaders.

The Lisbon objectives are particularly important for education. European education policy came of age at Lisbon. Never before in the history of European integration had it been singled as the true driver for success, as the main enabler for social and economic development. Building the knowledge society, realising the lifelong learning paradigm means transforming European education and training systems; making them better, more accessible, and more responsive to societal needs.

The use of information and communication technologies and the development of Internet as a backbone for social interaction at all levels are key characteristics of this new society. This is why one of the most urgent and far-reaching demands in education policy is a solid and effective integration of ICT in education theory and practice, and this, a well thought and socially responsive integration of ICT in education is what the European Commission aims to facilitate with the eLearning initiative.

E-Learning is an essential aspect of change, and a historical opportunity. Past the time of technological push, past the time of marketing hype, we can see today e-learning as a new frontier for education quality. It is more than a tool to do better what was already done. It is more than making learning opportunities independent of time and of space. It is more than putting

Alexandria at our fingertips. It is an opportunity for re-thinking and re-designing education, for a quantum leap in supporting learning.

It is also a fundamental challenge for Europe. The "e-learning revolution" started its development beyond Europe, and there is still a certain reticence, a whiff of mistrust in attitudes towards e-learning in Europe. Excess and irrationality in the initial years of the Internet revolution explain this; but it is time to leave them behind. Europe has mature education systems, and it is with maturity and wisdom that e-learning can, and must, be addressed. European education systems cannot ignore e-learning.

This is why a book addressing key topics for the development of e-learning in Europe in such a way is good news. The combination of long experience and untainted energy in the authors is a happy one, and it promises worthwhile reading. The book covers a wide range of issues: all are important. From a European point of view, two are particularly relevant: standards and keeping up a technological edge. They are the two sides of the success we want for the development of e-learning in Europe.

Standards are the only way to ensure wide interoperability; to achieve the critical mass of supply and demand required for a healthy market; to encourage investment in new solutions. Users and decision-makers need to be made aware of the need for standards, and of ways and means to test and implement them. In particular, their application to mobile services, building up on successful European initiatives, and on a dynamic European market of mobile solutions, looks very promising. Ambient learning has always been a very important kind of learning; technology enhanced ambient learning can take it to a new dimension.

And at the same time, while promoting the tools for rapid take-up, such as interoperability, while trying to interconnect tools and services, to mainstream collaborative e-learning; or to re-use learning objects, we must foster research and experimentation at the cutting edge of technology. Grid computing, P2P approaches open fascinating possibilities. Creativity has always been a hallmark of European art and science, and fostering creativity in the field of e-learning is essential.

With all the importance that technological progress in e-learning has, it would be wrong to stop here. There is more to the importance of developing e-learning in Europe. There are other traits of the knowledge society than pervasive and ubiquitous ICT. There is the European dimension. Again, nothing new. It is not by chance that the star education programme of the European Union is called Erasmus. Erasmus life is a powerful message of a frontier-free career. Universities are by their own nature free and frontier-less environments. There is an intrinsic value in this community of science beyond frontiers, and e-learning can do much to facilitate co-operation and contact, to build up an European dimension for all students, to make of virtual mobility a reality accessible to all.

There is, last but not least, globalisation. E-learning is a powerful tool for asserting the role of European universities in the global arena. It is also a powerful tool for extending and improving European co-operation for development. The conclusions of the recent World Summit for Information Society stress the important role that ICT-based developments (eGovernment, eHealth, eLearning) have for social and economic development, and the need for a worldwide effort for competence building. E-learning can be seen as an enabler for citizenship in the knowledge society.

The development of quality European e-learning is a crucial challenge. I hope that this book makes a good contribution to it.

Maruja Gutiérrez Díaz
Head of Unit MULTIMEDIA
Education and Culture Directorate-General
European Commission

Acknowledgments

We would like to thank all who have contributed to make this workshop a reality. First of all, the colleagues of IFIP WG 10.5 and TC 10, where the concept originated. The idea was welcome by TC 3, WG 3.6 and supported by their chairs and members.

The Programme Committee has been mainly composed by people from IFIP WG 10.5 and WG 3.6, but also includes other renowned experts in the field:

- Vassil Alexandrov, U. Reading, UK
- Oscar Bonilla, Northface U., USA
- Giorgio da Bormida, Giunti Interactive Labs, I
- Martin Curley, Intel, IRL
- Carlos Delgado Kloos, U. Carlos III de Madrid, E (PC Chair)
- Karl-Heinz Diener, Fraunhofer Gesellschaft Dresden, D
- Dudley Dolan, Trinity College Dublin, IRL
- Tina Ebey, Pacific Research Center, USA
- Baltasar Fernández, U. Complutense de Madrid, E
- Anna Grabowska, Gdansk U. of Technology, PL
- Piet Kommers, U. Twente, NL
- Martín Llamas Nistal, U. Vigo, E
- Giovanni de Micheli, Stanford. U., USA
- Iliana Nikolova, U. Sofia, BG
- Abelardo Pardo, U. Carlos III de Madrid, E
- Ricardo Reis, U. Federal do Rio Grande do Sul, BR
- Donatella Sciuto, Politecnico di Milano, I
- Peter Schwarz, Fraunhofer Gesellschaft Dresden, D

We would also like to thank authors, panellists and invited speakers, without whom this workshop couldn't have been possible.

IFIP WCC staff is also thanked for taking care of all organizational aspects. In particular, we thank Jean-Claude Laprie, Congress Chair, Michel Diaz, Workshop Chair, and Leon Strous, Publication Chair. Many thanks go also to Kluwer staff, in particular, Yana Lambert, IFIP Publishing Editor.

Sergio Gutiérrez and Raquel Crespo from Universidad Carlos III de Madrid have been helping with the setting up of the workshop web site and the preparation of the manuscript for Kluwer. Many thanks to them.

And last but not least we acknowledge the participation of the delegates to the workshop.

Carlos Delgado Kloos, Abelardo Pardo
Universidad Carlos III de Madrid
Leganés, May 2004

PART ONE

INVITED CONTRIBUTIONS

OPEN SOURCE APPROACHES TO EDUCTIONAL TECHNOLOGY INNOVATION

An MIT Perspective

Alfred Essa
Sloan School, Massachusetts Institute of Technology

Abstract: Universities have a mission to create, preserve, and disseminate knowledge. In realizing that mission, we face significant cultural, legal, economic, and technical pressures. The intellectual commons can be defined as "that shared wellspring of ideas and innovation from which all may freely draw" and its intent is to counteract regimes of control and replace them with regimes of opportunity. The approach to educational technology innovation at MIT seeks to advance the intellectual commons by developing and freely sharing "open content" and "open code". This talk describes MIT's approach to educational technology innovation by examining underlying principles, specifying technical architecture, and demonstrating specific projects. We focus in particular on .LRN, an open source project and platform for supporting innovation in collaborative education and learning and research communities. Originally developed at MIT as part of the intellectual commons, .LRN is now backed by a worldwide consortium of educational institutions, non-profit organizations, industry partners and open source developers.

Key words: open source, intellectual commons, .LRN

1. OPEN SOURCE

The original design for the Internet was both a technical architecture and a value. Known as the end-to-end principle, it specified that network designers should place intelligence at the ends, keep the network stupid, and allow for smart applications. The end-to-end principle along with open software was the original intellectual commons that created the Internet. The new intellectual commons seeks both to preserve the original vision against encroachments and to extend the public domain in ways that promote knowledge and freedom.

2. .LRN

.LRN is an open source platform for e-learning, providing support for course management, online communities, learning management, and content management applications. In addition, .LRN is a powerful framework and tools for quickly innovating on these applications and building customized solutions. Together these capabilities support the complete "online learning" environment for learning communities and communities of practice in higher education, K-12, government, and non-profit organizations.

The .LRN technology originated at MIT and is rapidly evolving from the collective experience and rigor of hundreds of talented software developers worldwide. The underlying kernel has been in production use for nearly a decade in hundreds of web sites worldwide. Elements of the underlying software infrastructure are at the backbone of the largest and most demanding production environments in the world, including aol.com, mapquest.com, and netscape.com.

.LRN is only one among several initiatives emerging out of MIT as part of the intellectual commons. MIT Open CourseWare (OCW) is another educational initiative which makes core teaching materials for all MIT graduate and undergraduate classes available at no cost to Internet users around the world. Currently, course materials from 700 courses are available on the MIT web site. DSpace is another groundbreaking digital library system to capture, store, index, preserve, and redistribute the intellectual output of a university's research faculty in digital format. The base platform is being extended so that it can serve also as a transactional repository for learning objects.

.LRN development is moving simultaneously along four dimensions. First, the base platform is being scaled so that it can be easily deployed and used by organizations small and large. Second, the .LRN technical infrastructure is being extended to allow exchange of learning and research content through intermediate digital repositories such as DSpace. Third, .LRN-based applications are being developed that illustrate the power of shared interactive learning and online communities. Finally, .LRN is being coupled with content initiatives such as MIT Open Course Ware so that organizations can quickly and easily draw on the wealth of free course and research content being developed worldwide.

3. CONCLUSION

The open source movement is moving to a new and exciting phase where end users will now begin to benefit from applications that go beyond the infrastructure examples we are all familiar with, such as Linux and Apache. As Aristotle recognized, knowledge is the central activity of man. It is an end in itself but also a requisite for liberty. MIT's intellectual commons initiatives are intended to promote knowledge by freely sharing content and tools which in turn can be extended by others, thereby becoming a wellspring of continuing innovation.

TOWARDS AMBIENT SCHOOLING
A European Research and Development Agenda

Frans Van Assche
European Schoolnet

Abstract: Ambient schooling creates a schooling environment 'surrounding' the pupil in a non-intrusive way. It is part of a ten-year vision of ministries of education in Europe in response to a changing information society. The realization of this vision will require substantive research and development. Critical success factors are the provision of the right infrastructure, the implementation of a school-grid allowing exchange of data and services beyond content, intelligent support for the learning process also in terms of knowledge building, better support for teachers, a different way of developing supporting tools, adaptation of buildings, and a clear migration strategy.

Key words: E-learning systems; learning technology; ambient intelligence; Europe; ambient schooling; grid; knowledge building; personalized learning.

1. AMBIENT SCHOOLING

The concept for ambient schooling was developed by the European Schoolnet as part of a ten-year vision of 26 ministries of education in Europe. It should be understood in context of a changing European society. As Matti Sinko, Finnish Ministry of Education observes[1]:

> "The whole notion of school used to be based on the idea that it is easier to organise learning when it takes place separated from the distractions of everyday social and business life. In recent years this paradigm has been completely changed in favour of increased and intensified communication and interaction between the school and the surrounding community and society. New concepts like a school without walls or a virtual school have emerged and become popular at least in school development rhetoric. Parents used to leave their children to school for

education, now parents and other adult members from various walks of life are more and more encouraged to assist in tutoring and even in teaching. And all this takes place not only in the classrooms and homes but in libraries, leisure centers and other public places, in shops, in workplaces, and businesses. This all makes learning much more natural, flexible and less distanced from realities of life, but at the same time it addresses more complex and genuine problems of life."

The re-organization of learning has been largely overlooked, even though there has been a recognition that national ICT strategies will only achieve their objectives once there is a "fundamental change in the way learning is constructed within schools"[2]. In 2004, the vision still remains more a part of what Sinko calls "school development rhetoric" than something that is visible in the majority of Europe's schools. Moreover, the original vision is under threat as society begins to question the return on investment for ICT in schools. There are signs of a 'disconnect' between ICT use in and out of schools with pupils being increasingly critical of the former[3]. Most worryingly, scenarios are seriously being considered where ICT simply fails to deliver and there is "technology meltdown".[4] In short, having failed to address fundamental issues related to the re-organization of learning, the future of e-learning for schools in the Information Society is being questioned.

Against this background the concept of **ambient schooling** is developed and represents a Copernican revolution. While in the past ICT has been used to bring content and services to schools, ambient schooling brings the school to the learner. Ambient means 'surrounding' and refers to the fact that a learner is surrounded by his/her school. This should be done in a non-intrusive way. The availability of the 'school functionality' should be managed and it can be turned off, much like a mobile phone.

Ambient schooling is a dynamic process where, via the appropriate use of advanced technologies, pupils are supported as they continue to learn in formal institutions but are presented with increasing opportunities to learn in the home, libraries, museums and the wider community. New, next-generation technologies are particularly required for ambient schooling in order to help pupils to navigate between a variety of learning environments and to ensure a high degree of interoperability between the learning services provided by each of the settings.

2. INFRASTRUCTURE FOR AMBIENT SCHOOLING

The key infrastructure components for ambient schooling are mobile technology, broadband, and one-on-one, i.e. one computer per pupil.

Mobile technology must involve ubiquitous wireless access and new devices. Typically these devices will be light and with adequate capabilities in terms on wireless communication. However, with the advent of organic light emitter technology, the shape may be quite different from the tablet PCs, palmtops or smart phones we know now.

Broadband technology provided must go all the way to the device that the user is using. In addition it will need to be wireless with ubiquitous access points much like mobile phones work today.

While schools have equipped some of their classrooms with computers, their use remains limited. Typically computers are only used when pupils are in the computer lab. Extensive research[5,6] has shown that (a) when pupils can 'own' their personal computer the usage increases dramatically and (b) along with the increased use, the learning is more effective. Currently only small computers such as palmtops are affordable. But even when prices drop, the mere fact that handhelds are so portable makes them an interesting choice. In the foreseeable future, personal computers will become a commodity and pupils will start to use their own portable devices in and out of the school premises.

3. OBJECTS FOR AMBIENT SCHOOLING

Currently, there exist quite a number of learning object repositories and recently the first federated brokerage system for learning objects using asynchronous messaging in a heterogeneous environment was demonstrated[7]. However, in order to realize the ambient schooling vision, interoperability of other data and services is required. For instance, where can a teacher or pupil in France find an expert of cartography of the middle ages, or a hotseat[1], or an interesting project, or a school in Queensland for twinning, etc. How can a user propagate a discussion to other forums, if s/he does not get an answer in his or her own environment?

[1] A hotseat is a mechanism where an expert is available for a specific period of time (e.g. a week) to answer queries from students. This is often done in an asynchronous way. The experts answers when s/he has time.

In technical terms this means that data, content, tools and services should be shared on a European and even global level. Four areas are of particular interest: Learning Content, Learning Management, Learning communities, and School management.

Learning content

Standards and specifications exist to support various aspects of the exchange of learning objects in an effective way. The IEEE LOM is a standard issued by an accredited standardization body and supports the description of Learning Objects. A subset of the LOM can also be used for the description of Learning Assets. For packaging content, the IMS content packaging specification can be used. The Dublin Core Metadata Initiative (DCMI) specification will support the description of other resources.

Learning management

In the field of learning management and learning content management we are dealing with objects such as student, learning progress, assessment, activity flow, etc.

Learning communities.

In the field of learning communities we are dealing with announcements of events (such as workshops, conferences, chats), users, user groups, schools, special interest groups, networks, news, projects, bulletin boards. Existing standards and specifications in this field are: vCard, vCalendar, RSS, NewsML.

School management.

In the field of school management we are dealing with issues such as transportation, libraries, student attendance, meals, gradebooks, human resources, financial, etc. In this area the specification of the Schools Interoperability Framework (SIF) and its adaptation to the European situation as developed in the OASIS project[2] and the work of CEN/ISSS WSLT[3] is of great importance.

4. THE SCHOOLGRID

During the last years we have seen the emergence of grid architectures from computing grids to data and application grids. For ambient schooling it is especially the latter kind of grid which is important. The schoolGRID can be seen as a further evolution of learning object brokerage systems currently being developed around the world. As in a LO brokerage system, the

[2] http://oasis.cnice.mecd.es/

[3] http://www.cenorm.be/isss/Workshop/lt/

purpose is to match demand with supply. However the data and services requested and delivered extend far beyond content and include the diverse object types as elaborated in section 3.

4.1 Architecture

At the heart of the SchoolGRID architecture (see figure 1) is a catalogue describing the services available. The catalogue is more than just a UDDI directory. The catalogue should contain at least:

- What service is delivered and under what conditions. This would include a textual description of the service, costs, rights, quality assurance measures from the provider, etc
- Where to access the service
- In what format the service can be requested. This would include the API and how to use it
- In what format the results are obtained.

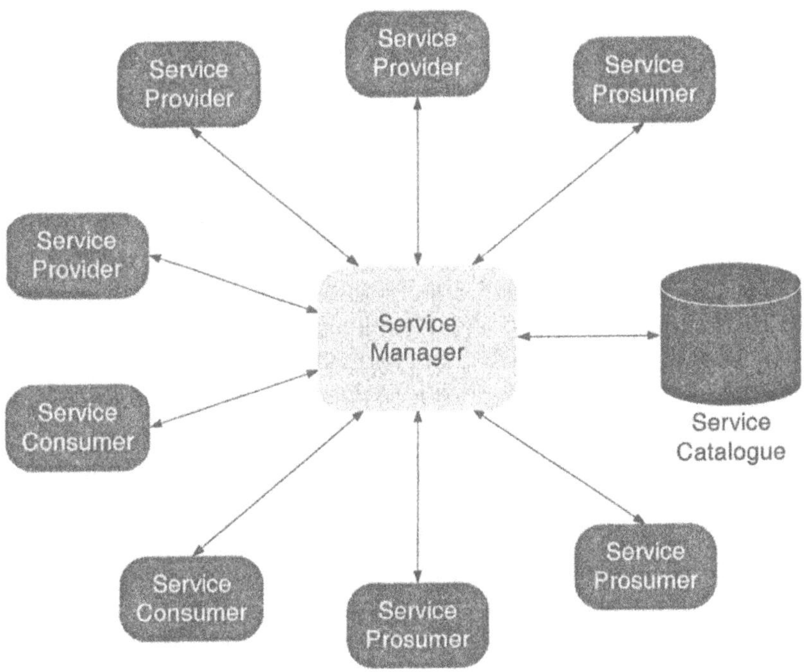

Figure 1. The Learning Grid architecture

As an example in the learning resource area, service prosumers (a service provider that is at the same time a service consumer) could be LMSs,

LCMSs; service providers could be learning object repositories; and service consumers could be some eLearning portals. An example service is the discovery and delivery of learning objects. The learning objects are organized in collections and the catalogue describes the collections. This fits well with the concepts of Collection Level Descriptors as developed in the field of metadata. A collection may be distributed over more than one repository and a repository may hold more than one collection (even several collections that are overlapping).

The important point is that collection level descriptions not only describe the collection as a whole but that many data elements will be inherited by the elements of this collection. As an example take the data element 'Quality Selection Policy' that describes the selection policy that is followed for resources to be included in the collection. By doing so it is not necessary to have the quality selection policy repeated over and over again with each resource. Not only does this facilitate the initial metadata tagging but also this ensures that changes to the policy are dealt with consistently.

Further work on collection level descriptors should be directed towards unification and standardization. While application profiles are necessary in order to meet the needs of the different communities, this is not so much the case for collection level descriptors.

A second example in the area of community objects goes as follows: in Austria, Switzerland, Northern Italy, and Germany are lively discussion groups dealing with physics. The discussion group in Austria is discussing something on which they would like to have a second opinion. The SchoolGRID would allow any member (teacher) of this discussion group to search whether there are other discussion groups of teachers discussing physics in German. After having identified such discussion groups, the Austrian teacher can post his/her question to a selected number of other discussion groups. Alternatively, this selection process could be automatic.

4.2 Services

From the examples it should be clear that the SchoolGRID will provide different kinds of services, but a large majority of these will be **discovery services**, providing answers to questions such as: are there interesting events, calls for proposals, projects, schools, LOs, etc. These discovery services may follow a drilling down pattern. For example, there is first a search of the catalogue to determine whether there are any interesting collections, and then a federated search is launched to search in these collections.

The SchoolGRID provides intelligent brokerage functionality in addition to a number of central services. This brokerage functionality is hierarchically structured. For example, take the search and exchange of learning objects. This can happen at different levels. LOs can be exchanged at the school level, at the regional level, at the national level, and at the international level. When a teacher using his/her own VLE would like to search outside his/her own school environment s/he should be able to do so either as the result of a conscious choice or automatically. In any case, the technical and rights negotiations between the different levels and the partners should be entirely transparent. Likewise, this teacher may decide to make a learning object available at a regional level. The regional administrator could decide to publish it at the country level, and the country administrator could decide to make it available at the European level.

While a single SchoolGRID will suffice in Europe, it is unlikely that it will be the only educational GRID in the world or even in Europe. Therefore the SchoolGRID should also be able to talk to the other GRIDs and exchange catalogue information such that services can also be exchanged. Moreover, because of performance issues, any such GRID will require mirroring of its basic services.

5. AMBIENT LEARNING

Ambient schooling will increasingly take place within an environment that can be tailored on-the-fly with regard to the personal learning style, preferences, competencies, dynamic learner profile, or learning needs of the pupils, and taking into account the available tools, digital resources, and human support. While customization possibilities exist in most currently available VLEs, adaptation of the learning process poses additional, major challenges.

The learning process in the ambient schooling vision is specific to any human learner, is suspended and resumed at his/her will, and may appear in quite different forms that adhere to the educational plan, but adapt to the progress of the learner, to his/her options, to the recommendations of other stakeholders, and to the availability of humans and digital resources.

One of the key components is this process is the Adaptive Learning Unit (ALU) that represents the "Educational Plans". While these might be represented by, e.g., a human teacher or even the learner, the aim is to support extensive reuse of digitally encoded educational plans that carry the expertise of eminently talented human educational experts. ALUs represent digitally encoded educational expertise, carry the rules for composing and organizing learning activities, and use descriptive information for decision making. Typical descriptive information is related to humans (e.g., current and desired competencies and many categories of preferences) and to digital resources (i.e. metadata for all kinds of digitally encoded expertise like learning objects, educational plans, information and resource brokering services, etc.). The ALU approach is capable of bringing diverse educational concepts into action, like IMS Learning Design but constructed on-the-fly.

For authoring ALUs, one should make extensive use of "lessons learnt" in formats of templates, wizards (for frequently used genres) and even generators (for regularly used and well approved genres) will provide effective support to authors who lack specific IT expertise. Authoring may be influenced by feedback from the users as part of a knowledge building process.

6. KNOWLEDGE BUILDING IN AN AMBIENT SCHOOLING CONTEXT

Knowledge building in an ambient schooling context deals with (a) further research on the knowledge building process and its support through ICT beyond current practice in computer supported collaborative learning (CSCL), (b) new ways of knowledge building assessment, (c) investigating the harnessing of new devices, and (d) shaping the supporting environment for the specific needs of ambient schooling. Recent research shows that ICT enhanced learning as implemented currently has a number of shortcomings. Scardamalia and Bereiter already in 1992 in their *knowledge building* theory proposed that schools should be restructured towards knowledge-building organizations, in which students and teachers participate in the construction of collective knowledge as in professional research groups where the object of activity is solving knowledge-problems. Currently we are only at the beginning of supporting this vision in schools through implementation of ICT.

7. ADVANCED FEATURES FOR TEACHERS

While ICT in education yields many benefits, they also come at a cost especially for the teacher. Currently, the cost for the teacher (measured in additional workload) frequently cancels out the benefit he or she perceives. The ambient schooling vision puts high emphasis on making the work of the teacher as easy as possible. The technologies used should therefore provide utmost transparency and user-friendliness for teachers and must be affordable and easily maintained/assimilated by the institutions that use them. This is well in line with the view of the ISTAG group[4] which states that:

> "[Ambient Intelligence] system will "know itself", adapt easily to the needs to the individual, actively look for ways to optimize its workings, be able to protect itself and recover from routine malfunctions etc. – all with a view towards making life easier for the individual who is engaged with the system but may not even know that s/he is consciously 'interacting' with it"

At least the following three research areas should be addressed. First, authoring support should improve or be newly developed, including for the earlier expounded ALUs. The required skills of authors should reflect their expected range of expertise. As currently only few experts have noteworthy experience with Educational Modeling Languages and IMS Learning Design, measures should be taken that will reduce the construction effort. Among these measures should be well-tested templates and wizard support in the construction of executable educational plans, based on the recognition of a variety of learner profiles. The necessary tools to create and modify these digital resources in various ways are needed.

Second, new ways should be promoted to ease the burden of meta-data tagging as much as possible including automated tagging based on semantic analysis, predictive tagging, tagging by placement in a repository taxonomy, and other techniques.

Third, concepts and tools for ontology mapping should be developed. Metadata are currently in a form that does not fully reflect the needs of teachers and pupils. For example, teachers and pupils do not instinctively think in the terms of the value spaces of metadata. Ideally they should be able to develop their own system of concepts (ontology) or choose some they like and have their concepts automatically mapped to the available metadata or metadata templates. By doing so, ontologies for the semantic web can also be provided.

8. AN OPEN FRAMEWORK

When providing ICT tools for supporting the field of learning, education, and knowledge building one has to deal with two conflicting requirements: diversity and standardization. Firstly, there is the requirement for many different kinds of support for different communities and categories of users.

[4] ftp://ftp.cordis.lu/pub/ist/docs/istag-wg1-final_en.pdf

The need for a diverse range of support is due to the large diversity of scenarios that is, in turn, dependent on the type of application, on personal and institutional habits, and on broader social and cultural factors. Secondly, there is a strong requirement for extensive interoperability across these communities.

The concept of an Open Component Framework proposed here is well able to comply with these seemingly conflicting requirements, mainly by decomposing platform functionalities to very fine-grained components. Requirement specifications can be derived from the analysis of a number of important scenarios for ambient schooling. Based on these specifications, components can be designed and implemented as needed. Components comprise various information object types, information processing software, interfaces, and protocols. The separation of component specification and technology binding is crucial for the 'longevity' of the framework. Following this approach a VLE can be built by assembling components. As VLE providers may provide their own versions of aggregations, in order to add value for specific clients and users, (using, e.g., an avatar for human-computer interaction), many VLEs will be able to co-exist.

The implementation should be open in two respects. Firstly the framework should be open for people to join in by picking the services they need and using them. Secondly, the implementation of the component framework should be open source to a large extent. The advantage of open source is that it fosters a basis of trust for a growing user community, a large experimenting community for fast feedback and high productivity, and a sustainable community infrastructure that on the long term is not dependent on a small group of developers. In this way, it allows any tailoring as needed (see for instance also the IDA study[8]).

9. FURTHER IMPLEMENTATION ISSUES

While a lot of the learning will also happen outside the school buildings, the implementation of the ambient schooling vision will probably require other building structures or at least other uses of existing buildings. An interesting study was done in a small school in Iceland where, due to inaccessibility, a lot of the learning was organized outside the classroom. The classical notion of a classroom was abandoned in favor of more flexible study and meeting places.

One of the major challenges will be the organizational change that the implementation requires. Scenarios and models for implementing next-generation technology combined with strategies for change management and the re-organization of learning in schools and other settings are required. Key actions are:

- To monitor and describe trends and issues in national education systems across Europe as the societal needs concerning education, as well as technological and organizational possibilities will change. The way that national educational systems are dealing with it needs to be closely followed and described.
- To provide demonstrations of implemented models of significant organizational change in schools and learning that takes place in a variety of settings (schools, the home, museums, libraries and the wider community), underpinned by next generation technologies.
- To evaluate progress in these areas against benchmarks for each of the participating municipalities given their current level of ICT implementation at the start of the demonstration phase.
- To establish an in-service teacher training initiative and associated materials related to change management, taking into account the wider visions of the role of the teacher in the ambient school, using online services, content and collaborative tools developed by Release.
- To describe and analyze current models of schooling and develop roadmaps for change to ambient schooling. When new models suitable for ambient schooling have been developed, the current state of schooling needs to be understood in order to develop the necessary roadmaps for teachers, schools, policy makers, and industry.

The ambient schooling vision must include the strong possibility that the provision of infrastructure will become less of a State responsibility as pupils increasingly carry their own personal information/communication device Though measures will need to be taken to support the 'have-nots' and combat a digital divide. Currently pupils in Europe are typically required to turn off their mobile phones when they enter the school but this will soon become nonsensical. Why should pupils turn off their next generation PDA/smart phones/computers at the school gates in order to use (probably older/inferior) equipment provided by the State solely for use in the classroom?

Ambient schooling will only succeed if social change and leveraging the increasing ubiquity of computing devices and networks is properly recognized.

ACKNOWLEDGMENT

I wish to thank Jim Ayre, Rolf Lindner, and Ulf Lundin for their contribution to the development of the ideas presented in this paper.

REFERENCES

1. Matti Sinko, Ministry of Education Finland, Tips for Making an Educational ICT Project a Success, 1999, http://np.ipc.lt/projektai/01-02_en.html.
2. Furlong J, Furlong R, Facer K and Sutherland R, *The National Grid for Learning: a curriculum without walls?* Cambridge Journal of Education 2000 30(1), p102.
3. Downes, T., and Reddacliff, C. *Young Children Talking about Computers in their Homes.* in Papers of the Australian Computers in Education Conference, Sydney, 1996.
4 David Wood, *The THINK Report: Technology in Education Futures* for Policy, EUN, February 2002, http://eminent.eun.org/THINK_FULL_DRAFT_2pp.doc.
5 Soloway, E., Norris, C., Blumenfeld, P., Fishman, B., Krajcik, J., Marx, R. *Log on Education Column: Palm-Computing Devices are Ready-at-Hand.* Communications of the ACM, (June 2001).
6. Norris, C., Soloway, E., and Sullivan, T. *Examining 25 years of technology in U.S. education.* Communications of the ACM (2002) 45(8): 15-18.
7. Van Assche F., Massart D., *Federation and Brokerage of Learning Objects and Their Metadata,* Proceedings of the I-CALT 2004 conference, to appear.
8. *POOLING OPEN SOURCE SOFTWARE.* An IDA Feasibility Study. Interchange of Data between Administrations, European Commission, DG Enterprise, June 2002, http://europa.eu.int/ISPO/ida/export/files/en/1115.pdf, page 7.

CAN LEARNING OBJECTS BE REUSED – AND HOW?

Lessons from ARIADNE

Erik Duval

Katholieke Universiteit Leuven, http://www.cs.kuleuven.ac.be/~erikd

Abstract: This presentation will outline how many of the current efforts to work with learning objects are misguided and will present some alternative approaches that will make it possible to realize the goal of "share and reuse" that the ARIADNE Foundation has been pursuing for more than 8 years.

Key words: learning objects, metadata, standardization, ARIADNE

1. WE'VE COME A LONG WAY

Over the past 8 years or so, we have made solid progress in developing some of the basic standards and specifications that are needed in order to realize an *open infrastructure for learning*, where components from different sources can interoperate more or less seamlessly (Duval, 2004):

- the Learning Object Metadata standard enables the description of learning objects in an interchangeable way;
- the content packaging specification allows us to aggregate several learning objects together;
- content sequencing can be used to express navigational structures over the components in a package;
- through the Course Managed Instruction specification, learning objects can exchange data with Learning Management Systems,
- etc.

The SCORM reference model clarifies how these specifications and standards can work together in a coherent way. Most importantly, this set of basic agreements is broadly accepted, so that a state of de facto standardization is achieved.

Thus, components (authoring tools, content, management systems, instructional designs, etc.) from different vendors or non-commercial developers can work together, so that we can realize the open infrastructure mentioned above, rather than developing isolated technology islands from scratch every time anew, as used to be the case until all too recently.

2. WE HAVE A LONG WAY TO GO

However, it is clear that we still have a large number of issues to tackle in more advanced ways than most developers do at this moment if we want to realize the full potential of "share and reuse" as we've labeled it in the ARIADNE Foundation (Ariadne, 2004; Duval and Hodgins, 2003).

2.1 We need more standards

Many of the basic agreements for interoperability are at the moment not finalized standards: rather, they have the status of specifications, and, as such, cannot be guaranteed to remain available for the long periods of time that are required – remember that the TCP/IP RFC (the basic specification underlying the Internet) dates from 1981!

ADL, the organization that maintains the SCORM model, has committed to rely only on specifications that are either open standards, or on their way to becoming such standards. This is very important, as it enforces an open and fair process in the definition and an ongoing commitment to maintenance of the basic technical definitions that underpin the global learning infrastructure.

At the moment, only the IEEE LTSC Learning Object Metadata (LOM) standard is a fully finalized standard. Even for LOM, the binding in XML is not final yet. Besides metadata, the core specifications for sequencing, packaging, repository interaction, etc. are at various points in their lifecycle.

It is vital that we maintain momentum in the development of these standards, and that we embed them in more systematic support for the communities that adopt them, in the form of good practice guidelines and application profiles.

Also, it is important that we clarify what exactly are the specific requirements on the technical level for learning applications and that we rely on more general standards where appropriate, i.e. when there are no specific requirements. At the very least, we should develop interoperability gateways between standards for learning technology and other, more generic standards where appropriate: for instance, how does packaging relate to MPEG-21, how does sequencing relate to SMIL, etc.

2.2 We need better tools

It is extremely important to understand that standards are meant to enable developers to realize interoperable technical components: standards are *not* meant to be visible to end users! It is understandable that early implementations of new standards and specifications focus on the implementation of the functionality required. However, it is obvious that evaluations of the actual experience of end users with these tools will show the failure of this approach.

Indeed, just like web browsers do not disclose the hairy details of HTML or HTTP, sophisticated tools should not expose for instance detailed Learning Object Metadata. We should hide those details and develop tools that do not unnecessarily burden or complicate the life of the end user. I have launched the slogan that "electronic forms must die!" in order to encourage the development of tools and infrastructure that fit well with the workflow of the end user.

As an example, in Leuven, we have integrated the ARIADNE learning object repository, called the "Knowledge Pool System", with the Blackboard Learning Management System, and we have been able to capture a detailed set of Learning Object Metadata, without requiring the end user to provide these metadata manually! Rather, we mine the data already present in the administrative system of the university, we exploit the context of operation and information about the user, etc. to deduce all the relevant data automatically behind the scenes. We believe that much more work along these lines is urgently needed, and we predict that, if such work is not undertaken, practitioners in the field will start to quickly lose interest in applying standards in reality!

Actually, we need to take this line of research much further. Our team has started to work on information visualization approaches as a radically different way of enabling access to relevant learning objects (Klerkx, J., Duval, E., and Meire, M., 2004). Similarly, social recommending techniques may help to suggest appropriate resources at the right time. Newer technologies for content syndication, like RSS, could be applied in this context as well. The overall goal is to provide flexible access to advanced functionalities for end users, without putting any additional burden on their side.

2.3 We need to go beyond content

Much of the work on interoperable learning technologies has focused up to now on content and the role it plays to "deliver" learning. This was for sure the first area that needed our attention, as interoperable learning content is a basic requirement for large-scale deployment.

However, it is now time to look beyond basic content building blocks and to consider for instance how content can be "glued together" at a higher level of abstraction that current packaging and sequencing approaches allow for. It is possible that, in doing so, we will start to capture some of the instructional design aspects that are supposed to enable us to realize quality learning.

Moreover, we also need to be more serious about addressing the social aspects of learning. This includes collaborative learning support, but is much broader than that: indeed, almost all learning includes important social dynamics, and we may be able to support that aspect in a far better way, both on a personal level, as well as on that of the organization(s) that the individual belongs to.

Finally, there are important emotional aspects to learning: these relate to the social aspects already mentioned, but also include facets that are directly linked to the experience of beauty and the construction of meaning. Little attention has been spent so far on how we can provide more advanced support in this domain through technology.

3. RECONSIDERING LEARNING

In fact, if we consider our research field more seriously, it seems like we may have a more fundamental problem… It would be hard to argue that we have made the same sort of progress that has been made in such diverse fields as medicine, physics, biology, etc. In fact, it is not even clear that we would have consensus within the field on how to measure "progress": is the number of publications or PhD's a good indicator? Or the budgets spent, or the profits made? Where is the "learning" and how do we know that we have improved it through our efforts?

In the ProLearn Network of Excellence, I am coordinating work on precisely these questions, and on the "grand challenges" that we will need to tackle in research if we want to understand better what it is we are trying to achieve and how we can distinguish real progress from "delta research" and fashionable statements-with-all-todays-buzzwords-in-them (Prolearn, 2004). Only in this way can we get better at getting better.

4. CONCLUSION

In conclusion, I believe that we have made substantial progress in the realization of an open global technical infrastructure for learning. Further work is needed in this area, and we must also shift our attention to usability issues that will determine how well our results can be put to practice. Moreover, we need to enlarge our scope to also include aspects that have been neglected so far. This will not be a small undertaking, but the potential benefits are huge: the result could be better learning for everyone (globally – really!) at any time (24/7 – really!).

ACKNOWLEDGEMENT

We gratefully acknowledge the financial support of the K.U.Leuven Research Fund, in the context of the BALO project on "BAsic research on Learning Objects".

REFERENCES

Ariadne, 2004 (May 2, 2004); http://www.ariadne-eu.org/.

Duval, E., 2004, *Learning technology standardization: making sense of it all*, International Journal on Computer Science and Information Systems, 1(1):33-43; http://www.comsis.fon.bg.ac.yu/ComSISpdf/Volume01/InvitedPapers/ErikDuval.htm.

Duval, E., and Hodgins, W., 2003, *A LOM research agenda*, Proceedings of WWW2003 - Twelfth International World Wide Web Conference; http://www2003.org/cdrom/papers/alternate/P659/p659-duval.html

Klerkx, J., Duval, E., and Meire, M., 2004, *Using Information Visualization for Accessing Learning Object Repositories*, Proceedings of IV04 - 8th International Conference on Information Visualization.

ProLearn, 2004 (May 2, 2004); http://www.prolearn-project.org/.

PART TWO

E-LEARNING STANDARDS

TOWARDS AN ENHANCED LEARNING DESIGN LANGUAGE

A Pattern-based Approach

Manuel Caeiro Rodríguez, Martín Llamas Nistal and Luis Anido Rifón
Departamento de Enxeñería Telemática, Campus Universitario s/n E-36200 Vigo (Pontevedra) SPAIN. E-mail: {mcaeiro;martin;lanido}@det.uvigo.es

Abstract: The objective of the IMS Learning Design (LD) Specification is to provide a containment framework of elements that can describe any design of a teaching-learning process in a formal way. It is pedagogical independent and does not impose any learning approach. In previous works we analyzed this specification from a structural perspective and proposed some extensions. In this paper, we consider the tasks and difficulties of learning designers, e.g. teachers, in order to compose courses and learning experiences. We investigate how already existing patterns and possibly pattern languages for learning and pedagogic can be used to improve IMS LD usability. Patterns are used in other domains to describe generic solutions to common problems. Pattern languages structure and relate patterns to each other forming a network of interconnected patterns, providing in this way an enhanced support to design.

Key words: E-learning; Educational Modeling Languages; Design Pattern; Pattern Language.

1. INTRODUCTION

Over the last years many E-learning systems have been built. However, in these systems, the learning logic, such as those for establishing the learning experiences and activities, is often hard-coded into the system components. In general, traditional learning systems are complex to build and do not easily accommodate changes. But, learning activities are usually sensitive to the learning approach and context. In addition, not only different learning approaches have different needs, but the same learning style or pedagogy may require different kind of activities in different phases of its development. Therefore, it is important for E-learning system support to be flexible and adaptable.

Our interest is to separate learning logic from applications in building learning systems. The first part of the solution is to find an executable language that supports the description of learning designs, independently of the learning approach and technology. These learning designs would be enforced at runtime by an appropriate infrastructure that generates the services, support, and control prescribed by the learning design. As a result, the design and implementation of learning applications are greatly simplified.

To overcome the differences between different pedagogies and learning styles the IMS Global Consortium published the Learning Design (IMS LD) specification [1]. This IMS proposal is a meta-language that allows to codify the pedagogic values of learning objects as *units-of-study* (e.g. courses, course components, study programs), associating each element of content (e.g. texts, tasks, tests, assignments) with information describing its instructional strategy (e.g., roles, relations, interactions and activities of students and teachers), that is, the activities that have to be carried out in order to achieve intended learning goals.

IMS LD language is mainly concerned with interoperability and reusability issues. It is not devoted to be used by final users (e.g. teachers, learning designers) to create courses directly. The language demands management of a huge amount of low-level concepts, coordination, and control mechanisms. In this way, as Spector [2] argues in general for the field of educational technology, the current situation is one of *technification.* That is, a domain largely controlled by and accessible to only those with special knowledge and skill. To solve this problem, our work is devoted to facilitate the labor of learning designers, e.g. teachers, to compose courses and general learning experiences, facilitating their reuse and interoperability.

In order to solve the usability problem we have followed a pattern based approach. The use of patterns in E-learning systems and related domains, e.g. pedagogy or coordination, is gaining an increasingly popularity, but to gain truly advantage of its use they need to be organized properly. We present the first steps towards a language of design patterns for learning hierarchical structured in three aggregation layers.

The rest of the paper is organized as follows. In the next section we introduce the IMS Learning Design Specification and analyze its structure, considering the usability problems for learning designers. In section 3 we present a pattern based development in order to structure and organize a pattern language for learning design. We finish the paper with some conclusions.

2. IMS LEARNING DESIGN

The main rationale of the IMS LD specification is to provide a framework that supports a wide range of pedagogical approaches. Rather than attempting to capture the specifics of each pedagogy, it considers their commonalities: "*regardless of the pedagogy involved, in practice every learning design comes down to a set of prescribed activities for the actors involved (learner and staff roles) that should be executed in a certain order*".

A *unit-of-study* represents more than just a collection of ordered resources to learn. It includes a variety of activities (problem solving activities, search activities, discussion activities, peer assessment activities, etc.) for the learners, together with assessments, services and support facilities provided by teachers, trainers and other staff members. Which activities, which resources, which roles and which workflow is dependent on the learning design.

This provides a means of expressing many different pedagogical approaches in a relatively succinct language. A learning design instance might involve a single user or multiple users; take a behaviorist, cognitive, constructivist or some other approach, or it might require learners to work separately or collaboratively.

In this way IMS LD enables the description of a great variety of learning experiences. These learning designs are executable and they may be enforced at runtime by an infrastructure. In this way, it is possible to separate learning logic from applications in building learning systems. Such descriptions can be executed by a runtime environment that provides the services, support, and control specified in the learning design. As a result, the design and implementation of learning applications are greatly simplified.

2.1 IMS Learning Design analysis

IMS LD can be considered as a process-based language. A learning design is a process that coordinates the execution of several activities. We have analyzed the IMS LD proposal from the Activity Theory (AT) [3] perspective, c.f. Figure 1, considering its relationship with workflow and Computer Supported Cooperative Work (CSCW) paradigms. These technologies are concerned with protocols, policies, coordination, and prescription mechanisms that are used to support people working individually or in collaboration in different contexts.

We analyzed IMS LD and found several problems related to its modularity and flexibility [3]. Then we considered the possibility to enhance IMS LD with the introduction of several modifications and extensions [4].

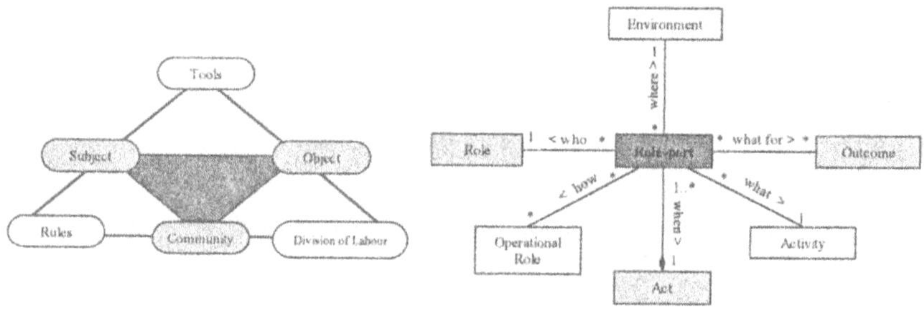

Figure 1. The AT Expanded Meditional Model (left), and the new proposal for the IMS LD Act Model (right)

The final learning design specification can be described considering several aspects: entities, environment, and method.

2.1.1 Entities

The entities model comprises all the artifacts supporting the learning experience along with their structure, usage, and intend. It comprises:

- Roles used to specify the conditions of participation for each user in a learning design. It should be possible to define different classes of roles, with specialization.
- Objects comprise the documents, resources, and any other element used during the learning experience.
- Applications are the tools and services used. It is necessary to describe the provided and required interfaces, events generated, etc.
- Activities are performed by users to achieve a certain learning goal. Activities may have properties such as preconditions, completion conditions, duration, etc.
- Activity structure. Activity structure is related to the hierarchical structure of complex activities in a tree. The tree forms a hierarchy where the high level activities are found at the top of the tree and the most basic activities are at the leaf nodes.

2.1.2 Environment

The environment represents the tools and resources where activities have to be carried out. They provide services and facilities that can be used by the actors to achieve the intended learning goal. An abstract description of the different tools and applications that may appear in an environment is very interesting to facilitate automatic and reuse.

The environment must contain some dynamic elements:

- Coordination policies are devoted to the description of the ways in which roles can participate in the environment and cooperate with other roles.
- Communication mechanisms, that characterize the way users can communicate with others and gather information from their actions.

2.1.3 Method

The method comprises the coordination and interaction necessary to carry out the intended learning experience managing the entities and environments. Definitions of these mechanisms depend on several factors, such as the current group of participants, environment, tasks, and goals. It may be necessary to consider the following mechanisms:

- Control Flow indicates the order in which tasks are executed. It also determines the assignment of roles to activities and environments.
- Data Flow is concerned with the transfer of documents and objects among different tasks. It is needed to consider concurrency issues.

2.2 Additional support is needed

IMS LD may be considered as a powerful tool to lead e-learning towards the future. It proposes a new model to develop final e-learning systems, more flexible and adaptable, providing the more appropriate solution to each particular learning requirement and situation. But this future would be not real if users do not use the IMS LD specification to describe their courses and learning experiences.

In the current form, IMS LD is devoted to promote interoperability and reusability; but not to be used by final users. Final learning designers, not experts in the use of technology, would require help in order to use the language. Currently, a year after the publication of the specification, there is no commercial runtime environment or authoring tool that supports the specification. If software designers do not achieve an easy understanding of the specification we consider that final users (e.g. teachers, professors) will experience more difficulties.

Our purpose is to provide a high-level language that supports a similar kind of properties. It should support the specification of different pedagogies and learning experiences. The ideal situation would be to provide a mapping from top level constructions to IMS LD descriptions. Patterns have been used to facilitate the design of activities by non expert users in other domains; in the next section we provide an introduction to this approach.

3. A PATTERN-BASED APPROACH

The main problem is that IMS LD is concerned with relatively low level language elements for the requirements of a typical learning designer. These people require other kind of constructions.

Generally speaking, the primary goal of patterns is to create an inventory of solutions to help learning designers resolve learning development problems that are common, difficult and frequently encountered (adapted from [5]). The use of patterns in learning, and other related fields of activity support, such as workflow [6] or CSCW [7], is gaining relevance in practice. Currently there are several collections of learning and pedagogical patterns, but they are not related: collaborative learning [8], pedagogical [9], etc.

3.1 Architecture and design patterns

The term 'pattern' has the meaning given initially by C. Alexander for architectural patterns [10]: "*each pattern describes a problem which occurs over and over again in our environment, and then describes the core of the solution to that problem, in such a way you can use this solution a million times over, without ever doing it the same way twice*". In other terms, a pattern is an abstract solution to a problem in a context.

Patterns have been a successful tool to model design experience in architecture, software design, Human-Computer Interaction (HCI), business process, etc. Alexander's goal in publishing architectural patterns was, above all, to provide a didactic medium for human readers, even (and specifically) for non-architects. In software engineering design patterns have been used in a different fashion. Software design patterns are considered a useful language for communication among software developers, and a practical vehicle for introducing less experienced developers into the field. Our purpose is to adopt the architectural pattern approach in the learning domain. The idea of final users (e.g. teachers) designing learning experiences must be taken over.

3.2 A language of patterns

A pattern by itself is just a small piece of the entire design "puzzle". Each pattern describes a proven solution to a problem in a certain design context. When all the pieces of the puzzle are "put together", it is possible to construct a complete body of design.

A pattern language is a set of patterns that work together to generate complex behavior and complex artifacts. An individual pattern may already be very valuable for designers but when patterns are related to each other we can potentially reach a far more valuable thing. Such a set of connected patterns is called a *pattern language*. When Alexander wrote his book on architecture design patterns [10], it did not just contain patterns, the patterns formed a language. His language was hierarchical and started out on the level of cities, then neighborhoods, houses, until the level of windows or seats was reached. In Alexander's idea, the language actually "generated" the design by traversing from high level patterns to the lowest level ones.

The patterns community realized that patterns in isolation provided only incremental improvements to software systems, organizations and processes. Pattern languages promise to drive fundamental and lasting improvements. The question is whether a similar language for learning design can be created or not.

3.3 A pattern language for learning design

We follow a similar approach to the one adopted in [11] for Interaction Design. They interpret the hierarchical nature of architectural patterns as a hierarchy of problems. The highest level problems are broken up in smaller problems for which solutions seem to exist. They also adopt the interpretation that *scale* means *scale* of problems. In learning design there is certainly a *scale hierarchical* of problems. Although it may not be visible it is always there behind the top-down design.

Usually learning design of a course is a top-down activity that start with the teacher gaining understanding of the learners and their goals, the resources and services available, the pedagogical approach, etc. Taking the example of a course design, the design continues organizing the activities that have to been carried out by learners and academic staff. In the next step it is necessary to define the control flow and document flow between the different activities. Then for each activity it is necessary to describe the actors involved, the environment (with its resources and services, and the properties, conditions and events associated), the way in which the actors are going to interact, communicate, etc. Such a top-down approach will generate an enhanced Learning Design language where patterns are at all levels.

Therefore it is possible to define layers of patterns. These layers are rough delineations of the typical levels that are encountered in learning design. The levels identified so far are: *pedagogical, learning experiences*, and *activity.*

The different levels and associated patterns can be shown in a graph of connected patterns as the one represented in Figure 2. In the figure arrows represent connections among patterns. These relationships are at the heart of the pattern language because they create actual additional value over single patterns. In [11] three kinds of connections are identified: *aggregation, specialization*, and *association.*

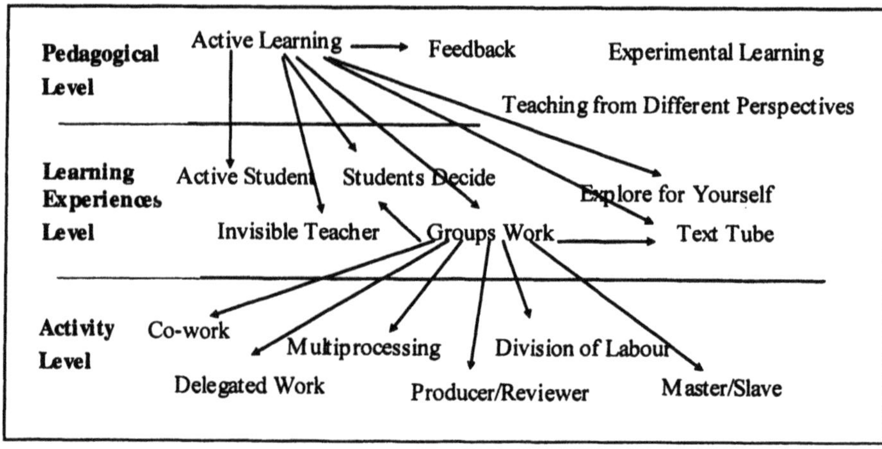

Figure 1. Structure of the pattern language for learning design

3.3.1 Pedagogical patterns

Every course, or learning application, has its own purpose; there are usually learning goals to be achieved and context conditions that prescribe its rationale. Proper learning design has its foundations in understanding why the learning design has been required and its purpose. A pedagogical pattern describes what the essentials of that pedagogic are: what kind of learning experiences are practiced, contents and applications involved, etc.

The Pedagogical Patterns Project (PPP) [9] collect many types of patterns that can help teachers to teach and students to learn. Pedagogical patterns try to capture expert knowledge of the practice of teaching and learning. They describe each learning approach introducing its particular learning experiences patterns. Currently, these are the published proposals:

- **Teaching from Different Perspectives.** This is a collection of patterns focused in providing learners with different perspectives. It describes patterns such as: *Wider Perspective*, *Team Teaching*, *Tool Box*, etc.
- **Patterns for Active Learning.** This collection focuses on empowering the student through active learning. It describes patterns such as: *Active Student*, *Students Decide*, *Real World Experience*, *Groups Work*, etc.
- **Feedback Patterns.** It focuses in a feedback oriented teaching environment. It describes patterns such as: *Feedback*, *Try It Yourself*, *Own Words*, *Peer Grading*, *Embrace Correction*, etc.
- **Patterns for Experimental Learning.** It proposes patterns such as: *See Before Hear*, *One Concept Several Implementations*, *Built in Failure*, etc.

3.3.2 Learning experiences patterns

From the basic pedagogic and from user research, learning designers will have to determine what the main learning experiences need to be supported and to what extent. A learning experience is not just about tasks and goals but also about how the learners reach their goals using a certain environment, how they communicate and cooperate with their peers, and how they are supported by academic staff (e.g. teachers, tutors, examiners). This kind of pattern describes a collection of general techniques, actions, and/or tasks for describing a particular learning experience. Learning experiences should therefore be understood as a broader goal for which we are designing. The learning experience-level patterns describe common experiences and which lower level patterns can be used to create such experience. Typical learning experiences were introduced in the previous section: *Team Teaching*, *Active Student*, *Try it Yourself*, etc.

3.3.3 Activity patterns

At this level we consider the patterns related to the constructs with IMS LD descriptions. This involves low level activities (such as *Produce a Document in Collaboration*, or *Communicate with Peer*) that are needed in high level experience patterns. These patterns are relatively pedagogic independent. The pedagogic and learning experience patterns set the context specifics and the activity patterns are used to fill in the blanks. These patterns describe series of user interactions in an environment for solving a certain problem. Such a series corresponds to a task sequence or a controlled interaction needed to achieve a certain goal.

An important feature of a process pattern in object oriented software engineering [12] is that it has to describe what should be done but not the exact details of how it is done. We plan to work in a different way, providing descriptions of how to express these patterns using current IMS LD language.

4. CONCLUSIONS

Patterns are used implicitly by many learning designers who have found solutions that have worked for them in the past. Using patterns for capturing and documenting design knowledge in other domains is a hot topic. There are many reasons for adopting this approach in learning design [13]:

- Patterns provide a lingua franca that can be read and understood by all.
- Patterns offer a way of capturing and transferring design knowledge.
- They promote reuse.
- Patterns are a valuable source of information, supporting both the analysis of the current situation and the design of the new system.

We look for a pattern language with proper support for learning design, relating it to the current IMS LD specification. The final purpose is to facilitate the usability of final users.

ACKNOWLEDGMENTS

We want to thank *Ministerio de Ciencia y Tecnología* for its partial support to this work under grant *CORBALearn: Interfaz de Dominio guiada por Estándares para Aprendizaje Electrónico* (TIC2001-3767).

REFERENCES

1. Koper, R., Olivier, B. & Anderson, T. (Editors), *IMS Learning Design Information Model.* Version 1.0. (IMS Global Learning Consortium, 2003).
2. Spector, J.M. 2001, An Overview of Progress and Problems in Educational Technology (1) *Interactive Educational Multimedia*, 27-37, (2001).
3. Caeiro, M., Anido, L., Llamas, M., A Critical Analysis of IMS Learning Design, (Proceedings of the CSCL, 2003).
4. Caeiro, M., Mikic, F., Anido, L., Llamas, M., (in spanish) Análisis de Componentes para un Modelo de Descripción de Unidades de Aprendizaje Heterogéneas, (CITA, 2003).
5. Loureiro, K. and Plummer, D., AD Patterns: Beyond Objects and Components, (Research Note # COM-08-0111, Gartnet Group, 1999).
6. van der Aalst, W.M.P., ter Hofstede, A.H.M., Kiepuszewski, B., Barros, A.P., Workflow Patterns, (Eindhoven University of Technology, 2000).

7. Herrmann, T., Hoffmann, M., Jahnke, I., Kienle, A., Kunau, G., Loser, K., Menold, N., Concepts for Usable Patterns of Groupware Applications (Proceedings of the 2003 International ACM SIGGROUP Conference on Supporting Group Work, 2003).
8. Asensio Pérez, J.I., Dimitriadis, Y., Heredia Rodríguez, M., Martínez Monés, A., Álvarez Rabanal, F.J., Blasco, M.T., Osuna Gómez, C., Collaborative Learning Patterns: Assisting the development of component-based CSCL applications (Proceedings of the International Conference on Parallel Distributed Conference (PDP'04), Workshop: Web-based systems, PDP'04, February 2004).
9. The Pedagogical Patterns Project, Pedagogical Patterns (April 2004) http://www.pedagogicalpatterns.org.
10. Alexander, C., Pattern Language: Towns, Buildings, Construction, (Oxford University Press, New York, 1977).
11. van Welie, M., van der Veer, G.C., Pattern Languages in Interaction Design: Structure and Organization, (Proceedings of Interact 2003).
12. Ambler, S.W., Process Patterns: Building Large-Scale Systems Using Object Technology, (Cambridge University Press/SIGS Books, July 1998).
13. Erickson, T., Interaction Pattern Languages: A Lingua Franca for Interaction Design? (UPA 98 Conference, Washington, DC., 1998).

A TYPE-BASED TAXONOMY OF ITEMS IN ASSESSMENTS

C. Delgado Kloos, A. Pardo, P. Muñoz Merino, N. Pérez Pérez
Departamento de Ingeniería Telemática, Universidad Carlos III de Madrid
{cdk,abel,pedmume,nperper}@it.uc3m.es

Abstract: The IMS Consortium in its QTI (Question & Test Interoperability) specification [1] presents a collection of question types that are useful to be used in an e-learning context. Standardization on the items and test types eases reusing them throughout LMSs, hence its importance. The IMS QTI question catalogue includes some items that are specializations of others. Others just differ in the rendering model. The goal of this paper is to categorize and put all those items in context, thus producing a new taxonomy. We do this by giving a type to each of the items. So, this work could be also understood a defining a type system for items. As a by-product, we include some new kinds of items and re-categorize others.

Key words: E-Learning, Standards, assessment, IMS QTI, type system

1. INTRODUCTION

The IMS Question and Test Interoperability specification [1] defines a catalogue of items that can be used in a variety on e-learning settings for assessment. It is good to have them defined in a standard way, because this permits the reusability of these items and their interoperability across Learning Management Systems. In IMS QTI terminology, an item consists of a question and in some cases a list of possible answers, from which the student has to select one or more. A section can contain one or more sections and one or more items. An assessment contains one or more sections. The OKI initiative [2] (which defines a behavioural model instead of a data model) also uses the same terminology for item, section and assessment. IMS QTI specifies a catalogue of items. In this paper, we study and classify them by finding a clearer taxonomy, and in particular one that separates concerns clearly. We include some additional items that are not covered by IMS QTI, but are used by several tools (some of them are Canvas Learning Course Builder [4], QuestionMark Perception [5], Respondus [6], IMS Assesst Designer [7]. Not all these tools have all types of items). The new taxonomy defined is useful both for better understanding the items, as well as for implementation purposes.

An item can be understood as a function, where the possible answers are the arguments and the evaluation, the result. Therefore, we can give a type to items. For convenience, we give them a type in a domain of polymorphic, dependent types. We use a functional-like notation. Three steps can be identified when processing items answered by a student:

1. Data validation (e.g. is the data inserted in a fill-in-the-blank item of the type expected, integer, string, etc.?). This is type checking. Additional range checking could be needed at run-time. The use of dependent types reduces this additional checking. Dependent types are types that can depend on values. They can be used to assign more accurate types to programs, thus improving error detection at compile-time, and they allow one to assign types to a range of programs that do not type check in traditional type systems but produce a "reasonable" result.
2. There might be data dependent questions, e.g. a question posed may depend on the response given by the student earlier. This notion is also well captured by a theory of dependent types.
3. Evaluation, i.e. interpretation of the function: giving scores and feedback to the item for some particular data collected.

Let **S** = type of scores, for example, **[0..10]** (in Spain), **[1..6]** (in Germany), **[A..F]** (in USA), **B** (the type of Booleans, passed/not passed) or the number of points given to a correctly responded item. The scores of the items in a section or assessment are combined to give an overall score. Analogously, if we are using this notation to specify a survey we could compute some statistics.

Let **F** = type of feedbacks, which would typically be **String**, the type of strings. The result type of a question could be **(SxF)**, a score and some feedback. Let's call **R = SxF**

In an assessment without feedback, we have **F = U** (unit type).

In the following sections, we study first choice-based items (section 2), then text-based items (section 3), and then the composition of items (section 4). We finish by discussing the rendering options (section 5) and giving some conclusions (section 6).

2. CHOICE-BASED ITEMS

2.1 True/false items

A true/false item is a function of type **B->R**. We will call it a 1-from-2 item (2 possible answers, of which 1 is correct).

```
parisFrance :: B -> R
parisFrance true  = (1, "right, congratulations!")
parisFrance false = (0, "wrong, travel more!")
```

A typical rendering could make use of radio buttons in an html form.

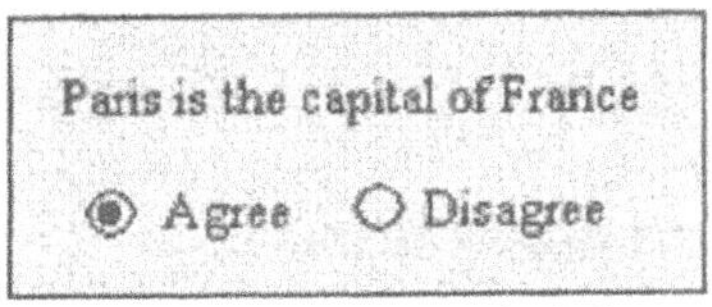

But we want to separate the value responded from the position the user has to click. We introduce an indirection step by defining a bijective function **order** that maps ordinals to Booleans (in QTI this is handled with the **ident** attribute of the **response_label** tag):

```
order :: [0..1] -> B
order 0 = true
order 1 = false
```

then, the composition of both functions is of type:

```
parisFrance o order :: [0..1]->R
```

Using a different ordering function produces a reshuffling of the same item answers. There are many more indirection steps in IMS QTI, which we ignore. This item is a special case of the multiple choice item (next).

2.2 Multiple choice items

A multiple choice item has type **Enum(α) => α->R**, where α is a type variable. α should be an enumeration type. We will call this a 1-from-n item (n possible answers, of which 1 is correct).

```
parisLyonNoneFrance :: (Paris, Lyon, None) -> R
parisLyonNoneFrance Paris = (1, "well done!")
parisLyonNoneFrance Lyon  = (0, "wrong, try again!")
```

```
parisLyonNoneFrance None   = (0, "wrong, try again!")
```

Again applying an ordering function, in this particular example of type `[0..2]->String`, would give us an item with ordered responses. A typical rendering could make use of radio buttons in an html form:

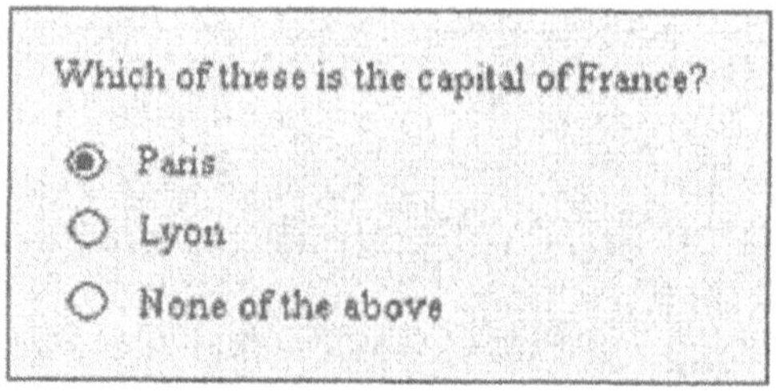

This item is a special case of the multiple response item (next).

2.3 Multiple response items

We call a multiple response item an m-from-n item (n possible answers, of which m are correct). Its type should be `℘(α)->R` (where ℘ is the powerset constructor), because the user has to get the set of correct answers.

```
inh1MFrance :: ℘(Paris, Nice, Lyon) -> R
inh1MFrance {Paris,Lyon}= (10, "very good!")
inh1MFrance {Paris}     = (5, "got one!")
inh1MFrance {Lyon}      = (5, "got one!")
inh1MFrance else        = (0, "not quite!")
```

A typical rendering could make use of checkboxes in an html form. An ordering function would map response positions to response values.

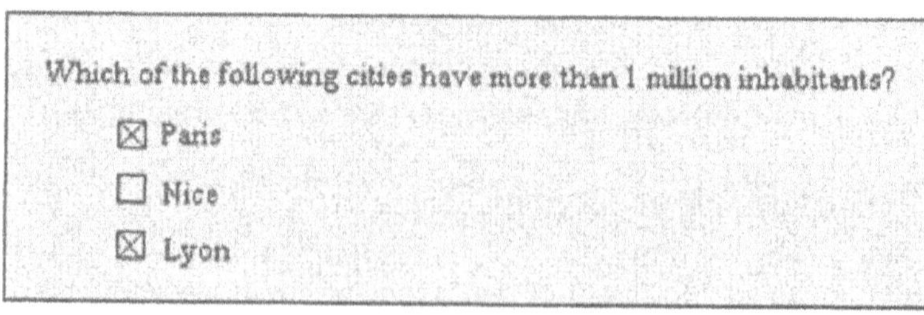

2.4 Summary

The choice-based items are related as follows:

$$\{1\text{-from-}2\} \subseteq \{1\text{-from-n}\} \subseteq \{\text{m-from-n}\}$$

After applying ordering functions, the true/false items are a subset of the multiple-choice items, and these a subset of the multiple-response items.

3. TEXT-BASED ITEMS

3.1 Fill-in-the-blank items

A fill-in-the-blank item is of type `α->R`. A typical rendering could make use of input elements of type text in an html form.

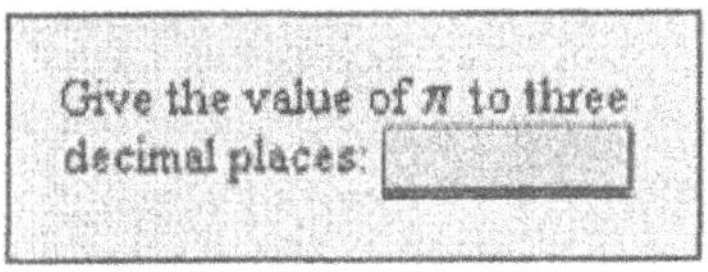


```
pi3Decimals :: Num -> R
pi3Decimals 3,141 = (1, "very good!")
pi3Decimals else  = (0, "not quite!")
```

In general there might be several correct answers (if there is logically just one, one might allow different spellings or upper/lower case alternatives).

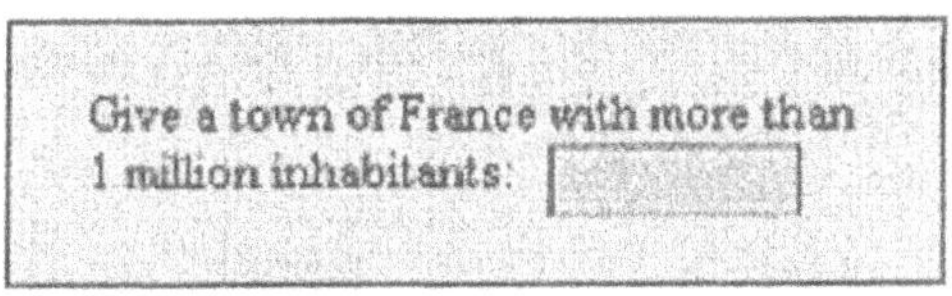


```
inhab1MFrance :: String -> R
inhab1MFrance "Paris "     = (1, "very good!")
inhab1MFrance "Lyon"       = (1, "very good!")
inhab1MFrance "Marseille"  = (1, "very good!")
inhab1MFrance "Toulouse"   = (1, "very good!")
inhab1MFrance else         = (0, "not quite!")
```

3.2 Short answers

A short answer is a kind of item whose evaluation cannot be fully automated in general. Whereas in a fill-in-the-blank item, one can list all the possible valid answers, this is normally not the case for short answers or full essays in general. Thus, this type of items needs intervention by a grader. We model this with an additional argument that reflects the (sometimes not formalizable) criteria of the grader. Let's call its type `C`:

```
short-answer :: (C -> String -> R)
```

A rendering could make use of a text-area element in an html form.

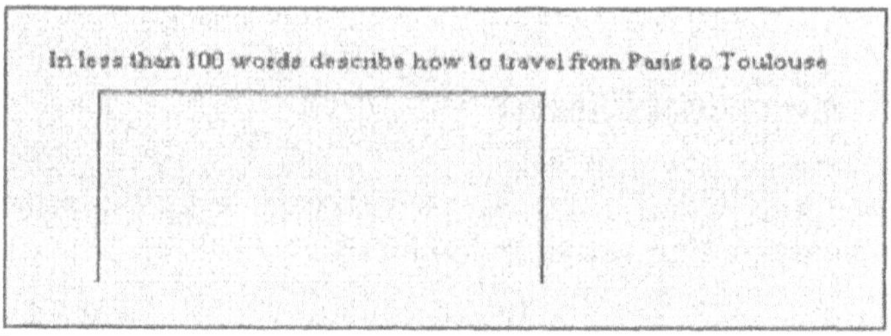

Some item generation tools have another kind called "essay". We subsume it under the same kind as "short answer".

3.3 File upload

When the text to be delivered is even lengthier, it is more reasonable to have the student create it using some editor and them save it in a file. The grader criteria again are needed in order to evaluate the results. This type (which is not included in the IMS QTI specification) is similar to the one of the short answer, except, that the string is interpreted as a file name. There is an indirection step to get the submitted text:

```
file-upload :: (C -> String -> R)
```

A rendering could make use of input elements of type text in an html form in which one could write the name of the file to be uploaded. It would be useful to have a window in which to browse through the local directory.

3.4 Summary

The text-based items are related as follows:

$$\{\text{fill-in-the-blank}\} \subseteq \{\text{short-answer}\} \approx \{\text{file-upload}\}$$

Fill-in-the-blank is a subset of short-answer, where the length is limited. Short-answer and file-upload are equivalent. The difference is whether the text has to be typed in online or stored previously in a file. Choice-based items are a special case of text-based items. Instead of typing in the answers, they are selected from a list of possible values. We move from a finite set of possible answers to a (theoretically) infinite set for the text-based items.

4. COMPOSITION OF ITEMS

4.1 Simple sequential composition of items

We can compose items sequentially, by just putting one after the other in the same way as we compose two sentences in an imperative programming language (by using the ";" symbol): one sentence is executed after the other. There the result is a composite sentence and here, a composite item. Its type is the product of the types of the individual items, but some type operations can be performed. A item composed sequentially by two ordered true/false items with the same result type would be of type **([0..1]->R) x ([0..1]->R)**, which is equivalent for our purposes to **([0..1]^2->R^2)**.

There should be a function the converts the result of type **R**^{2} of the individual items to an overall result of type **R**. This kind of sequentially composed item is a special case of the one presented in the next section, in which the second item depends on the answer of the first item.

IMS QTI considers what they call a Matrix-based Multiple Response a composite item type. This is an example:

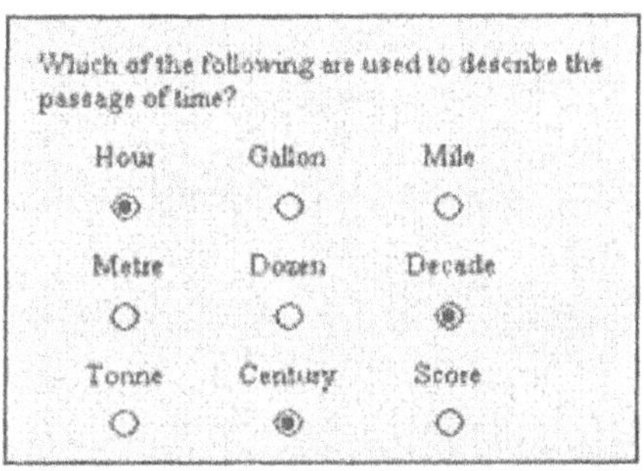

We consider this a sequential composition of items, in this case, multiple choice items that share the questions, and therefore can be skipped. We use the name Matrix-based for the two-dimensional composition (see below).

4.2 Dependent sequential composition of items

In this type of sequential composition, the second item may be one or another depending on the user's behaviour. Here is a simple example with an initial true/false item and a second one that depends on the value given to the first one by the user. We use a functional notation to capture the result of the item and an ad-hoc notation for dependent types, to make the point clearer:

```
depSeqQuest (x,y) =
let (s,f) = (lyonFrance(x)) in
  let (s',f') in if s then (londonUK (y))
                    else (parisLyonNoneFrance (y))) in
    (scorecomb(s,s'), feedbcomb(f,f'))
```

scorecomb and **feedbcomb** combine the scores and feedback of the individual items to the result of the composed item. Its type happens to be dependent. Here are the types of all the items:

```
lyonFrance :: B->R
londonUK :: B->R
parisLyonNoneFrance :: (Paris, Lyon, None) -> R
depSeqQuest ::
    (B∋b x (if b then B else (Paris, Lyon, None)))->R
```

4.3 Matching item

This type of item is not included in IMS QTI, but is available in several assessment systems. Therefore, it is of interest to include it in this taxonomy. In a matching item we have two sets of elements (A and B) that can be of different cardinality (|A| and |B|). The student has to link each element in A with one or several of the elements in B. There are several variants now:

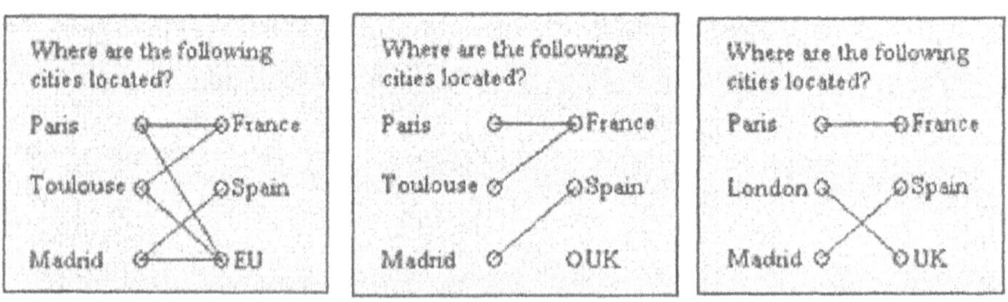

1. M_1: each element in A can be linked to one or more in B, without restriction. This is like having |A| multiple response items that share the response set (B). Type: **℘(℘ (α)->R)**.
2. M_2: each element in A can be linked to one and only one in B, where those in B can be reused (the inverse is a partial function). This is like having |A| multiple choice items that share the response set (B). Type: **℘(α->R)**
3. M_3: each element in A can be linked to one and only one in B, without the possibility of reusing those in B (we have a bijection, if

$|A|=|B|$). This can be understood as an extension of the true/false item to cardinality $|A|$. Type: $\wp\ (\alpha\text{->}\mathbf{R})$

The matching items are related to the choice-based items as follows:

$$\begin{array}{ccccc} \{1\text{-from-}2\} & \subseteq & \{1\text{-from-}n\} & \subseteq & \{m\text{-from-}n\} \\ & & \in & & \in \\ M_3 & \subseteq & M_2 & \subseteq & M_1 \end{array}$$

4.4 Two-dimensional composition of items

A two-dimensional item is a tabular or matrix-based arrangement of items. An example is a crossword puzzle. This is also not a type defined in IMS QTI, but is a nice example of composite item. A crossword puzzle is a two-dimensional composition of fill-in-the-blank items. Type: $\wp\ (\alpha\text{->}\mathbf{R})$

	A.	B.	C.
1.	Q		A
2.	T	I	M
3.	I	M	S

Horizontal:
1. A. Question
   C. Answer
2. A. Berners-Lee
3. A. Instructional Metadata Specification

Vertical:
A. 1. Question and Test Interoperability
B. 2. Instant Messaging
C. 1. American Mathematical Society

5. RENDERING

We separate the type of item from the way it is presented or rendered. A true/false item can be rendered with radio buttons or with an image map, conceptually it is the same. Not all renderings are possible for all types of items. Here is a table that captures the reasonable possibilities:

RENDERING	Radio	Checkbox	Text	TextArea	Slider	Image
True/False	X		X		X	X
Multiple Choice	X		X		X	X
Multiple Response		X				X
Fill-in-the-Blank			X			
Short Answer				X		
File Upload			X			

6. CONCLUSION

We have used a powerful type system when giving types to items for convenience. This exercise just shows the complexity that is inherent in this topic. When implementing a system that handles these item types, it is clear that a polymorphic, dependent type system is not needed; instead more variants of functions have to be implemented.

We have separated elements which are conceptually orthogonal on the one hand, and identified those which are related on the other one. The rendering issue has to be clearly separated from the basic types of items. We have distinguished basic items from those that can be obtained through composition. For instance, matrix-based multiple response items or matching items are really composite ones. A section is just a composite item with some selection and ordering functions. We think that with the definition of this taxonomy, the different types of items can be better understood and put into context. While defining the taxonomy we have identified some additional types of items, which are not part of IMS QTI, but are of interest.

ACKNOWLEDGEMENTS

This work has been partially sponsored by the E-LANE project [3] (EU @LIS Programme) and the SIEMPRE project (Spanish Ministry of Science and Technology, TIC2002-03635). In the E-LANE project, work is being carried out to extend the .LRN Learning Management System [8] (based on the OpenACS platform [9]) to cope with IMS QTI based assessments.

REFERENCES

[1] IMS QTI, http://www.imsglobal.org/question
[2] OKI, Open Knowledge Initiative, http://web.mit.edu/oki
[3] E-LANE project, http://www.e-lane.org
[4] Canvas Learning, http://www.canvaslearning.com
[5] QuestionMark, http://www.questionmark.com
[6] Respondus, http://www.respondus.com
[7] IMS Assesst Designer, http://www.xdlsoft.com/ad
[8] .LRN, http://www.dotlrn.org
[9] OpenACS, http://www.openacs.org

PART THREE

USE OF STANDARDS IN A TECHNICAL SETTING

IMPLICATIONS OF LEARNING TECHNOLOGY STANDARDIZATION IN ELECTRONIC DESIGN

Luis Anido (panel chair)
Departamento de Ingeniería Telemática, Campus Universitario s/n E-36200 Vigo (Pontevedra) Spain. E-mail: lanido@det.uvigo.es

Abstract: The e-learning domain is involved in a deep standardization process. Several topics related to e-learning authoring, delivering, and management are being discussed to obtain general accepted recommendations. This panel will discuss the main standardization activities from a general perspective but also will analyse its implications in a specific field: the electronic design.

Key words: E-learning systems; standardization; electronic design; CAD; semiconductor industry.

1. INTRODUCTION

Advances in information and communication technologies, and specially in Multimedia, Networking and Software Engineering allow the apparition of a new generation of computer-based training systems. Internet is today the ubiquitous supporting environment for virtual and distributed learning environments. As a consequence, many institutions, both public and private, take advantage of new technologies to offer training products and services at all levels.

In this situation, educational systems and resources proliferate, and a need for standardization becomes apparent. Like in other standard-driven initiatives, standardization applied to learning technologies will enable reuse and interoperation among heterogeneous software systems. To achieve this, a consensus is needed on architectures, services, protocols, data models and open interfaces.

Thus, institutional users of educational software are joining their efforts to achieve standards and recommendations to support the interoperation of heterogeneous learning systems. This is an active, continuously evolving process that will last for years to come, until a clear, precise and generally accepted set of standards for educational-related systems is developed. This is a complex process, which occurs at several levels and is supported by many different related initiatives.

2. SOME LT STANDARDIZATION ACTIVITIES

A basic aspect subject to standardization is educational content organization, that is, data models to describe static and dynamic course structure. Static course structure defines the *a priori* relations among course contents (lessons, sections, exercises, etc.), whereas course dynamics determines the particular vision that users have depending on their attributes and previous interactions. To be able to implement both static course organization and dynamic behavior as defined by course developers, a clear and precise definition of the supporting data models is needed.

Going a step further, more elaborated learning designs can be specified using EMLs. An Educational Modelling Language (EML) is a semantic notation to create units of learning to support the reuse of pedagogical entities like learning designs, learning objectives, learning activities, etc. They are used to create highly-structured course material. An EML-based course might offer features such as: re-useable course material, personalised interaction for individual students, media independence, etc.

As common agreements on course structure and design enables the migration of educational contents to different software platforms, data models on final users will facilitate the sharing of student records and other personal information among educational institutions. An agreement is needed on contents (i.e. which information should be provided) and formats. Student data include static information, like name and affiliation, and dynamic information generated as a result of their interaction with educational resources, like grades or completed courses.

In fact, student evaluation and grading is also subject to standardization. Some recommendations about testing and grading are already available. They define taxonomies and vocabularies to be used to de.ne tests. The corresponding data models define aspects ranging from question formatting to evaluation and assessment criteria.

A key aspect in networked educational systems is to define, as precisely as possible, the services offered to potential users. Information on offered courses, related contents, target audience or technical requirements should be made available in a way that permits searching, location and, eventually, access. The trend is to describe this information using metadata. Metadata recommendations for educational systems are one of the most productive activities in the standardization of computer-based learning systems.

Besides commonly accepted data models, an agreement is needed on course encapsulation to facilitate course transfer among institutions. Packaging models define how to encapsulate all elements belonging to a course (educational contents, organizational information, metadata, etc.) in a single entity to be easily transferred from system to system.

To permit content reuse, course contents should be clearly separated from the runtime environment. Runtime environments deliver educational contents, supervise student interaction with contents, and decide the next content to be delivered depending on course statics and dynamics, and previous student interactions. Institutions involved in this standardization process recommend that all logic needed for the runtime environment should be implemented independently from the logic used to define, handle or store educational contents. For this, clear open interfaces are needed. This is another field where standardization efforts have been remarkable.

There are also some proposals identifying common software components and their interfaces for distributed educational systems. As in the case of runtime environments, these components should offer open interfaces to permit peers in other institutions to locate and access offered services. A general agreement on interfaces for distributed systems will permit software and content reuse and interoperability, and incremental distributed system design.

Additional standardization fields include: accessibility, collaboration, glossary and vocabulary, intellectual property and digital rights, localization and internationalization, competency definitions, user interfaces, platform and media or quality standards.

The e-learning standardization process was initiated by several unrelated groups to arrange formats for data interchange. Nowadays, the standardization is mainly driven by a few bodies (c.f. Table 1). These institutions and other organizations and bodies that also participate in this process have a close relationship among them and collaboration is very common. Involved actor include official standardization bodies, massive consumers of learning objects and educational software and other consortiums of both public and private institutions, including individuals, that are interested in the promotion of learning objects and software reuse and interoperation.

Table 1. Main learning standardization bodies

Acronym	Initiative	URL
DoD ADL	US Department of Defense Advanced Distributed Learning	http://www.adlnet.org
AICC	Aviation Industry CBT Committee	http://www.aicc.org
CEN/ISSS/LT	European Committee for Standardization / Information Society Standardization System / Learning Technologies Workshop	http://www.cenorm.be/sh/lt
IEEE LTSC	IEEE Learning Technologies Standardization Committee	http://ltsc.ieee.org
IMS	IMS Project &Consortium	http://www.imsproject.org
ISO/IEC JTC12 SC36	ISO/IEC Joint Committee for the Standardization of Learning Technologies	http://www.jtc1sc36.org

3. THE PANEL

This panel will present LT standardization activities both in Europe and at a world-wide context. For this special attention will be given to specific needs of the electronic design area. Two experts in this field will participate and offer the perspective of learning objects and educational software consumers: Mr. Martin Curley, director of IT Innovation at Intel Corporation, who will bring the needs from the semiconductor industry and Mr. Ricardo Reis, IFIP vice president and professor at the *Universidade Federal do Rio Grande do Sul*, Brazil.

Expertise on LT standardization will be provided by Mr. Frans van Assche, from the European SchoolNet and current vice-chair of CEN/ISSS Workshop on Learning Technologies, and Mr. Rolf Lindner, from the Darmstadt University of Technology, Germany, active member in several communities like CEN/ISSS WS on Learning Technologies and the corresponding group in ISO (ISO/JTC1/SC36).

As a result of the panel discussion we will answer the following questions: Is there a real need for LT standardization in the electronic design domain? Is there any specific need in electronic design different from other areas as far as LT standardization is concerned? Can these needs be overcome with the current outcomes from the LT standardization process? Do we need to open new standardization work to cover specific needs for education in electronic design?

REVIEW OF STANDARDS AND STANDARDISATION ACTIVITIES

Rolf Lindner
Computer Science Department, TU Darmstadt, Germany

Abstract: An short review of standards and standardisation activities in the field of employing information and communication technology for learning, education, and training is provided.

Key words: Learning; Education; Training; Information; Communication; Technology; Standard; Specification

1. INTRODUCTION

Today's electronic design means first of all the design of highly integrated electronic circuits. This design is supported through the use of specific descriptive languages (like VHDL – Very High-level Design Language), tools for VLSI synthesis (like the Synopsis software), and simulators (like HSPICE). Considering Learning, Education and Training (LET) in this field will also include basic knowledge and skills like electrical engineering, computer science, and mathematics. In this panel, the state-of-the-art of education in these fields will be discussed in the context of how they can be further supported and advanced by the use of Information and Communication Technology (ICT), and how learning technology standards can be of help here.

2. EXISTING AND EXPECTED LT STANDARDS

There is a small number of standards which have been developed particularly for the LET field. Below, those existing standards and standards projects are listed and briefly described which are of obvious importance for the support of LET applications.

2.1 Computer Managed Instruction

The most popular approach for ICT LET support is found in the field of Computer Managed Instruction (CMI). These activities can be traced back to the time long before the advent of the World Wide Web and powerful computers like they are at hand to everybody today.

The basic idea of CMI is using computers as multiplicators for human topical and educational expertise. This is done by transforming the human expertise into diverse formats that can be put into operation by machines and that are able to communicate with humans through the help of machines.

Huge amounts of material of this kind have been produced, spending hours and hours of experts' work. Cost-effectiveness is sought through all kinds of multiple use and adaptation to multiple purposes. Interoperability between operational platforms (so-called Learning Management Systems) and domains of learning material is essential for efficiency in this field.

The Content Communication (IEEE 1484.11.x) activities of the IEEE LTSC[1] WG11 comprise a set of correlated standards for the CMI field. This set will contain at least standards for:

- Data Model for Content to Learning Management System Communication (IEEE P1484.11.1)
- ECMAScript Application Programming Interface for Content to Runtime Services Communication (IEEE Std 1484.11.2™-2003)
- XML Binding for Content to Learning Management System Communication

These standards specify the rules how learning material interacts (communicates) with the operational software that provides the material objects. They concern the basic level of interoperability and are therefore of extremely high importance.

2.2 Learning Resource Metadata

Learning Resource Metadata (LRM) comprise semantical, technical and organisational information on learning resources (such as the addressed subject and method of systematic identification, the intended educational use, the technical format and object size, the intellectual property and usage conditions, etc). LRM provide categories and values for search attributes and all the same contextual information related to the use of the resources (e.g. a fraction of the context associated with a learning progress report).

There exists one international standard in this field that arose from the Learning Objects Metadata (LOM - IEEE 1484.12.x) activities of the IEEE LTSC WG12 and has its sources in several previous European initiatives. It comprises a set of correlated standards that will contain at least standards for:

- Learning Object Metadata (IEEE Std 1484.12.1™-2002)
- ISO/IEC 11404 binding for Learning Object Metadata data model (IEEE P1484.12.2)
- XML binding for Learning Object Metadata data model (IEEE P1484.12.3)
- Resource Description Framework (RDF) binding for Learning Object Metadata data model (IEEE P1484.12.4)

Learning resource metadata can be seen as the "conceptional language" of the machines that are engaged to cooperate with humans. LRM are understood by humans and they can be evaluated and processed by machines.

2.3 Participant Information

The term *participant* denotes all kinds of actors in an application environment. In the LET field, typical participants are individuals or groupings of learners, tutors, teachers and authors, but as well software agents that may act as technically implemented substitutes (such as an automatic helpdesk that may substitute a human helper).

Participant information is of the same information category as LRM is. The term "metadata" is, however, not used here.

The only already existing international standard in this group is providing just the data type for a login-string:

- ISO/IEC IS 24703:[2] Information technology — Participant identifiers. The purpose of this Standard is to define the datatype of an identifier for the purposes of identifying participants in learning, education and training. Participants may be users, teachers, agents, groups, organisations, institutions, etc.

This standard was sufficiently simple for achieving international consensus within a short period of time. This is not the case with other standards projects in the field of Information Technology (IT) for LET (ITLET):

- ISO/IEC project 19786: ITLET -- Participant accommodation information

- Proposal ITLET -- Description of language capabilities
- ISO/IEC project 19787: ITLET -- Participant performance information
- ISO/IEC project 24726 ITLET -- Data Model for Specifying Performance Metrics

Accommodation information is provided for the purpose of supporting the adaptation of services to particular preferences, capabilities, disabilities, etc. of participants (e.g.: preferring graphical representation of information for those humans who are particularly gifted to make use of this kind of representation). In this context, the description of language capabilities is part of this approach. There are other initiatives that are important in this field like the recommendations of the World Wide Web Consortium (W3C)[3] related to Web-based material and user interfaces.

The slowness of achieving consensus on information models (and data models) in the field of participant information results from the complexity of these attributes and their structuring inside the information models. Plans for handling these attributes in smaller, coherent groupings reflects the attempt of digesting these issues in smaller bits.

Performance information is provided for the purpose of supporting the adaptation of services to the expectable knowledge, expertise, skill, talent, etc. of participants (e.g. filling particular knowledge gaps, avoiding repetition of information that is apparently known). There are many initiatives doing specification work in this field. As Learning Resource Metadata also address competency (that might arise from making use of a learning resource) it is evident that competency specification is important for both, LRM and Participant Information.

The project on a data model for specifying performance metrics is another attempt of breaking complex information models into fractions, to speed up harmonisation processes, and to allow multiple use of the fractions in diverse standards.

2.4 Conceptual Frameworks

Supporting LET by ICT is an issue that is controversially discussed in and across the diverse disciplines that are involved. Educators are suspicious of technically oriented experts and tend to accuse them of being ignorant regarding educational facts and findings. Technologists are suspicious of educationally oriented experts and tend to accuse them of having no ideas what technology might provide them and how this is related to cost and values added. Conceptual frameworks contribute to this discussion and aim at providing conceptual models and terminology that help the experts of different disciplines to articulate themselves and develop a common understanding of the involved educational and technical phenomena.

The only international standard existing in this field is the IEEE Standard for Learning Technology—Learning Technology Systems Architecture (LTSA) (IEEE Std 1484.1™-2003). This standard focuses mainly on the delivery process of CMI-like educational services. Educators, facing the technically oriented terminology of this standard, do hard to understand its very high abstraction level and are not really willing to accept it and to make intelligent use of it.

Vocabulary and terminology work might well be seen as central contributors to conceptual work. Descriptive formats are planned for communicating the potential of learning environments and their components to all involved stakeholders as well as specifying approaches for quality assurance and management. See e.g.:

- ISO/IEC 19796: ITLET -- Quality Management, Assurance and Metrics

3. APPLICABLE SPECIFICATIONS

Important specifications exist in several further important fields that still need time to enter international standardisation. The following list can only indicate the multitude of standards expected in medium or long terms:

- Education modeling initiatives. These initiatives aim at reflecting educational expertise and experience by specifying rules for organising educational processes and providing appropriate support or orientation where this is advantageous. This may include the provision and operation of any kinds of resources and the set up of appropriate infrastructures for handling them.
  Typical representatives of such initiatives are the IMS[4] Manifests like Simple Sequencing or the IMS Learning Design (derived from a European Educational Modeling Language initiative).
- Harmonisation initiatives for particular kinds of learning material. A typical representative is the IMS Question & Test Interoperability Specification.
- Initiatives for aggregating resources for delivery purposes. The archetype of such initiatives is the AICC[5] Content Packaging, now available as an IMS specification. The Content Aggregation Model in the SCORM specifications is in this group as well as diverse Digital Repositories projects that contribute to these initiatives.

It is not at all possible to be exhaustive here and to list all kinds of initiatives that currently exist and are planned.

4. APPLICABLE INTEGRATIONS

The value of standards is implied by their use. Making efforts of bringing standards into action is of highest importance. There are many regional, national and international activities that do work of this kind and that cannot all be listed here. The currently most prominent initiative of this kind is the ADLs[6] Sharable Content Object Reference Model (SCORM) initiative that currently focuses on the CMI kinds of LET applications.

4.1 SCORM – Sharable Content Object Reference Model

In a previous version (version 1.3), SCORM is denoted to be an "Application Profile". This denotation comes really near to what SCORM represents. The SCORM initiative provides a basic application suite for a community of developers, integrates the most important and recent standards, makes use of prominent specifications that are required for the overall operation, and provides a SCORM-specific, experimental runtime system and very helpful documentation.

The standards, projected standards, and specifications that are integrated into SCORM have been introduced above and are:

- IEEE Data Model For Content Object Communication
- IEEE ECMAScript Application Programming Interface for Content to Runtime Services Communication
- IEEE Learning Object Metadata (LOM)
- IEEE Extensible Markup Language (XML) Schema Binding for Learning Object Metadata Data Model
- IMS Content Packaging
- IMS Simple Sequencing

The main advantage of the SCORM initiative (and of further initiatives of this kind) over individual research and development projects is that of deploying the LT standards by building communities of practice.

5. SUMMARY

Harmonisation in LET means building common agreement on how to make use of ICT support for these applications. This is done in order to enable multiple and modifying use of the results from distributed efforts and thus mark down the cost and increase the quality of this support. Achieving this harmonization without causing unacceptable implications to LET applications is the challenge to be met in standardisation.

6. REFERENCES

1. IEEE Learning Technology Standards Committee (LTSC), http://ltsc.ieee.org/
2. ISO/IEC JTC1 SC36 Information Technology for Learning, Education, and Training, http://jtc1sc36.org/
3. World Wide Web Consortium (W3C), http://www.w3.org/
4. IMS Global Learning Consortium, http://www.imsproject.org/
5. Aviation Industry CBT Committee, http://aicc.org/
6. Advanced Distributed Learning (ADL) Initiative, http://www.adlnet.org/

REQUIREMENTS FOR COMPUTER-AIDED LEARNING FROM THE POINT OF VIEW OF ELECTRONIC DESIGN

Ricardo Reis
Instituto de Informática – Universidade Federal do Rio Grande do Sul, C.P 15064- CEP 91501-970 Porto Alegre, Brazil. E-mail: reis@inf.ufrgs.br

Abstract: The main challenge to set up an computer environment for microelectronics education (design or CAD) is to have a resourceful and specific framework and to made a consortium to fill this framework with tools that really use the advantages and facilities that a computer provides. Comparing to printed books, any figure should be transformed in a tool that could simulate the problem related. It also should allow the student interaction with. The learning flow of a computer-based course should also be different from traditional learning flows. The paper shortly extends this point proposing a new learning flow.

Key words: Electronic design education; CAD; computer aided learning; e-learning systems; standardization; semiconductor industry

1. INTRODUCTION

The existent information and communication technology provide the opportunity to supply tools to improve the learning process. But the availability of a new generation of computer-based education systems, that really use the available technology, is still fare away. Also, when we talk about computer-based education we should consider two situations: the first one, e-learning as a remote or self-learning system and a second situation where the computer-based system is used in a regular learning process inside an education institution. In both situations we have some similar specifications and needs, but we have also different ones. For example, in a remote education procedure where it is needed student evaluation or grading, it is needed a system that can do the certification that the right student is doing the exams. If we are using a computer-based system in a regular course in an educational institution we don't need a similar system, because the exams can be done in a specific room and time.

2. ELECTRONIC DESIGN LEARNING

The two main challenges in the development of an educational learning system are the learning framework itself and the development of the course contents. The learning framework can be divided in two parts: the administrative framework (that handles, for example, student access, student progress supervision) and the learning framework. The learning framework should control the learning flow by giving access to the modules related to a specific step of learning or to a specific learning module. The construction of the learning framework needs the definition of a standard for this framework. This standard should also guide the educators responsible for the development of the learning material. This a major task when we really construct a learning system that really use the computational facilities that are available nowadays. The development of the contents of a course must be divided between a large number of educators because the authoring of each learning module demands an enormous amount of work. We can easily conclude this if we compare a good learning system with a didactic book. We can accept that each static figure of a book could be replaced by an animated one when it is part of a computer-based learning system. For example, a figure of an atom in a book can be replaced by a simulation tool that emulates how an atom works. This "animated figure" can improve the learning process because it gives to the student a more real information of how an atom is composed and how it works. Another example, a figure of a transistor cut from a book should be replaced by an animated figure constructed as a simulation tool that shows how the p and n carriers moves in function of changes in the transistor input signal (gate signal). This tool could give an interactive experience for the student that could change the values of the gate signal and observe the possible changes in the flow of carriers.

So, for example, if we only consider the development of a basic computer-based microelectronic course based on a traditional book and if we change the figures by animated and interactive ones, the amount of authoring work is enormous and should be divided between several educators. As consequence, we need a standard to organize the process of construction and authoring a course that is made by different educators. It is also needs tools to help course construction by the educators (Indrusiak et al, 2003). A point that is not easy to solve is the different vocabulary between educators, but a tool could guide educators to construct texts with a more common vocabulary.

We also face another problem, how to set up a team of educators to construct a course, educators that probably work in different institutions around the world. The course framework must also consider that the educators and students could use different computer and operating system platforms. So, the standards must consider these different environments.

An Educational Modelling Language (EML) is also important to help educators to customize a course to a specific curriculum or to a specific student.

In the Electronic Design area we could divide the learning contents in several major modules. As example, one possible and simple division could be:

- microelectronic basics
- digital design
- analog design
- test
- CAD

Each one of these modules has some specific needs or characteristics. For example, the design of an integrated circuit demands the use of a big set of CAD tools. So, the students must have a good experience with the use of these CAD tools. The challenge is that the professional CAD systems are composed by a big set of tools that were developed during years by different teams of professionals, several times in different companies that were acquired along the years. There is also a lack of good tutorials to guide the student and designers in the learning process of how to use the CAD tools.

3. COMPUTER-BASED LEARNING METHODS

The use of computer-based learning systems in a regular course can change the approach or flow of learning. One of the problems that we can face in a course is the presence of students with different backgrounds. If we use a learning flow where as first step the student must do a self-learning procedure, with the use of a computer-based learning system, then the student with different backgrounds will take less or more time to learn the lesson but all the student could reach a same level of knowledge at the end of the lesson. This could be certified by a self-test done by the student himself. The professor could also remotely monitor the learning flow of each student. This an important feedback to the professor because he can know which points he should improve in the learning material, as well which parts he need to strengthen in the second step of the course. As a second step, the students could attend a course with the participation of a professor. In this second step the professor can consider that the students have the same knowledge about the subject. The students can put questions about the lessons they have studied by themselves and the educator can also go deep in the subject.

4. LEARNING MODULE ANIMATION EXAMPLE

One example of the substitution of a book figure by an animated object is the substitution of a figure representing a schematic at logic level by an animated object. It is possible to identify by colours the values of the inputs as well the voltage values in the connections (Fig. 1) (Casacurta et al, 2003). So, the student can change the value of an input by a click over it and he can observe the propagation of this input over the logic circuit by a change in the color of the connections belonging to a node which value changes in function of the input change.

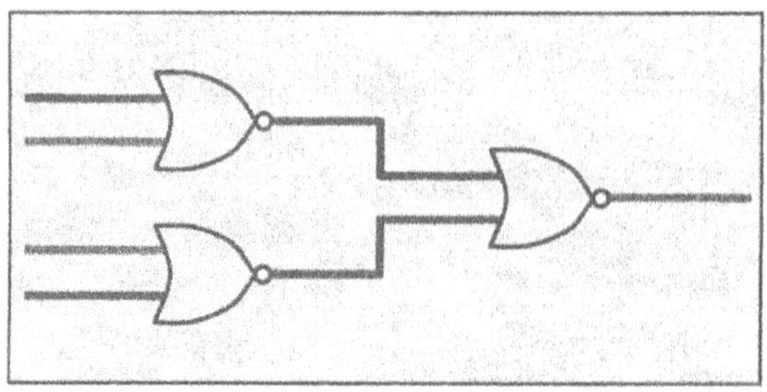

Figure 1. Example of logic circuit with inputs, output and connections colors related to voltage value (Casacurta et al, 2003)

Some features can be associated to this animated figure. It is possible to change the view of a logic cell or a group of logic cells to see its layout, where the colors of lines and regions are set in function of their voltage value (Fig. 2). This layout view simulates the view provide by an Electron-Beam microscope, but in color. It is also possible to control the velocity of propagation of input changes to help the understanding of signals propagation. This small example shows that a computer-based course can provide to the student a much better understanding when he has the help of animated objects that he can interact with.

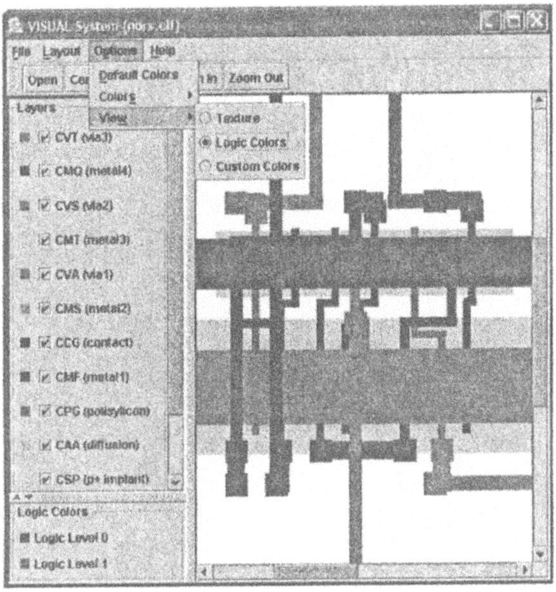

Figure 2. Example of circuit layout where connections and regions have colors related to their voltage value (Casacurta et al, 2003)

5. CONCLUSIONS

The development of computer-based learning systems demands standards as well frameworks to plug learning materials and to manage the learning flow. It is also necessary to define standards and tools to guide educators in the development and authoring of learning materials. These learning materials should really use the facilities that a computer can provide, like simulations and interactions with animated objects. A big challenge is to put together a large group of educators to prepare a course using a large set of animated figures and simulated objects.

A learning framework should work with any computer or operating system platform.

ACNOWLEDGEMENTS

We want to acknowledge Casacurta and Almeida for the work that they have done and that is used as example in section 4.

REFERENCES

Indrusiak, L. S., Reis, R. A. L., Glesner, M., Alcántara G., Hörmann S., Steinmetz, R. Reducing Authoring Costs of Online Training in Microelectronics Design by Reusing Design Documentation Content. In: IEEE Microelectronics System Education, Anaheim, June 1-2, 2003. pp 57-58.

Casacurta, A., Almeida, M., Reis, R. , 2003, A Visual Simulation Tool at Layout Level, in: IEEE Microelectronics System Education, Anaheim, June 1-2, 2003, pp. 110-111.

LEARNING TECHNOLOGY STANDARDIZATION IN EUROPE

Implications in electronic design

Frans Van Assche
European Schoolnet. E-mail: frans.van.assche@eun.org

Abstract: Learning Technology Standardization in Europe addresses some specific issues which are complementary to worldwide standardization activities.

Key words: E-learning systems; Learning Technology; Standardization; Europe

1. INTRODUCTION

E-Learning has many aspects including learning related, content related, data and metadata, infrastructure, systems and environments, administration, teacher and student communities. Each of these aspects is subject to standardization one way or another and the effective and efficient operation of any educational system is greatly affected by the degree of interoperability reached. Indeed interoperability is an enabler for sharing pedagogy, infrastructures, tools and resources (digital and non-digital including human resources). It has been well documented that interoperability and the use of standards has a number of benefits in terms of lower costs, greater supply, higher accessibility and availability, higher quality, and a shorter delivery time. However, sharing of data, content, tools and services can only be achieved when clear technical agreements are made between all parties concerned. The more global this agreement is, the greater the benefit. In this respect, Europe standardization and pre-standardization efforts seek adoption of European work at the global level and vice-versa. Because of its multicultural and multilingual nature, Europe puts great emphasis on internationalization and localization of standards and specifications.

2. STANDARDIZATION BODIES AND CONSORTIA

The European standardization body is CEN/ISSS. In addition Europe has a number of standardization consortia and organizations which represent European user communities. The most important ones are presented in section 2.2.

2.1 CEN/ISSS

The European standardization body, also in the field of education, is CEN/ISSS. CEN stands for 'Commité Europ€en de Normalisation' or the European Committee for Standardization. CEN was founded in 1961 by the national standards bodies in the European Economic Community and EFTA countries.

Today CEN is contributing to the objectives of the European Union and European Economic Area with voluntary technical standards which promote free trade, the safety of workers and consumers, interoperability of networks, environmental protection, exploitation of research and development programmes, and public procurement. CEN/ISSS is important because it is an accredited standardisation body. This means that its members, currently 28 European Countries are legally obliged to implement the standards issued by CEN/ISSS. In the field of e-learning, there are two workshops (i.e. working groups): the Workshop on Learning Technologies and the Workshop on ICT Skills and Profiles.

The Workshop on Learning Technologies (WSLT) was established in February 1999. Its objective is to encourage the effective development and use of relevant and appropriate standards for learning technologies for Europe.

The WSLT decided, as a matter of principle, not to duplicate work already being done elsewhere, but to ensure that diverse European requirements are properly addressed by global initiatives. Specifications, agreements, guidelines or recommendations are developed when no initiative addressing the identified requirements is in place yet or when global solutions developed elsewhere need to be localized to European requirements.

Finally, in the domain of eLearning and eTraining, considerable efforts are invested under the IST programme of the European Commission as well as via many national or European initiatives. Projects producing specifications, architectures, reference models, etc., with the intention of attracting broader support and recognition of their work, can use the Workshop as a useful tool for reaching a European-wide consensus on their deliverables.

The Workshop on ICT Skills and Profiles was established in April 2003 and addresses initially two subject areas:

For IT practitioners' profiles at professional level the objectives are:

- Validate the skill/competence profiles developed so far by the Career Space (Industry) Consortium
- Recommend respective industry standards for skills and competencies profiles
- Encourage the effective use and wider application of the respective professional and occupational profiles for IT practitioners as standards for employment and careers in Europe

For curriculum development guidelines for Higher Education Providers the objective is to validate the curricula development profiles developed so far by the Career Space (Industry) Consortium.

2.2 Other European standardization players

First of all there are the national standardization bodies such as DIN (Germany), AFNOR (France), BSI (UK), UNI (Italy). They organize standardization activities is different ways. They often organize standardization in conjunction with e-government. Other countries would look at e-standards as a whole while some would have different standardization structures for dealing with standards in education. For example in the UK, CETIS deals with Higher and Further Education, while other institutions will deal with vocational training, schools, etc. Countries may choose to have a representation at the standardization bodies ISO and/or CEN/ISSS.

The ARIADNE (Alliance of Remote Instructional Authoring and Distribution Networks for Europe) Foundation for the European Knowledge Pool was created to exploit and further develop the results of the ARIADNE and ARIADNE II European Projects, which created tools and methodologies for producing, managing and reusing computer-based pedagogical elements and telematics supported training curricula. Together with the IMS Global consortium it is at the basis of the Learning Object Metadata standards issued by IEEE. Validation of the tools and concepts took place in various academic and corporate sites across Europe and was encouraging enough to go ahead with this idea of non-commercial exploitation.

European Schoolnet (EUN) is an international partnership of 26 European Ministries of Education developing learning for schools, teachers and pupils across Europe. EUN provides insight into educational use of ICT (information and communications technology) in Europe for policy-makers and education professionals. EUN is actively involved in the work of CEN/ISSS WSLT, IMS Global consortium, IMS Europe, and the Schools Interoperability Framework. The EUN has organized its standardization work in an international action on the Learning Interoperability Framework for Europe (LIFE).

The eLearning Industry Group, eLIG, is an open consortium of leading ICT (information and communications technology) companies and eLearning content providers who seek to promote eLearning throughout Europe, in schools, universities, the workplace and homes. The eLearning Industry Group was launched on 25 April 2002. ELIG has a project group on Open Standards. Its objective is to encourage the adoption of and participation in the development of open technical standards for eLearning, so that international open standards, together with technological innovation and free market competition will deliver solutions that encourage broad participation in eLearning.

Recently, European IMS, was incorporated in the Netherlands as a separate non-profit organisation. European IMS is an offshoot of the IMS Global consortium and seeks to ensure participation and use by Europe in open specifications, support adoption of specifications by European vendors, promote an inclusive, open, accessible, European and Global elearning market (i.e. "level the playing field"), and promote the development of open source libraries to foster implementation and innovation.

The European Commission is last but not least an important player in the field of standardisation. The European Commission is organised in different directorates which each have a specific emphasis and strategy for supporting standardisation work. For example, the Directorate for industry supports the standardisation work through direct funding of work items proposed by CEN/ISSS; the Directorate for Information Society Technologies requires for research projects to explicitly describe the contribution to national or international standards; the Directorate for Education and Culture stimulates the contribution and adoption by the user communities.

3. STANDARDIZATION ACTIVITIES IN EUROPE

The European organizations dealing with standardization, pre-standardization, and adoption of standards and specifications are active in a number of areas related to learning resources, learning management, learning communities, and institutional administration. In addition some standards and specifications address issues across these areas. The activities are too numerous to be elaborated in the context of this paper and the ones listed are merely examples of the work being carried out.

In the area of learning resources we find the only standard in the field of education, the IEEE Standard for Learning Object Metadata (LOM). Apart from delivering the basis for this standard through the ARIADNE project, Europe contributes in this area, through work on internationalization and localization (including translation) of the LOM, multi-linguality aspects, the relationship to national curriculums, copy-rights and digital rights, and more adoption issues in general. Furthermore, much work has been done on a more comprehensive model for education resulting in various educational modeling languages which eventual find their way in specifications such as IMS learning design.

The field of learning management addresses issues such as student information, student progress, the learner information package, gradebooks, etc. In short everything necessary to manage the learning process. In this area European institutions contribute by activities such as providing a European Model for Learner Competencies, elaborating the concept of an ePortfolio, and elaborating a method of recording the training carried out and skills acquired during a period of work experience, undertaken as part of an on-going training programme, in another European country (EuroPass).

Apart from resources and learning management, the field of education requires substantial support in establishing different communities. This encompasses communication and collaboration tools for learning, authoring material, exchanging technical expertise. In this area one can build upon quite a number of existing standards and specifications ranging from vCard to the whole IMS enterprise specifications. However very little work has been done on harnessing existing technologies and standards for the benefit of the education community.

A prominent institution administration specification is the School Interoperability Framework (SIF). SIF is an initiative of North-American industry. In Europe a European version of the SIF has been elaborated in the OASIS project which was reviewed by CEN/ISSS. The CEN/ISSS WSLT reviewed the SIF Infrastructure, Architecture, Message Processing Layer, the Transport Layer, the SIF Data model, and elaborated internationalisation and harmonisation recommendations.

Apart from the four areas above, Europe addresses a number of topics that support those areas including work on application profiling, harmonization of vocabularies, quality issues with respect to all processes related to education, accessibility to resources and software tools, interoperability and brokerage of resources and services. Many of these activities happen in close collaboration with international standards bodies and consortia.

PART FOUR

E-LEARNING IN SYSTEM DESIGN

OPTIMILLER: AN INTERACTIVE ENVIRONMENT THAT HELPS STUDENTS IN THE UNDERSTANDING, DESIGN AND OPTIMIZATION OF MILLER ELECTRONIC OSCILLATOR CIRCUITS FOR QCM SENSORS

L. Rodríguez-Pardo, J. Fariña, C. Gabrielli[1], H. Perrot, R. Brendel[2] and M. J. González

Dpto. T. Electrónica, IEA Barrié de la Maza, Univ. Vigo, Spain.. E-mail: jfarina@uvigo.es; [1]Lab. Interfaces et Systèmes Electrochimiques, LISE-CNRS, Paris, France; [2]Lab. Physique et Métrologie des Oscillateurs, CNRS, Besancon, France

Abstract: The quartz crystal oscillator used as mass sensor in damping media suffers significant losses implying the need to adapt the oscillator design to compensate them. In this paper, a CAD tool to help students in the understanding, design and optimization of Miller oscillators for the realization of high sensitivity quartz crystal microbalance (QCM) sensors for liquid media is presented. This tool is oriented not only to the practical teaching of advanced Thickness Shear Mode (TSM) acoustic wave sensors for mass changes detection, but also to aid designers in the development of QCM sensors.

Key words: CAD tool; Miller oscillator; QCM

1. INTRODUCTION

The quartz crystal microbalance is a thin plate of piezoelectric crystal with one rigidly attached metal film electrode on each side. The crystal is made to vibrate at its resonant frequency by inserting it in the feedback path of an oscillator circuit. In gravimetric applications, the crystal is in direct contact with its environment and the changes in the crystal resonant frequency, caused by environmental changes, are used as analytical signal.

In particular, the changes of mass deposited on the crystal surface, are directly reflected in frequency changes in such a way that an increase in mass, will cause the circuit oscillate more slowly.

Despite the long history of quartz crystal electronic oscillators circuits, the success of their use as mass sensors in damping media, still depends strongly on the designer's ability and experience. The design must be adapted so that the oscillation remains in spite of the large reduction that the quality factor of the quartz experiences in those media. Although it is not difficult assemble an oscillator that works, the procedure required to build an oscillator that meets some predetermined requirements is not so simple. In the case of oscillators to be used as mass sensors in damping media, this kind of procedure has not been sufficiently developed.

With the objective of providing a tool that allows students to understand the operation of the quartz crystal oscillators, the software system OptiMiller has been developed. OptiMiller is a CAD tool that aims at helping not only students but also users in the design and optimization of Miller electronic oscillator circuits for QCM sensors [8].

Different oscillator circuit topologies are used in QCM. This tool is based on Miller oscillator topology. The basic structure of a Miller oscillator is represented in Fig. 1 [1,2,3].

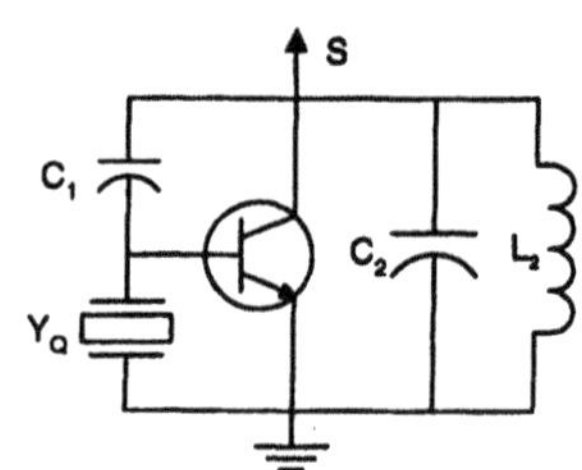

Figure 1. Basic structure of Miller oscillator circuit

This tool allows the tasks indicated in the Fig. 2 to be automated. These tasks are described in the next point.

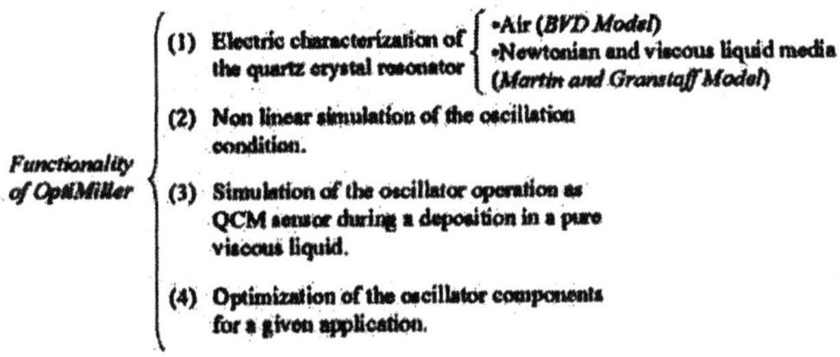

Figure 2. Tasks carried out by OptiMiller

2. OPTIMILLER FACILITIES

The interaction with the user is carried out through the main window of the program, which consists of a menu and a button bar that enable the use of different tools. This window is represented in Fig. 3.

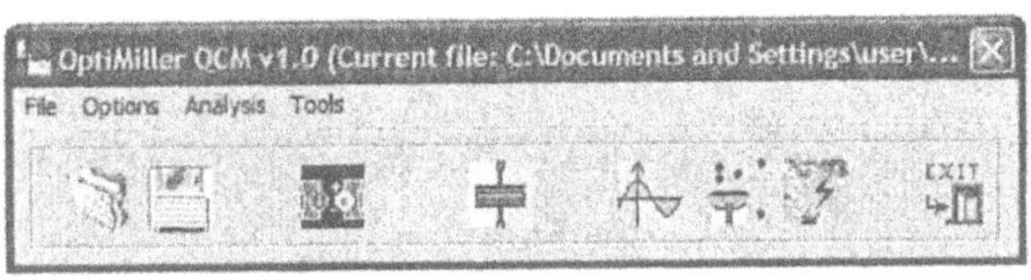

Figure 3. Main window of OptiMiller

2.1 BVD equivalent circuit

The quartz impedance Window allows students the quartz crystals performance to be understood in different environments (e.g. air or damping media).

OptiMiller enables users the electric characterization of the quartz crystal resonator to be executed. The user has to introduce the experimental values for the Butterworth Van Dyke (BVD) equivalent circuit, measured by means of an impedance analyzer, or the crystal physical characteristics and the working environment characteristics, defining the quartz. In Fig. 4, the quartz impedance window has been represented. Through this window, the user can do the following tasks:

- Obtain the BVD equivalent circuit of the quartz resonator.
- Obtain the characteristic frequencies of the resonator.

- Obtain the graphical visualization of the impedance according to the frequency.
- Store the results in a text file.

OptiMiller enables the student to obtain the BVD equivalent circuit of an AT quartz resonator starting from its dimensions and physical parameters, as much as in air as in a newtonian and purely viscous liquid medium. In the last case, the density and viscosity of the liquid characterize the influence of the medium in the behavior of the resonator. The tool calculates the BVD equivalent circuit modified by Martin and Granstaff for a quartz crystal loaded by a liquid [4]. The application also facilitates that the experimental values obtained by means of impedance analyzer can be introduced, for its later use in the simulations of the behavior of the oscillator.

Once the electric circuit of the quartz has been defined, the program allows calculating series and parallel frequencies, minimum and maximum phase frequencies, and minimum module frequencies, as well as the resonator quality factor, in order to define the operation point of the sensor [5].

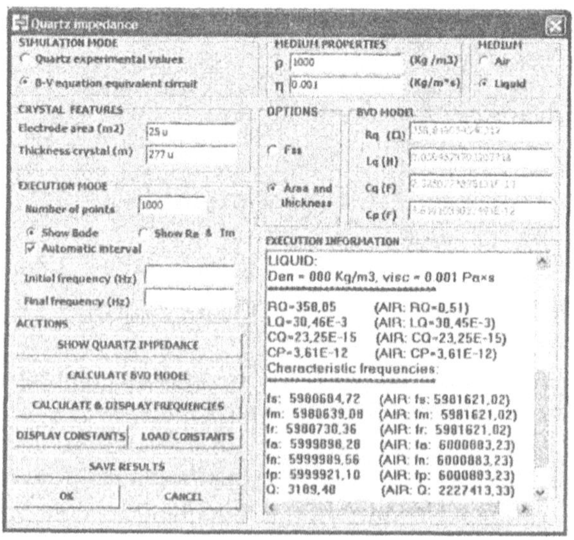

Figure 4. Quartz Impedance Window of OptiMiller

In Fig. 4, an example of obtaining the BVD equivalent circuit and the characteristic frequencies of a quartz resonator is shown. In this case, the calculation was made for a quartz resonator of thickness 277μm and area of electrode 25 mm^2, in air and submerged in distilled water at 25°C (density 1000 Kg/m^3, viscosity 0.001 Pa·s). The obtained values are summarized in

Table 1. In this way, the student can easily compare the values obtained in both media, and to observe the influence of the liquid in the behavior of the resonator.

Table 1. OptiMiller results for BVD equivalent circuit and characteristic frequencies in the case of quartz thickness 277μm and area of electrode 25 mm^2, in air and submerged in distilled water at 25°C (density 1000 Kg/m3, viscosity 0.001 Pa·s)

	Air	Distilled water
R_Q (Ω)	0.51	358.8
C_Q (fF)	23.25	23.25
L_Q (mH)	30.45	30.46
C_P (pF)	3.61	3.61
f_s (MHz)	5.981621	5.980685
f_m (MHz)	5.981621	5.980639
f_r (MHz)	5.981621	5.980730
f_a (MHz)	6.000883	5.999898
f_n (MHz)	6.000883	5.999990
f_p (MHz)	6.000883	5.999921
Q	2227413	3189.5

Another utility contributed by OptiMiller for the understanding of the quartz resonators operation is the possibility to have a graphical visualization of its impedance according to the frequency, so that student can appreciate visually the damping of the resonator when it works in a liquid medium. This graphic representation of the impedance can be shown through the Bode diagram (module and phase), or by means of the observation of the real and imaginary part. The graphic resolution and the interval of frequencies to be represented can be selected. To obtain the graphic representations, the program connects with the mathematical simulation tool Matlab (MathWorks Inc.), sending it the data to be represented which undertakes the graphic realization as it is shown in Fig. 5.

Moreover, OptiMiller enables the storage of calculations done in a text file in code ASCII: the values of the elements of the resonator BVD equivalent circuit, the characteristic frequencies and the impedance values. In this way, the student can use them in other simulation environments.

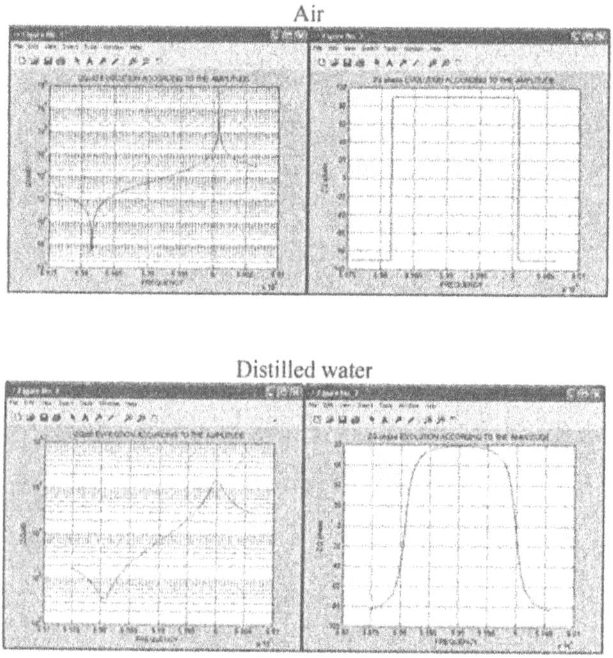

Figure 5. Graphic representation of the impedance resonator bode diagram for the example of Fig. 4 and Table 1

2.2 Active device model

The active device model Window allows students the amplifier non-linear performance to be shown by means of different graphics.To carry out the non-linear simulation of the oscillation condition of a Miller oscillator circuit it is necessary to characterize the amplifier. In order to do this, the non-linear behaviour of the active device is described by using non-linear admittance parameters (y parameters) whose values are a function of the input signal level. For this reason, the user has to introduce these parameters in relation to the oscillation amplitude. The introduction of the data is made by means of a text file that contains a table with the values in ASCII. These parameters are obtained by using an electrical simulator like SPICE or from an impedance analyzer. These values will be used later by OptiMiller in the simulation of the oscillation condition to obtain the frequency and amplitude of the output signal of the circuit [6].In addition, once the amplifier data have been introduced, OptiMiller allows student the graphical visualization of the amplifier Y parameters according to the amplitude, in logarithmic or linear scale, connecting with Matlab. In Fig. 6 an example of the variation of the transconductance of an OTA660 amplifier for 6MHz is represented.

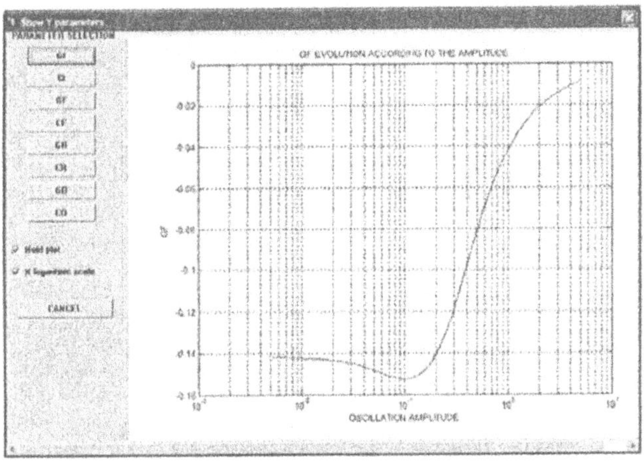

Figure 6. Admittance parameters visualization Window. Variation of the transconductance of an OTA660 amplifier working at 6MHz

2.3 Oscillation condition: non-linear simulation

Once the values both the BVD equivalent circuit and the amplifier admittance parameters according to the amplitude have been introduced, OptiMiller enables the students to carry out the non linear simulation of the oscillation condition of a Miller oscillator circuit [6]. In order to do this, the tool provides the oscillator condition simulation Window, represented in Fig. 7. This window enables to specify the value of the passive components of the Miller oscillator circuit (feedback capacitor, C_1, and filter L_2C_2). Once these values are specified, the user can simulate the operation of the defined circuit in order to check the oscillation condition and to find both the frequency and amplitude that verify the oscillation condition. Moreover, OptiMiller enables the students to graphically study the transient state of the oscillator (values of frequency according to the amplitude), as well as to store the results of the simulation in an ASCII text file.

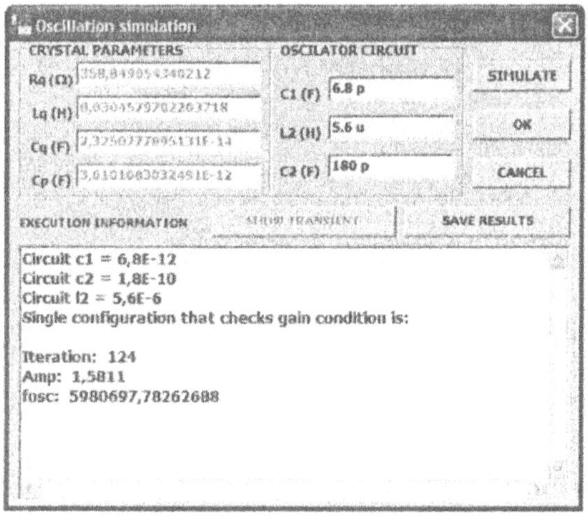

Figure 7. Simulation of oscillator condition Window

2.4 QCM sensor simulation

The OptiMiller deposition simulation Window allows students the behavior of the Miller oscillator as sensor QCM during a deposition of mass [7] to be understood, that is, it is possible simulating a mass deposition and showing the crystal oscillation frequency evolution during that deposition (see Fig. 8).

The user should specify the following parameters:

- *Deposition velocity*: quantity of mass that will be deposited in the electrode (in grams for unit of time and for square centimeter).
- *Velocity of change of the medium*: index that indicates the variation of the liquid medium in which the electrode is submerged for unit of time (product density for viscosity of the medium) [1].
- *Duration of the deposition*: expressed in units of time.

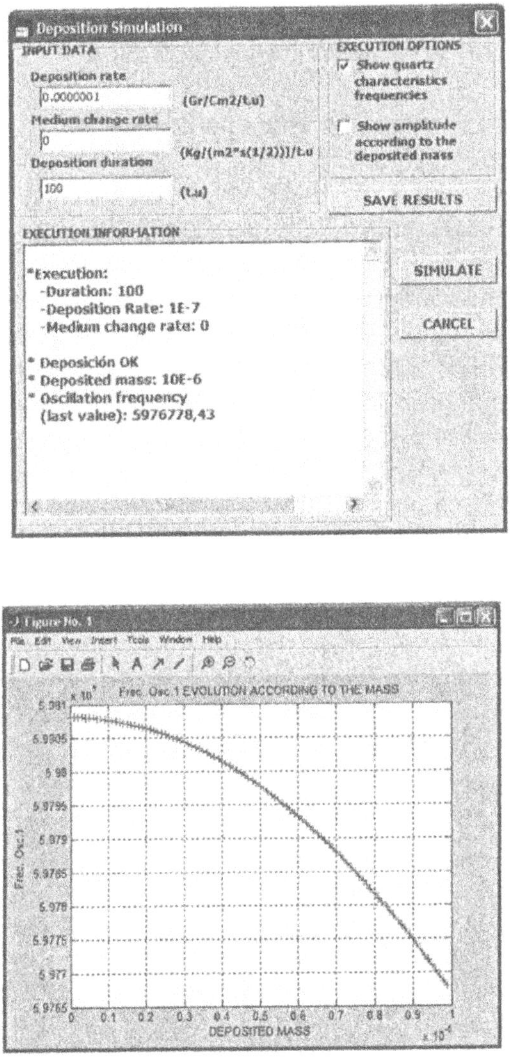

Figure 8. Window of simulation of the oscillator behavior during a mass deposition

OptiMiller modifies the quantity of deposited mass and the characteristics of the medium with respect to the time, and it carries out a non linear simulation of the oscillation condition at each instant to calculate both the oscillation amplitude and frequency that fulfill the gain condition. The tool indicates as a result whether the oscillation is stable or not along the whole deposition, and it enables to graphically observe the evolution of the oscillation frequency according to the deposited mass. In addition, OptiMiller enable the calculation of the new characteristic frequencies of the quartz to the end of the deposition, as well as observing the evolution of the oscillation amplitude according to the deposited mass.

2.5 Optimization of Miller oscillators for liquid media

OptiMiller provides a tool that helps the user in the design and optimization of Miller oscillators for its use as QCM sensor in liquid media [9].

The access to the optimization tool of is carried out through the window represented in the Fig. 9. This window enables the good values of the components of a Miller oscillator electronic circuit to be obtained for a given application. The optimization is carried out starting from the data of the quartz equivalent circuit, the characteristics of the active device and the initial values of the feedback capacitor C_1 and of the filter components C_2L_2. To characterize the sensor application and therefore the working operation conditions of the oscillator, it is necessary to indicate both the quantity of maximum mass that will be deposited in the sensor electrode, and the area of the same one (to calculate the superficial density of mass). Besides the characteristics of the liquid medium in which the deposition will be carried out must be indicated (by means of the density-viscosity product). The program redesigns the circuit by means of the execution of an optimization algorithm [9], and it calculates, should they exist, the values for the components (C_1, C_2 and L_2) such that the circuit is able to oscillate for the conditions of the suitable application.

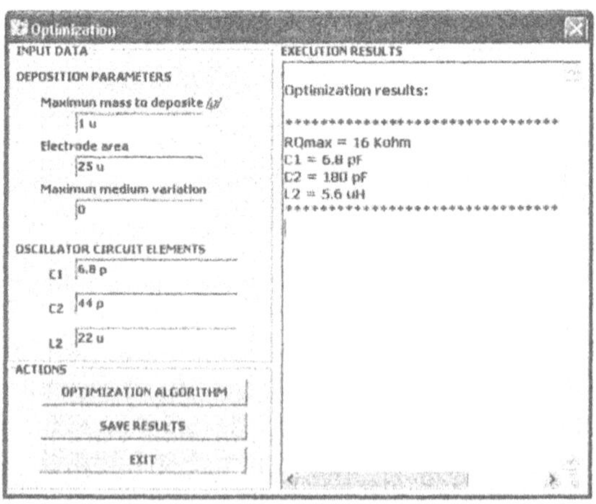

Figure 9. Optimization Window

3. SUMMARY

A computer program for QCM based on Miller oscillator circuit is presented. This tool allows students to understand and to analyze the performance quartz crystal microbalance based on Miller oscillator circuit. In addition, OptiMiller helps users in the design and the optimization of the Miller oscillator circuit. It gives to the designer the variation of the important parameters to work within the specifications under all conditions.

Which this tool can be obtained the BVD equivalent circuit of the AT quartz from its dimensions and physical parameters, both in air and in pure viscous and newtonian liquid media. In this last case, the density and viscosity of the liquid characterize the influence of the media. The program also enables the user to introduce experimental quartz values to be used in the simulations of the oscillator behavior. With the purpose of carrying out simulations taking into account the non linear behavior of the active device, the values of the admittance parameters of the active device as a function of the amplitude can be introduced. Once the values of the oscillator components were specified, the non linear simulation of the oscillation condition, the simulation of the oscillator operation as QCM sensor during a deposition in liquid, and the optimization of the circuit components for a given application can be carried out. This last process consists of calculating new values for the components, so that the new circuit is able to oscillate under conditions of maximum mass to deposit and viscosity of the media.

REFERENCES

1. R. Matthys, Crystal Oscillators Circuits, Ed. John Wiley & Sons, ISBN 0-471-87401-9, 1983.
2. S. Cosnier, H. Perrot, R. Wessel, Electroanal., 13 (2001) 971.
3. K. Bizet, C. Gabrielli, H. Perrot, Analusis Eur JAC, 7 (1999) 609.
4. V.E. Granstaff and S.J. Martin. Characterization of a thickness-shear mode quartz resonator with multiple nonpiezoelectric layers, J. Appl. Phys. 75(3), pp. 1319-1329, 1994.
5. Publication and Proposed Revision of IEEE Standard 177-1966 "Standard Definitions and Methods of Measurement for Piezoelectric Vibrators" IEEE Transactions on Ultrasonics, Ferroelectrics, and Frequency Control, Vol. 40. No. 1. pp. 1-20, january 1993.
6. Brendel, R. Marianneau, G., Blin, T.y Brunet, M. Computer Aided Design of Quartz Crystal Oscillators, IEEE Transactions on Ultrasonics, Ferroelectrics, and Frequency Control, Vol. 42, No. 4, pp. 700-708, july 1995.
7. G. Sauerbrey, Verwendung von Schwingquarzen zur Wägung dünner Schichten und zur Mikrowägung, Z. Phys. 155 (1959) 206.
8. L. Rodriguez-Pardo, J. Fariña, M.J. González-Braña, C. Gabrielli, H. Perrot and R. Brendel, *Ieee sensors*, 2003, 0-7803-8133-5/03 pp. 534-538.
9. L. Rodriguez-Pardo, J. Fariña, C. Gabrielli, H. Perrot and R. Brendel, *to be published*.

EDUCATIONAL TOOLS FOR INDUSTRIAL COMMUNICATION NETWORKS DESIGN

P. Marino, H. Hernandez, M.A. Dominguez, F. Poza, F. Machado
DTE, University of Vigo, Galicia, Spain.
{ pmarino, mdgomez, fpoza, fmachado } @uvigo.es, hhdez@nuyoo.utm.mx

Abstract In this paper it is presented the state-of-the-art in fieldbus technology, according with the authors' particular experience, giving diverse points of view about the necessary skills for using development tools and involved electronic devices, currently present in the training market. Given its growing impact all over automotive industry, an introduction about the CAN fieldbus is presented, along with the software and hardware tools that configure training environments for this protocol. Following the two different CAN nodes developed currently by the authors, using the aforementioned tools, are presented. Finally, future developments with great potential in the education of engineers, and fieldbus training applied to automotive industry and others, are also mentioned.

Keywords: Instructional design, Education of Information Technologies, Industrial Fieldbuses and Development.

1. Introduction

According to the definition of IEC (International Electrotechnical Commission) and ISA (Instrument Society of America) a fieldbus is a digital, serial, multidrop, data bus for communication with low-level industrial control and instrumentation devices such as transducers, actuators and local controllers. Fieldbuses are serial information transference buses used in the industry and orientated to data transmission in discrete and continuous processes. Before the appearance of fieldbuses, the connections between process units (PLCs, controllers, CNC machines, etc.) and field devices (sensors and actuators) were point-to-point links. It means complex (a lot of wires) and expensive (in time and money) installations. Also the maintenance and modification tasks were harder. These problems are solved with fieldbuses, because all devices are connected through a single physical medium (twisted pair, coaxial, two wires, optical fibre, etc.) extended over the whole area of the distributed control process system (cost reduction). So new devices can be added connecting it to the fieldbus without additional wiring (easy maintenance and modification). Other advantage of fieldbuses is that allow the distribution of the intelligence of the control process. So the intelligence comes close to the sensor devices (smart sensors with capability of computation and communication) [Mariño, 2003].

Fieldbuses represent the lower level of the communications networks in a flexible manufacturing system. In this way, a fieldbus like a LAN (Local Area Network), fulfils the two first layers of the OSI model (physical and data link) and the last layer (application). Besides it has a layer for the management of the previous ones. But fieldbuses offer shorter messages (commands, events, measures, etc.), with answer times between 100ms and 5ms (operation in real-time), and high security in the communication (reliability), over distances from 200m up to 2km, with data rates lower than 1Mbps. Usually the physical medium is a pair wire with EIA RS-485 interfaces, although applications with coaxial cable, optical fibre, radio a infrareds can be found.

Nowadays the total standardisation of fieldbuses is not reached, [Marsh, 1999] but some organisations have indicated configuration profiles that are useful as a guide for the different manufacturers in the design of their field equipment.

2. Curriculum design for fieldbus skills

The authors have been involved in research and development projects about fieldbus technology for seven years [Mariño et al., 1996]. Also, during that time, they have run curricula university programs and directed several Ph.D. thesis, about different topics in that area of knowledge [Mariño et al., 1999]. Their experience in the state-of-the-art has provided diverse points of view about the necessary skills for using development tools and involved electronic devices currently present in the training market. A curriculum about fieldbus knowledge was designed following several topics:

- Formal description languages in order to specify complex system requirements in an ambiguities free and complete way. Two languages were used: LOTOS and SDL.
- Complete specification of several fieldbus standards at the data link level of the OSI model, based on LOTOS and SDL, for making analysis and simulations of possible alternative solutions for a system. Thus it can be checked what alternative is more adequate and the right choice can be made at the design stage, which could bring important economic and time savings. For this specification two relevant European fieldbuses were selected: PROFIBUS and WorldFIP [Mariño et al., 1997].
- Design and implementation of nodes for the selected fieldbuses by means of development tools and prototype boards provided by manufacturers. An interesting line of research was opened when FPGA chips (Field

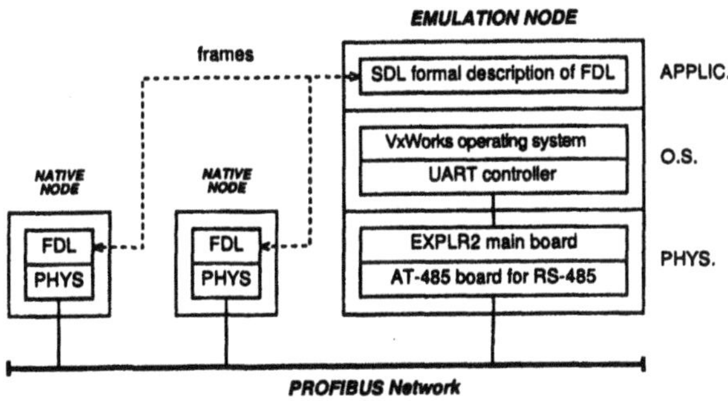

Figure 1. Profibus emulation node

Programmable Gate Array) were included for the design and implementation of that nodes [Lías et al., 2000].

- Design and implementation of nodes for the selected fieldbuses by means of RTOs (Real-Time Operating Systems). The growing interest in embedded systems, that can be reconfigured to use several fieldbus standards, gives another line of research in emulation nodes based on tools for developing environments (Fig. 1). For this purpose it was selected the Tornado tool which runs on the VxWorks real-time operating system, and is manufactured by Windriver Systems Inc.

In following sections it is made a short description about specification languages and fieldbuses used by the authors in their university lessons.

2.1 LOTOS language

LOTOS is a formal description technique (FDT) standardised by ISO to design services and protocols used in the communication of open systems (OSI). The system behaviour in LOTOS is specified as a succession of events or actions.

Using LOTOS the authors have specified the whole data link layer of the OSI model (level 2), for the two European fieldbuses PROFIBUS and WorldFIP.

2.2 SDL language

SDL is a standardised language used to specify and describe systems. It was developed by the ITU-T (International Telecommunications Union section Telecommunications), formerly CCITT (Comité Consultatif International Telégraphique et Teléfonique), and published as the Z.100 ITU-T Recommendation.

With SDL the authors have specified the whole data link layer of the European fieldbus PROFIBUS. Given that both FDTs where used to specify the same fieldbus (PROFIBUS), a comparative between both languages (LOTOS and SDL) based on achieved results was published by the authors [Mariño et al., 2001].

2.3 PROFIBUS reference

In 1987 a group of manufacturers and end users, along with the German Government, defined a fieldbus based on the OSI/ISO model named PROFIBUS. This description was later published as the German standard DIN 19 245 and as the European CENELEC IN 50170 [CENELEC EN 50170, 1996a]. PROFIBUS uses only three of the OSI layers: the physical layer (PHY), the data link layer (FDL) and the application layer, FMS/LLI (Fieldbus Message Specification/Lower Layer Interface).

A PROFIBUS network was implemented by the authors to test the specifications made from LOTOS and SDL languages (sections 2.1 and 2.2), and in addition the designed and implemented nodes, making use of the development tools and prototype boards provided by manufacturers, and the included RTOs based emulators (section 1.2).

2.4 WorldFIP reference

French manufacturers (Cegelec, Telemecanique, Efisystem, Gespac, etc.) promoted a protocol for industrial communications, that was standardised with the name of FIP (Factory Instrumentation Protocol). Its characteristics were recorded in the French standard NFC 46-601÷605. Later, this protocol was described by CENELEC into the standard EN 50170 vol. 3 with the name WorldFIP [CENELEC EN 50170, 1996b]. It was the same than the former French standard but with the adoption of the international standard IEC 1158-2 (now IEC 61158-2) for its physical layer.

A WorldFIP network was implemented by the authors to test both: the specification made from LOTOS language (section 2.1) and the nodes, which were designed and implemented using development tools and prototype boards provided by manufacturers, as well as the included FPGA chips (section 1.2).

3. CAN systems and devices classification

Communication protocols applied to automotive applications are valued by semiconductor manufacturers, standardisation organisations and the Society of Automotive Engineers (SAE).

CAN systems and devices can be classified attending to several criteria (ISO, protocol version, mailbox structure and integration degree) specified next.

The ISO classification is the simplest: low speed (< 125 Kbps) and high speed (> 125 Kbps).

CAN is a message passing protocol and follows a producer-consumer model [Etschberger, 2001], thus, only when an important event occurs, the producer accesses the medium to communicate this information to the other nodes sending a message. The medium access is resolved by means of the message identifier priority, so that the highest priority message takes the medium and transmits the messages, and the transmission of the lower priority messages is postponed. The size of this identifier depends on the CAN specification version: 11 bits for version 2.0A and 29 bits for version 2.0B [bos, 1991].

The communication is basically carried out by means of diffusion. All the nodes receive the message and filter it according to the identifier configured in the buffers (known as mailboxes), which are responsible to establish the identifiers of the transmitted and/or received messages. When a message is received and its identifier has been previously configured on the mailbox, the CAN node verifies its integrity. Only if this message is error free, it would be transfered to the node controller, and in the opposite case it would be rejected.

Depending on the mailbox structure, two implementations are possible: BasicCAN and FullCAN structure.

CAN systems and devices can also be classified by its hardware integration degree in: Stand alone and SLIO (Slave-IO).

4. CAN educational tools

In this section the hardware and software tools, which comprise the educational environment for CAN fieldbus learning, are described.

4.1 esd development system

The development system manufactured by esd GmbH (electronic system design) comprises: a PC-CAN interface board (model *CAN-PCI/331*), a digital input/output module *CAN-CBM-DIO8* with 8 channels, I/O wiring including terminations and T-connectors, drivers, *CANscope* application software for Windows NT/95/98/2000, and CAN introduction and operating manuals. All system nodes are electrically insulated and comply with the CiA standards [esd, 2000].

The PC-CAN interface board uses a microcontroller of type 68331, which takes care of the local CAN data management, and a *Philips SJA1000* CAN controller, that complies with the ISO 11898 [ISO 11519-2, 1994, ISO 11898, 1993], allowing a data transfer rate of 1 Mbit/s. This controller is also compatible with CAN 2.0A and CAN 2.0B.

The 8 digital I/O module is configurable and comprises a *SAB 80C515C* microcontroller as a SLIO-CAN device, and a *PCA82C250T* CAN transceiver.

The *CANscope* application software is based on the CANopen standard, and allows the configuration of the development system and the monitoring of CAN events. In addition, the software development tools for application layer solutions includes the CAN device controllers and the NTCAN Application Programming Interface (API), available for Windos and UNIX environments, as well as for embedded and real-time systems.

4.2 IXXAT development system

This development system comprises the following IXXAT GmbH manufactured devices: 3 intelligent PC-CAN interface boards (*iPC-I 320/PCI*) for PCI bus systems, and licenses for *canAnalyser/32*, *CANopen Configuration Studio*, *CANopen Node Manager*, *CANopen Master API* and *Programming Client* software.

The PC-CAN interface board includes a *Dallas DS80C320* microcontroller, and *Philips SJA1000* and *Intel 82527* CAN controllers. This CAN adapter board enables a data transfer rate of 1 Mbit/s, complies with the ISO 11898 and is compatible with CAN 2.0A and CAN 2.0B.

The IXXAT development system offers a very powerful software tool for the development, testing and service of CAN-based networks. Thus the *canAnalyser/32* software supports the functionality of layer 7 protocols (CAL, CANopen, DeviceNet and SDS), allowing the display and transmission of CAN objects with 11 and 29 bits identifiers. The *CANopen Configuration Studio* software is useful to configure and manage CAN networks (with the CANopen standard application layer implementation), and the other tools provide extended functions. Among the latter stand out, the protocol-specific representations of messages in CANopen based systems (*CANopen Client*), the transmission and reading of PDO- and SDO-objects (*CANopen Node Manager*), or individual programming of new functions with the aid of a programming module (*Programming Client* and *CANopen Master API*).

The development system also contains a modular I/O device manufactured by WAGO, with CANopen standard capabilities (*WAGO I/O System 750-307*), that works like a fieldbus node with CANopen standard support. This modular I/O device includes:

- A bus coupler, that constitutes the link between the fieldbus and the other modular devices with I/O capabilities.
- Special function modules, which capture and condition data to be processed. Particularly, they consist of two digital input modules (*750-402*) and two digital output modules (*750-504*), each one with 4 channels.
- Termination module, without I/O capabilities, but necessary to avoid failures.

5. Teaching environment for CAN networks

In this section two hardware projects are described: the design and development of CAN nodes (for general applications), and the development of an educational environment for CAN protocol teaching (including several devices communicated by means of this bus).

5.1 CAN nodes implementation

The CAN nodes are designed and developed as general application CAN devices, enabling the study of CAN and other derived protocols (i.e. TTCAN). The hardware implementation of these CAN nodes uses a *8751* microcontroller of the Intel MC-51 family to administrate the node, a *Philips SJA1000* CAN controller and a Texas Instruments CAN transceiver (*UC5350N*) to insulate the controller and bus voltages. The developed software presents a user interface that can directly establish connections to the microcontroller, and send messages to the CAN bus. This hardware implementation also allows the test and verification of the developed CAN hardware (section 1.5.2). On the top of figure 3 the CAN network based on the implemented nodes is depicted.

The educational environment for CAN protocol teaching consists of one monitoring station (protocol analyser) and four field devices that comply the CAN standard. The monitoring station captures frames going through the fieldbus to perform further processing on them. For this purpose, a personal computer with a high speed CAN interface board manufactured by NSI is used, along with the CAN board controller software. This board is based on the *Intel 82527* CAN controller and *Philips 82C250* transceiver, which enables a data transfer rate of 1 Mbit/s, complies with the ISO 11898 and is compatible with CAN 2.0A and CAN 2.0B. The protocol analyser software was developed using the Borland C++ Builder programming environment, running on Windows 2000/Nt/9x operating system.

The CAN devices are implemented on a printed circuit board that includes analog and digital inputs/outputs, a SLIO-CAN controller (*Philips P82C150*), and the required elements to configure the CAN controller and to attach the device to the bus.

5.2 Developed CAN hardware

The developed hardware is based on Programmable Logic Devices (PLDs) technology and implements a general purpose CAN device for control applications. Following the protocol description, the CAN functionality was implemented and executed on a Xilinx Field Programmable Gate Array (FPGA). This functionality was programmed using VHDL (VHSIC Hardware Description Language) by means of the Xilinx Foundation development kit, and im-

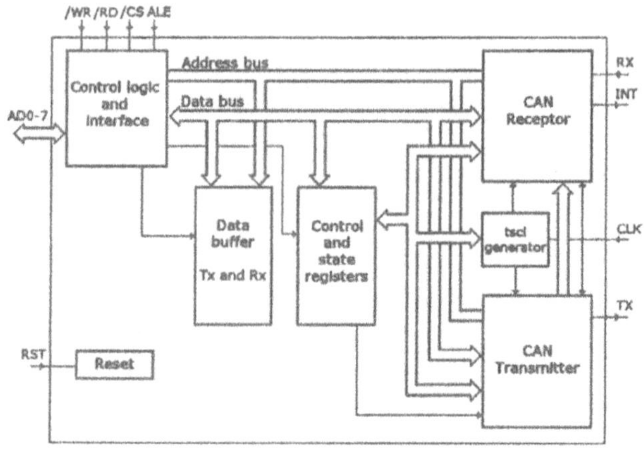

Figure 2. CAN protocol hardware description

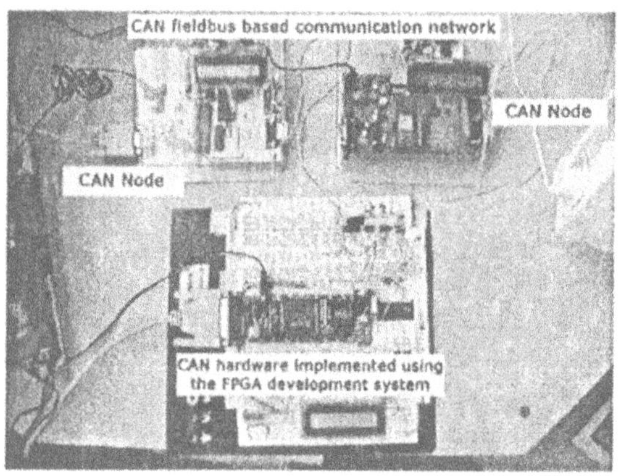

Figure 3. CAN fieldbus based communication network

plemented on a *XS40* prototyping board manufactured by Xess Corporation. This board includes a Xilinx 20,000-gate *XC4010XL* FPGA and an Intel *8051* microcontroller. Figure 2 shows the block diagram of the CAN protocol hardware description accomplished using the following Xilinx Foundation design tools: schematic design, LogiBLOX and VHDL. In addition, this hardware description of the CAN protocol can be easily adapted to other FPGAs.

The final system (Fig. 3) is formed by the CAN nodes (section 1.5) and the CAN hardware implemented using the FPGA development system.

6. Conclusions and future works

In this paper the state-of-the-art in fieldbus technology is presented, based on the authors' experience working with engineering students of information technology at university grades. Proposed curriculum topics are: the introduction of FDTs in the formal description of industrial communication protocols, and the design and implementation of nodes for selected fieldbuses (i.e.: PROFIBUS, WorldFIP and CAN) by means of development tools and prototype boards provided by manufacturers. Particular lines of research, about the implementation of fieldbus nodes using FPGA chips and RTOs for emulators, are also pointed out.

Given its growing impact all over the automotive industry, an introduction about the CAN fieldbus is presented, along with the software and hardware tools that configure training environments for this protocol. The authors' more recent work on fieldbus technology is shown through the two different CAN nodes, developed by them employing the previously presented tools.

Future developments with great potential in IT university education include fieldbus training applied to automotive industry and others, such as:

- Application of formal description techniques (FDTs) to the development of integrated circuits for fieldbus networks, based on the generation of VHDL code (language for hardware description) directly from their FDT's specification [Gauer, 2002].
- Current demands for installing automotive electronic devices for communication and control have opened a trend towards the use of more electric power aboard cars in order to satisfy the future needs. Current technical reports forecast a move from 12V batteries to 36V ones, for loads with high-power (42V) and low-power (12V) demands [Frank et al., 2001].
- The software integration of FDTs and new packets that provide new functionalities of fielbuses such as access networks, is an exciting area for new developments. Among them it is worth mentioning the work carried out by some European industrial groups such as IDA [Kaplan, 2001] and OSEK, that are devoted to integrate fieldbus technologies for Web/Internet and automotive software standards for embedded controls respectively.
- Another interesting area of research is the wireless fieldbus technology, not only in the fast moving sector of automotive industry where ITS (Intelligent Transportation Systems) programs are known worldwide, but also throughout every industrial sector [Pottie and Kaiser, 2000].

Acknowledgments

This work has been sponsored by two R&D projects from the following entities: Research General Directorate of the MCYT, Ref. TIC2001-3701-C02-01, Central Government (Madrid, Spain); and Presidency Department, Ref. PGIDT01TIC30301PR, Autonomous Government (Galicia, Spain).

References

(1991). *CAN Specification Version 2.0.* Robert Bosch GmbH.

(2000). *CAN-Starter-Kit for Windows NT/2000, Windows 95/98 Rev 1.2.* esd electronic system design GmbH.

CENELEC EN 50170 (1996a). *General Purpose Field Communications System*, volume 2/3 (PROFIBUS).

CENELEC EN 50170 (1996b). *General Purpose Field Communications System*, volume 3/3 (WorldFIP).

Etschberger, K. (2001). *Controller Area Network: Basics, Protocols, Chips and Applications.* IXXAT Press.

Frank, R., Kolanko, F., and Phillips, T. (2001). Higher-voltage vehicles generate new demands for power management. *Electronic Design*, pages 71–76.

Gauer, R. (2002). The SoC design platform and its application in the automotive industry. *Information quarterly of ARM*, 1(1):30–32.

ISO 11519-2 (1994). *Road Vehicles - Low-speed serial data communication - Part 2: Low-speed controller area network (CAN).* ISO 11519-2.

ISO 11898 (1993). *Road Vehicles - Interchange of digital information - Controller area network (CAN) for high-speed communication.* ISO 11898.

Kaplan, G. (2001). Ethernet's winning ways. *IEEE Spectrum*, pages 113–115.

Lías, G., Valdés, M., Domínguez, M., and Moure, M. (2000). *Field Programmable Logic and Applications (FPL 2000)*, volume 1896, chapter Implementing a fieldbus interface using a FPGA, pages 175–180. Springer-Verlag.

Mariño, P. (2003). *Enterprise Communications: Standards, Networks and Services.* RA-MA, 2nd edition.

Mariño, P., Domínguez, M., Poza, F., and Nogueira, J. (1999). *Fieldbus Technology (FET'99)*, chapter Formal Description Software for WorldFIP Industrial Fieldbus, pages 157–163. Springer-Verlag.

Mariño, P., Nogueira, J., Sigüenza, C., Poza, F., and Domínguez, M. (2001). The profibus formal specification: A comparison between two FDTs. *Computer Networks Journal, Elsevier Science*, 37:345–362.

Mariño, P., Poza, F., Domínguez, M., and Nogueira, J. (1997). *Transformation-Based Reactive Systems Development (ARTS'97)*, chapter Specification and Verification of a Real-Time Field Bus with Formal Description Languages, pages 415–429. Springer-Verlag.

Mariño, P., Poza, F., and Nogueira, J. (1996). *Balanced Automation Systems II (BASYS'96)*, chapter Information System Based on Industrial Standard Protocols, pages 201–208. Chapman & Hall.

Marsh, D. (1999). Surviving the fieldbus wars. *Electronic Design*, pages 34–46.

Pottie, G. and Kaiser, W. (2000). Wireless integrated network sensors. *Communications of the ACM*, 43:51–58.

REMOTE SYSTEM OF DESIGN AND TEST OF DC-DC CONVERTERS

L. Eguizabal, A Lago, C. Peñalver, J. Doval, J. Marcos and A. Nogueira
Electronic Technology Department, University of Vigo

Abstract: The increasing interest in remote test and experimentation has allowed the incorporation to the educative system of new tools that improve the classic methods of education. In the field of the Power Electronics, the possibility of access of the engineering student through the development of this type of tools to equipment generally of high cost, and therefore of low availability in the educational laboratories, is very important. This work shows a Remote System of Design and Test of DC/DC Converters (RSDTC) that can be used either locally or remotely. The developed system is based on a test bench manufactured by Hewlett-Packard. Taking as its starting point this equipment, a software application has been developed using the visual programming language "LabVIEW". This programming tool combined with CGI (Common Gateway Interface), allows the developed analysis system to be executed remotely using a web browser.

Key words: Automatic Test Software, DC-DC power conversion, Internet, Power system monitoring, LabVIEW programming.

1. INTRODUCTION

Nowadays, with the generalization of the use of PCs in education, new tools have appeared that are very helpful in improving the classic methods of education.

Among these new education tools developed around the use of PCs , it is possible to emphasize:

1. *The use of simulation software*, which allows multiple kinds of analysis in the study of circuits, thus obtaining results that in any other way would be very difficult to get.

2. *The possibility of improving the presentation methods*, as much the theoretical classes as the practical ones.
3. *New learning techniques of circuits in the practical classes*, based on the connection of programmable instrumentation equipment to a PC, by means of an instrumentation bus.
4. *The use of Internet*, to facilitate the access to the information available in the network, and also giving the possibility of making practical exercises at distance, which has come to be known as "Remote Experimentation".

This article present a System of Design and Test of DC/DC Converters (RSDTC), that tries to explore the possibilities shown in 3 y 4.

The RSDTC allows the study of this type of power converters in two ways:

a) *Design.* In this first step the students can use the developed system to determine the values of the passive components that form the circuit output filter of the converter.
b) *Test.* Once designed the topology, in this phase the quality of the converter is studied. To do this a series of tests have been defined: line regulation, load regulation, etc.

References [1-4] analyzed the main topics of this work.

2. THE TEST BENCH OF DC-DC CONVERTERS

The electronic hardware necessary to implement the test system is based on a set of programmable instruments interconnected using the GPIB bus. In order to be able to control and supervise these instruments, a PC is used. The PC sits in one of its PCI expansion buses a GPIB card of the manufacturer National Instruments. The main instruments that compound the test bench are shown in figure 1. It is interesting to emphasize the configuration and interconnection elements.

In order to interconnect the Unit Under Test (UUT) and the instruments, the following element has been used: HP75000. This instrument works like controller of the test bench. In addition it has connected in its VXI expansion slots: three 4*4 matrixes of contacts HPE136A cards, and 2 HPE1664 cards of 16 relays.

The relays are used for interconnecting the instruments and the UUT, and for modifying the operation mode of the topology; for example, changing between several inductances and capacitors connected to the converter.

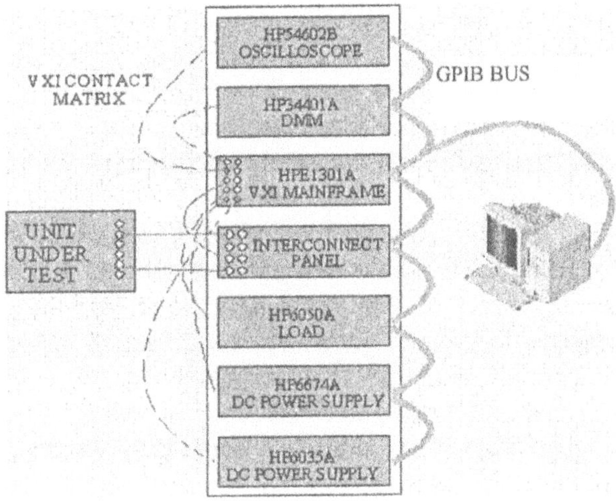

Figure 1. Block diagram RSDTC

3. SOFTWARE DESCRIPTION

The software developed has two main modules as shown in figure 2:

- Test Software: controls the instruments from the PC using GPIB commands.
- Network Software: communicates the host and different clients who receive information from the test bench.

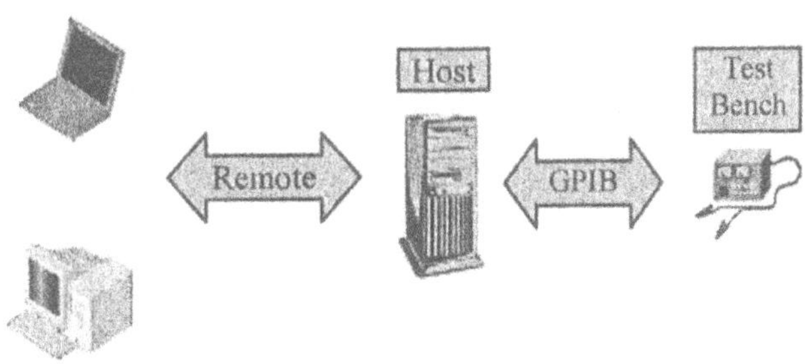

Figure 2. Software structure

3.1 Test software

In order to develop this module, the widely used graphical programming language LabVIEW (Laboratory Virtual Instrument Engineering Workbench), has been used. LabVIEW is a powerful and flexible programming language used for data acquisition, control of instruments and for analysis. [5]

The developed application is located in a personal computer that is connected to the test bench, allows the execution of tests in local and remote mode. In this last case, the PC works as a bridge between the test bench and the remote client.

Because of the instruments are controlled through a GPIB bus, the communication between the host and the instruments is based in text messages. The main part of the software is in charge to generate the necessary messages for the control of the different devices, and to understand the answer messages that are received; for it three Virtual Instruments (VI), basically related to GPIB protocol 488.2, will be used:

1. MakeAddr: generates GPIB compound addresses, necessary to control the matrix of contacts and the relays.
2. Send: it sends a text message to the element whose direction is indicated like parameter.
3. Receive: read from the GPIB bus a message of a certain length.

Following the structure of these three virtual instruments, two news virtual instrument were created: GPIBcommand and GPIBquery (show in figure 3). It's interesting to emphasize the second one, that is compounded of the Send and Receive commands. So that, in only one VI is used for request a information and then, the bus is scanned until the answer message is received. Therefore, with these two new virtual instruments, and once the addresses of the instruments included in the test bench are known, the control software automatizes the test process.

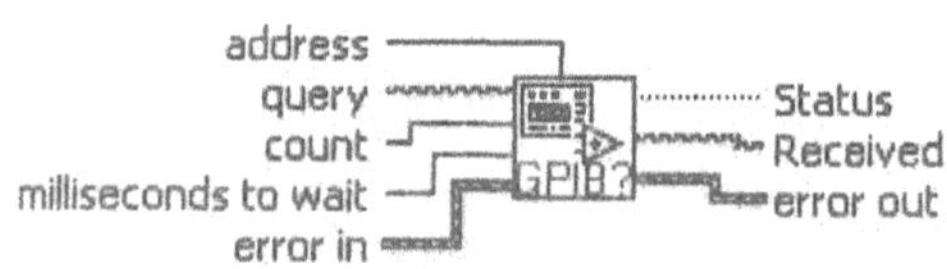

Figure 3. Virtual instrument GPIBquery

Once detailed the software that makes GPIB communication, it will be explained the two options used for the remote control of the test bench.

3.2 Remote access application

In this article are presented two possibilities to access to the test bench in remote way:

1. The first one is a client-server based on an application implemented by means of a communication protocol TCP/IP.

2. The second one is based on the programming of CGI applications, so the bench can be controlled through a web browser.

Both options follow a very similar operation philosophy that is indicated in the next paragraph.

The remote access application contains two modules:

a) A program developed in LabVIEW for controlling the instruments by means of GPIB. A virtual instrument of this module must be generated with the necessary inputs and outputs for controlling and executing.
b) The second module must link the requests for information from the client to the server. That is to say, when in a client computer a button of the designed application is clicked, the effect in the GPIB communication program is the same as this one were being executed in local way.

Therefore, the differences between both communication methods are in the sending of data between the client and the server, and the process of these data to connect them to the virtual instrument control.

This communication TCP/IP has two important disadvantages:

- Is mandatory that the LabVIEW program is installed in both computers (client and server), and the developed application.
- The transfer of data is slow due to the complexity of the virtual instrument used.

For these reasons, in this work the solution based on programming CGI is only described.

3.2.1 CGI programming

CGI is the acronym of Common Gateway Interface. CGI is based on a communication protocol by which a Web server communicates with other applications or databases. CGI only defines an interface, is not programming language. Fig 4 shows the interface relation.

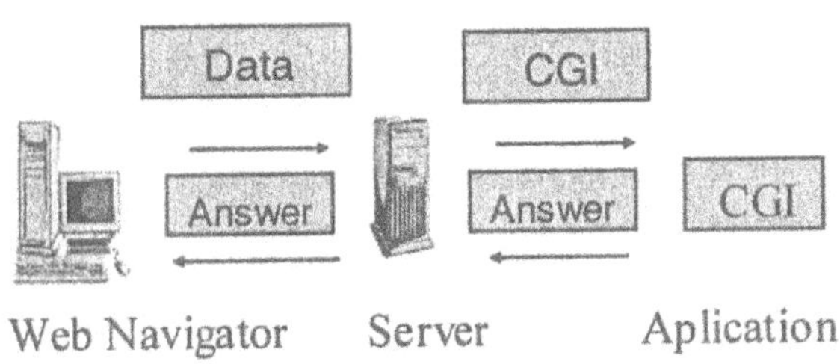

Figure 4. Interface relation

CGI applications can be written in most of the programming languages, although the most used it is the Perl language. In order to be able to use this communication interface in LabVIEW, the Internet tools for LabVIEW are needed. These Tools contain virtual instruments for the CGI communication [7].

When in a web browser the URL (Uniform Resource Locator) address of a CGI application is indicated, the communication process has the following steps:

- The browser sends the request to the web server. This request includes the name and the location of the CGI application, and all the input parameters of the application.
- The web server calls the CGI application, transferring all the input parameters and other available data as: the time, the client date and IP direction.
- When CGI application finalizes the execution, it gives back its output parameters to the browser.

The Internet tools of LabVIEW provide a virtual instrument called G Web server, see figure 5. It is the server who uses LabVIEW to be able to connect a VI to Internet.

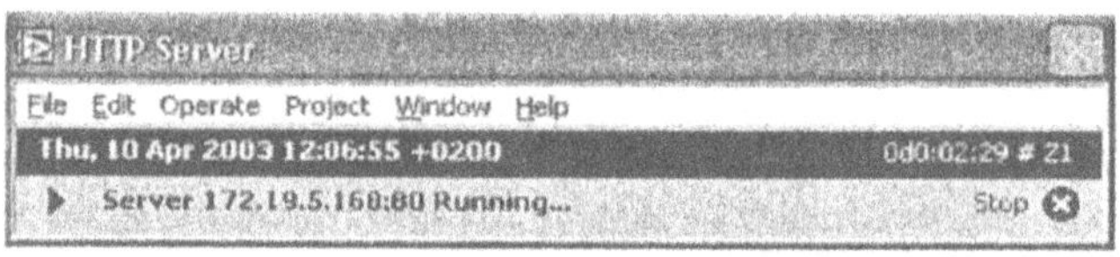

Figure 5. G Web Server

CGI application consists of three basic parts:

- A virtual instrument that makes the CGI communication between the server and the browser. Its function is to receive the request for information from the server, it sends this request to another virtual instrument that processes it, and finally, it sends the answer to the browser. The reception of this information is made by means of CGI instrument: Read Request.vi, and it is sent by CGI Release.vi.
- The virtual instrument that processes the request for information, have like main missions look for in the Keyed Array (see Table 1) with the help of the virtual instrument Keyed Array Index, the necessary inputs, and send them to the virtual instrument that is wanted to control. Finally, it is created the web page to send to the browser.
- The virtual instrument that the clients are going to be able to handle through the browser is the one in charge to communicate with the test bench.

Table 1. Example of a Keyed Array

Key	Value
Signature	Electronic
Credit	12
Course	1°

The virtual instruments more important to program this CGI communication are: CGI Read Request.vi, CGI Write Reply.vi, CGI Release.vi, CGI Parse URL-Encoded Param String.vi, and Keyed Array Index.vi.

Therefore, with this software that implements CGI communication, the students can use the system, from any connected computer to Internet and through any browser, without to have installed LabVIEW.

4. PROCEDURE FOR THE DEFINITION AND ACCOMPLISHMENT OF THE TEST

In this section is described the procedure to follow in order to use the test bench.

At the time of defining the tests sequence, it must be distinguished between local and remote execution.

4.1 Execution in local way

This work mode can only be used from the computer that is connected directly with the test bench, through the GPIB card. In this mode all the configuration windows are available. The steps to follow for the definition and accomplishment of a new test are:

a) Make physical connections between UUT and the test bench.

The following steps correspond to the definitions that must be introduced in the test software.

a) Step 1. *Information Editor.* The new model of the UUT is named.
b) Step 2. *Definition of connections.* The connections between the UUT and the test bench are defined.
c) Step 3. *Specifications Editor.* In this section is defined the maximum and minimum voltage and currents values, that can handle the converter.
d) Step 4. *Test definition.* In this section the test to be realized and its sequence are defined.

Step 5. *Limits and conditions test.*

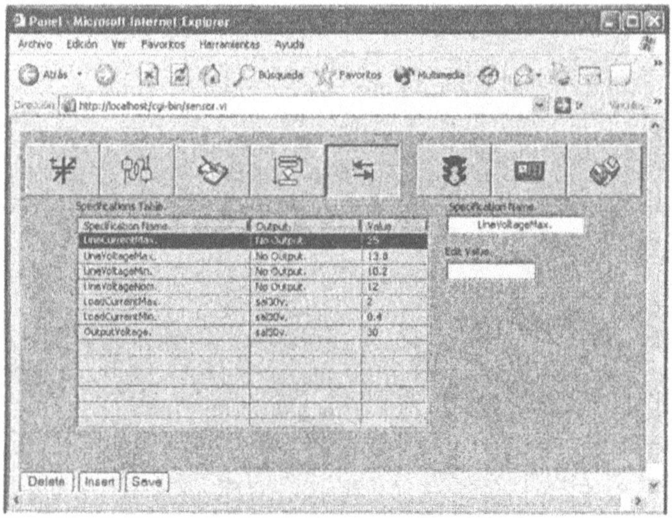

Figure 6. Remote access to the step 3 window

As an example in figure 6, is shown one of the windows in which is defined the limits values of circuit operation, obtained in remote way by means of a browser.

Once made these six steps, the system is ready for the execution of the test sequence. For it, software enables a new window in which there are a series of buttons to the tests execution, and a zone where the evolution of execution is observed. In figure 7, is shown this window when a tests sequence has finished.

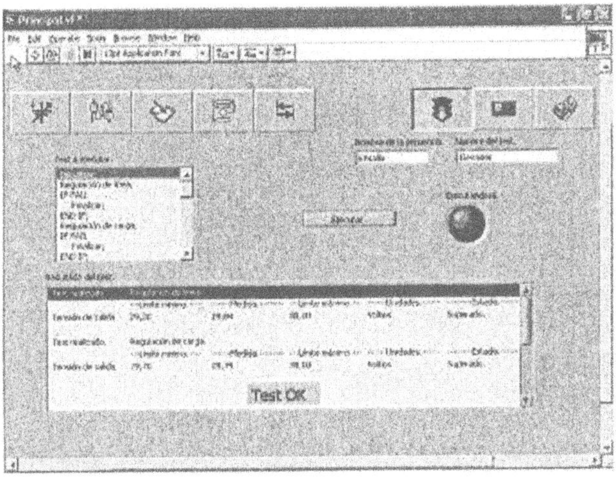

Figure 7. Test execution window

4.2 Execution in remote mode

If the tests are made in remote mode, the test software doesn't allow modifying the parameters as in local mode, it is only possible to visualize, the values of the three first steps. It solely allows to define a new test sequence, to introduce the tests values limits, and finally to execute the new sequence.

5. TOPOLOGY DESIGN AND RESULTS

As it was indicated in previous sections, the developed system is useful for the design and test of DC/DC converters.

From the design point of view, the software offers a window that allows access to all the instrumentation of the test bench. With this window, it shows in figure 8, it is possible perform a manual configuration of the bench, choosing the connection and waveform to measure. The possibility of changing the connections allows to modify the physical structure of the converter, it facilitates the analysis of the topology.

Thus in figure 8, it can be observed basic signals of the step-up converter: the upper waveform is the control signal to the switch, the middle represents the inductor current and the lower waveform is the output voltage.

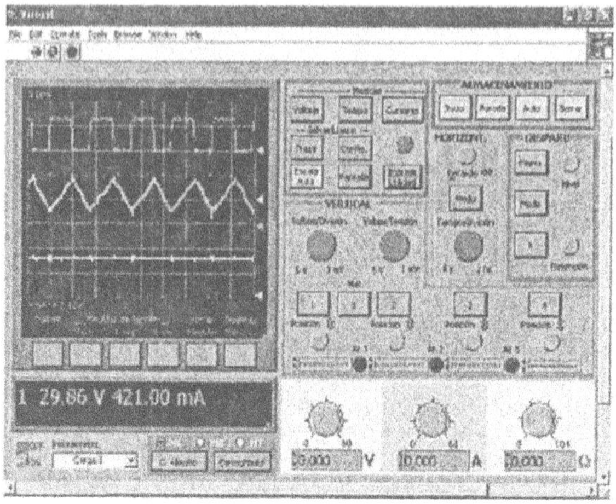

Figure 8. Circuit Operation in CCM

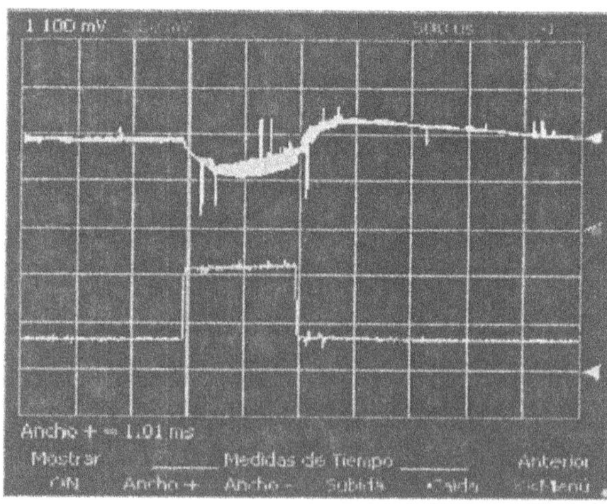

Figure 9. Result obtained with a load regulation test

In this analysis mode also is possible to visualize waveforms through the instrumentation window. As an example, in figure 18, is shown the obtained answer when executing an analysis of "current pulse in the load". The current pulse applied can be observed, that varies of 0.4 Amp. to 2 Amp. and the variation that experiences the output voltage is only of the order of 20mV. This last measurement is solely shown the AC component, to obtain a greater definition.

6. CONCLUSIONS

The tests system presented in this article can be used as a complement to the power electronics laboratory lessons, for the study and analysis of DC/DC converters. The solution that is shown here, allows to analyse the operation of this kind of circuits, obtain the basic parameters that define their answer quality: line regulation, load regulation, input impedance, output impedance, susceptibility, etc. Adding a set of switches that allow us to modify the circuit structure, it is possible to study how this changes affects the converter behaviour in: continuous and/or discontinuous operation mode. All it added to the possibility of making the tests through a browser increases the versatility and the system utility.

ACKNOWLEDGMENTS

This research work has been sponsored by Secretaría Xeral de I+D of Xunta de Galicia (Spain) in the project PGIDT01PX30304PR. This authors wish to thank the Xunta de Galicia for their financial support.

REFERENCES

[1] C. Salzmann, D. Gillet, and P. Huguenin, Introduction to real-time control using LabVIEW with an application to distance learning," Int. J. Eng. Eud. vol. 16, pp. 255-272, 2000.
[2] K.K. Tan, T. H. Lee, and F. M. Leu, "Development o a distant laboratory using LabVIEW", Int. J. Eng. Educ. vol. 16, pp. 273-282, 2000.
[3] Kok Kiong, tong Heng, and C. Y. Soh. "Internet-base monitoring of distributed control systems". IEEE Trans. Education. vol. 45 May 2002, page 128-134.
[4] ANSI/IEEE standard 488.2-1992. "IEEE standard codes, Formats, Protocols and Common Commands" The institute of Electrical an Electronics Engineers, Inc, 1988, 1993.
[5] Lisa K. Wells y Jeffrey Travis, "LabVIEW for everyone", Ed. Prentice Hall PTR.
[6] Comer, Douglas E. Y Stevens, David L. "Internetworking with TCP/IP", Ed. Prentice Hall, 2001.
[7] Jeffrey Travis, "Internet Applications in LabVIEW ", Ed. Prentice Hall PTR.

PART FIVE

MOBILE E-LEARNING

AN OPEN ABSTRACT FRAMEWORK FOR MODELING INTEROPERABILITY OF MOBILE LEARNING SERVICES

Developing the MobiLearn Arquitechture

Giorgio Da Bormida, Marco Di Girolamo, Ingo Dahn, Elena Murelli

GIUNTI Interactive Labs S.r.l., Via Portobello, Abbazia dell'Annunziata,16039 Sestri Levante (GE), Italy, Tel: +393356517013, g.dabormida@giuntilabs.com

Hewlett-Packard Italiana, Viale Europa 2, 24040 Stezzano (BG), Italy, Tel: +390292123218, marco.digirolamo@hp.com

University Koblenz-Landau, Knowledge Media Institute, Universitaetsstr. 1, 56070 Koblenz, Germany, Tel: +492612871552, dahn@uni-koblenz.de

Università Cattolica del Sacro Cuore, CRATOS, , Via Emilia Parmense 84, 29100 Piacenza, Italy, Tel. +390523599446, elena.murelli@unicatt.it

Abstract: The MOBIlearn project, co-funded by the European Commission, the National Science Foundation and AU Department of Education, Science and Training, is strategically positioned to provide relevant research outcomes in the field of innovative use of mobile environments to meet the needs of learners, working by themselves and with others. The objectives are achieved by defining a set of mobile services identified and specified through an open abstract framework. This assures proper interoperability between MOBIlearn services themselves and existing services provided by third parties, such as the Open Knowledge Initiative or the IMS Global Learning Consortium. The paper introduces the MOBIlearn project and its underlying approach describing the *Open Mobile Access Abstract Framework* (*OMAF*).

Keywords: mobile learning, abstract framework, service-oriented architecture, ambient learning

1. DEVELOPING THE MOBILEARN ARCHITECTURE

A key objective of the MOBIlearn Project is to improve the knowledge level of individuals by developing learning processes that are both time-efficient as well as being cost-effective. It is focusing on three representative groups: *workers* - to enable them to meet their job requirements and to update their knowledge continually; *citizens* as members of a culture, to improve their learning experience while visiting a cultural city and its museums and *citizens as family members* who need to have simple medical information for everyday needs.

Four scenarios have been identified by the project for testing out the learning processes and have been described in Issue 2 of this newsletter. Depending on availability, various mobile devices are being utilised with various communication systems. However, new devices and methods of communication are emerging all the time and existing ones over time are starting to become more viable in a learning context as costs go down. Therefore, in order to ensure "future proofing" the MOBilearn project is developing an architecture that is not dependent upon one type of device or communication system.

Taking the scenarios as a starting point it has identified a number of components or services that will be required by the various types of users – mobile learners, tutors, moderators, learning content authors and administrators. The top-level components and their associated services have been identified like the:

- Mobile Device – this could be a PDA, mobile phone, tablet PC, wearable PC or a laptop computer with an associated service.
- Portal – the central unique access point to services for the user. Associated services include those for authentication, authorization, billing, content delivery logging-in, user registration, a change of quality or an adaptive user interface service.
- Content – involving services for the management of content or learning objects and related features involving content creation and management, annotation, rendering, tracking, customization and personalization, information filtering and test creation and management services.
- Content and User – involving the management of user profiles.
- Location and Navigation – this could include a geographical information management service, indoor or outdoor positioning services.
- Collaboration and Communication – representing the umbrella of services related to collaboration and communications between two

or more persons, either in a synchronous manner or asynchronously and independent of the data nature, such as text, pictures, graphics, voice, video or applications. It also provides the session and user management functions for collaborative sessions.

- Context – this provides a means of gathering, maintaining, and processing a store of context data in order to produce recommendations (in the form of a ranked list) from the currently available content and options. Data can be gathered from other services, including automated data input such as sensors, manual input from the user, and generalised preferences.
- Multimedia Delivery – involving the delivery of content and annotations.
- Remote – involving the remote control of applications and devices.
- General – this could include a digital repository management, information package creation and management, seamless roaming or vocabulary creation and management services.

2. OPEN MOBILE ACCESS ABSTRACT FRAMEWORK

Each of these component services requires software tools to be developed and to enable them to interoperate with other service components, some of which could come from other suppliers. In order to drive forward developments towards interoperability the MOBIlearn Project is developing an "Open Mobile Access Abstract Framework" (OMAF). It is also aimed that this will help to encourage and exploit the usability of software through an object orientated software development approach. This will thus enable single re-usable services to be used on different mobile applications.

This approach is based on an extensive study of existing best practices including those from the Open Knowledge Initiative (OKI) and the IMS Abstract Learning Framework (ALF). The Open Knowledge Initiative is defining an open and extensible architecture for learning technology, although specifically targeted to the needs of the higher education community. OKI provides detailed specifications for interfaces among components of a learning management environment and open source examples of how these interfaces work. The OKI architecture is intended to be used both by commercial product vendors and by higher education product developers. It provides a stable; scalable base that supports the flexibility needed by higher education as learning technology is increasingly integrated into the education process.

The interface methods defined by OKI support the ongoing integration of three general categories of software:

- learning applications ranging from individual quizzing, authoring, and collaboration tools to suites of such tools that include course management and learning management capabilities;
- central administrative systems such as student information, human resource, and directory management;
- academic systems including library information systems, digital repositories of research and educational materials.

It is considered that once this architecture is fully adopted by the education market, new components may be plugged into the learning infrastructure using OKI's tightly defined and standardized application programming interfaces (APIs, Figure 1).

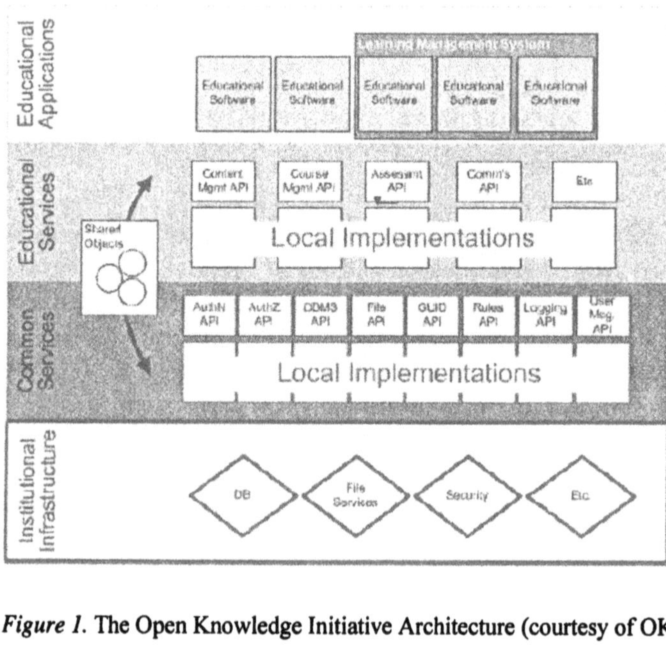

Figure 1. The Open Knowledge Initiative Architecture (courtesy of OKI)

IMS is developing an Abstract Learning Framework (Figure 2) that will guide the creation of future specifications – i.e. guidelines and suggestions for implementing something. They are a tool to help the developer, implementer, or administrator make decisions. Specifications, unlike standards, capture rough consensus and evolve rapidly. The framework is a device to enable the IMS to describe the context within which it will continue to develop its e-learning technology specifications, but it is not an attempt to define the IMS architecture, rather it is a mechanism to define the set of interfaces for which IMS may or may not produce a set of interoperability specifications.

In the cases where IMS does not produce a specification then every effort will be made to adopt or recommend a suitable specification from another organization. It is the intention of IMS that this Abstract Learning Framework and the associated IMS specifications produced to enable the exchange of information between the identified services will be adopted in a manner suitable for a particular system requirement.

Summarising, the IMS Abstract Learning Framework is an abstract representation of the services and their interfaces that are used to construct an e-learning system in its broadest sense; focused on the support of distributed electronic learning systems; a framework that covers the possible range of e-learning architectures that could be constructed from the set of defined services and interfaces.

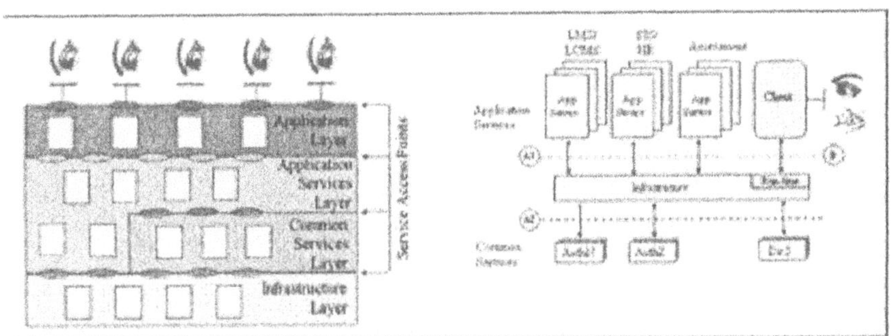

Figure 2. The IMS Abstract Learning Framework (courtesy of IMS)

In developing the MOBIlearn Open Mobile Access Abstract Framework a Unified Modelling Language (UML) methodology was adopted with the internal communication system completely XML-based.

The project is keen to get the views of others who are working in this area in order to reach a global consensus on the development of mobile learning systems and services. It is keen to avoid a situation that has already emerged in the mobile device industry of competing and often incomparable operating systems – that is slowing down the development of content across platforms.

On the basis of this Abstract Framework concept, a goal is set to create specifications of the different services, according to the 'open architecture' approach. OMAF will help also to exploit reusability of software according to the object oriented software development approach (Figure 3).

Following the User Centred Design and the UML frameworks methodologies, OMAF will address the conceptual layout of services to access knowledge and learning in a mobile environment, for example, via collaborative spaces, context aware and location based. In fact these are examples of possible services to be implemented in MOBIlearn. These represent also possible implementations of the conceptual framework specifications, but, the real value resides in the latter. Nevertheless, as described in chapter one, an instantiation of OMAF will be actually developed and tested in real users trials.

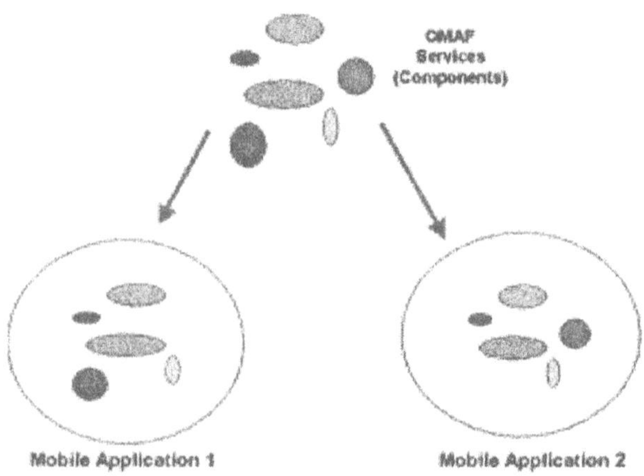

Figure 3. From single re-usable services to different mobile applications

The multi-layer model of OMAF, depicted in Figure 4, is composed by the following layers:

- The Mobile Meta-Applications Layer (MmAL): the set of systems, tools and applications obtained as a combination/integration of two or more mobile applications, to provide extended and more complex functionalities to users.
- The Mobile Applications Layer (MAL): the set of systems, tools and applications specifically designed and implemented to provide a particular mobile functionality. They are built starting from the suite of mobile services and common services.
- The Mobile Services Layer (MSL): the set of components able to provide mobile specific services, which are used by the mobile applications.
- The Generic Services Layer (GSL): the set of components that provide generic services to be used by the application services.

- The Infrastructure Services Layer (ISL): the underlying services that enable to exchange data in terms of communications, messaging and transactions.
- The Service Access Points (SAP): interface to the corresponding service. Each SAP provides access to one service capability. SAPs will be implemented through APIs (Application Programming Interfaces)
- The Components Store (CS): a set of components that has to be specified to support the Generic and Mobile services. For instance, it will be possible to find in the BSC the data models for images (BMP, GIF, etc.), user profile and location, geographical coordinates of objects, etc.

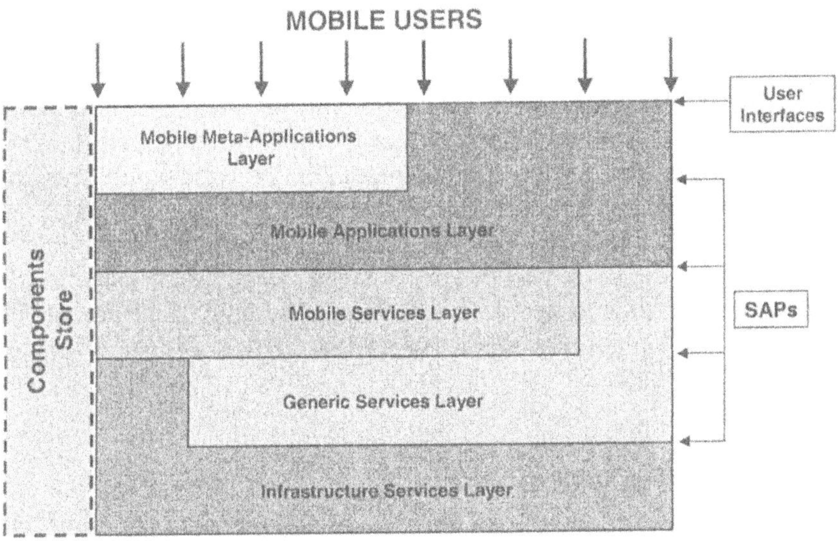

Figure 4. The OMAF layered-model

The services will be described using the Unified Modelling Language (UML) package diagrams. These graphical representations are suitable to map a complex system as a function, which is then broken down into sub-functions that can be further broken down into sub-sub-functions and so forth.

3. CONCLUSION

Having defined the OMAF model, the project will focus on activities for services identification, their functionalities and interface specifications. It is reviewing existing technologies for mobile applications and identifying the most suitable solutions for developing the OMAF instantiation, to be used in real users' trials during 2004.

The results of the first MOBIlearn Users Trials will be reported into the conference presentation, together with a demonstration of the MOBIlearn service-based architecture on mobile devices.

ACKNOWLEDGEMENTS

MOBIlearn is a 30-month, 8 MEURO, Research and Development (RTD) project co-funded by the European Commission (DG Information Society D/3-Education and Training), under the contract IST-2001-37187, within the Information Society Technologies (IST) programme of the Fifth Framework Programme of RTD. The participation of US partners (MIT and Stanford) is funded by US National Science Foundation (NSF), and its implementing arrangement between the European Commission and the NSF, specifically addressing co-operative activities in the field of e-learning. The participation of AU partners is funded by AU Department of Education, Science and Training.

REFERENCES

G. Da Bormida et al: MOBIlearn description of work, May 2002, http://www.mobilearn.org
M. Norton: Advances in Distance Learning Standards and their Adoption, Proceedings of the Educause 2002 Conference, Atlanta USA, October, 2002.

V. Kumar, J. Merriman, S. Thorne: What is the Open Knowledge Initiative? (A white paper prepared by Eduworks Corporation), September 20th, 2002, http://mit.edu/oki

IMS Abstract Learning Framework White Paper – Revision: 31st July, 2002. http://www.imsglobal.org

G. Da Bormida, R. Vaccaro, P. Lefrere, M. Sharples, Exploring next generation interfaces for mobile environments and devices to meet the needs of learners, working by themselves and with others: the MOBIlearn project, mlearn Workshop, 2002.

ISTAG (2001). Information Society Technologies Advisory Group: Scenarios for Ambient Intelligence in 2010, http://www.cordis.lu/ist/istag.htm.

PART SIX

DEVELOPMENT OF E-LEARNING TOOLS

VIRTUAL COMMUNITY IN THE CLASSROOM: AN INNOVATING TOOL FOR ELEARNING

F. Bruschi[1], P. Faverio[2], R. Hodges[2], L. Mari[2], D. Restelli[2] and D. Sciuto[1]
[1]*Politecnico di Milano, Dipartimento di Elettronica e Informazione, P.zza L. Da Vinci 32, 20133 Milano, ITALY;* [2]*LIUC, CETIC, C.so Matteotti 15, 21053 Castellanza, Varese, ITALY*

Abstract: This research in progress introduces a learning architecture where ICT tools complement the traditional models of formative process management through a moderated virtual community in the classroom. In particular, the research presents the main features of the conceptual framework leading to the implementation of such architecture in a web-based system. Among the several experiences of its usage, we report here the example of the application of this framework in a class of Information Systems Planning, to teach how to model the requirements of a system and it is being customized to teach modeling of hardware systems.

Key words: virtual community; e-learning framework; web-based system; community software architecture.

1. INTRODUCTION

The most typical use of the new information and communication technologies (ICT) in the learning processes is *substitutive* when the learner can't physically be where the lessons take place (Piccoli, 2001; Smith et al., 2001). The lack of the community dimension, which is so important in learning processes (Kaplan, 2002; Mitchell and Hope, 2000), justifies the usual denomination of "distance learning" for these scenarios. On the contrary, the learning architecture presented here is founded on the strategic choice of adopting ICT to *complement* the traditional management of learning processes. It is a technology-based approach, whose aim is to create new formative situations in the classroom (Girod and Cavanaugh, 2001; Marold et al, 2000).

This architecture differs from traditional supporting tools for another fundamental reason. Traditional learning processes are usually based on two very different formative configurations: classroom sessions and individual study. It is noticeable how these configurations diverge with respect to the media employed (see Table 1):

Table 1. The two possible configurations of traditional learning processes

Classroom sessions	**Individual study**
interaction person → person	interaction person → didactic material
greatly multimedial and broad band	unimedial and narrowband
not repeatable without a teacher	constantly repeated without a teacher

The "intermediate" formative situations (e.g. practice in laboratories) witness the importance of innovative training solutions as a middle course between these extremes of a potential *formative continuum* (Guttormsen Schär and Krueger, 2000; Levine, 2002; Saunders and Werner, 2000). This research in progress presents the fundamentals of the *moderated Virtual Community (*VC*) in the classroom*, a software-based environment that represents an attempt to experiment the educational potentialities of these "intermediate" formative situations.

2. THE MODEL OF THE MODERATED VIRTUAL COMMUNITY IN THE CLASSROOM

The idea of using ICT tools as a support for discussion among groups of students for teaching purposes is clearly not new: typical examples can be found in the so-called forum and chat systems, supporting the management of asynchronous and synchronous communication, respectively. In a communicational perspective, these systems are extremely poor: they do not carry any contents in themselves and they are weakly structured and structuring.

On the contrary, our model of the VC is based on the structuring of information according to the teaching purposes: that is why the VC is driven by a learning path organized through subsequent phases. Within each phase a discussion between the participants takes place, being defined both the subject and the planned outputs of the discussion (Simpson, 2002; Smith et al., 2001). Unlike what happens in forums and chats, in the VC the role of the moderator is neither accidental, nor banally censorious.

The choice of experimenting with this model of VC in the classroom, instead of among students interacting at a distance, originates from the interest in empirically testing one of the hypotheses which have inspired the eLearning project (http://elearning.liuc.it) where the VC took place: unlike what is often maintained, eLearning *is not synonymous with* distance learning; more specifically, distance learning supported by ICT tools represents just an example of eLearning. In particular, the usage of the VC has led us to verify the possibility of managing everybody-with-everybody discussions in the classroom, a communication setting that would be unfeasible with traditional modalities (Mitchell and Bacic, 2000).

The model of VC we have defined interprets a discussion as a game structured in a temporally linear sequence of *game phases*, each phase being characterized by the different involvement of three actors (see Table 2): the configurer (the *coach*), the student (the *player*) and the teacher/tutor (the *referee*).

Before the actual start of the game, in the *set* state the *coach* configures the VC system, by specifying the number of phases and for each phase:

- *its ordinal position within the play sequence;*
- *its information/communication structure*, defined according to the Composite View design pattern: the front end of the VC system with which the players interacts during the game is a table of one or more elements, each one of them being chosen among a set a pre-defined high-level configurable components, e.g., a read-only text box (used in particular by the *coach* himself to specify some descriptive characteristics of the phase, such as its title and aims), a read/write area, a chat subsystem, a forum subsystem, ...; as a further option, the *coach* can specify that the default contents of an element will be generated runtime, as a copy of the data introduced in a previous phase by the *players*;
- *the players' identity, role and permissions*: players can be impersonated by either single students, pre-defined groups, or groups established by the *referee*, according to the results of the previous phases); moreover, the coach sets the exclusive or concurrent access to each element of the front-end structure and, in the latter case, the corresponding read/write rights.

The second actor, the *player*, interacts with the VC previously configured (the *set*) by the *coach*, and the *referee* behaves as a player interacting with the participants. However, it is only up to the *referee* to establish the timing for the activation and the conclusion of the phases and to evaluate the contents provided by the players during each phase. This last operation is necessary in order to configure the next *runtime* phase, called "*hidden game*".

Table 2. The range of actions of each actor in the VC

	Actors		
State	**coach**	**referee**	**player**
Set	X		
Game		X	X
Hidden game		X	

A formal model for the Virtual Community can be represented as stack automaton, constituted by four states $Q = \{q_0,q_1,q_2,q_3\}$, where:

- q_0 = Set (initial state);
- q_1 = Hidden Game;
- q_2 = Game;
- q_3 = End of the Game (final state $F = \{q_3\}$).

The edges notation chosen is the following: $\alpha,\beta/\beta\gamma$, where the information carried out is the following:

- α: indicates the action performed on the Virtual Community;
- β: indicates the reading action of an information on the Virtual Community, stored in a previous action;
- γ: corresponds to the storing action of an information concerning the state of the Virtual Community.

The notation $\alpha,\beta/\beta\gamma$ describes the situation in which the character β is reported as read and the character γ is added to the stack. Furthermore the notation $\alpha,\beta/\beta$ shows that β is read and reported on the stack with or without an alteration done by an actor.

The set of characters allowed on the stack (β e γ) are:

- Z_0: default character for the initialization of the stack;
- A: character that identifies a *game* phase. The total number of characters in the stack identifies the number of phases for the given Virtual Community;
- B: character that defines the end of the state *set* and the possibility of beginning the Virtual Community;
- C: character that identifies the end of a *game* phase and the beginning of a *hidden game* phase.

The alphabet of characters on the input data stream is the following:

- a: corresponds to the insertion of an information during a phase;
- b: corresponds to the insertion of an information that ends a configuration to go from a *set* phase into a *hidden game* phase;
- c: corresponds to the insertion of an information that defines the transition from a *hidden game* phase to a *game* phase;
- d: corresponds to the insertion of an information during the *game* phase;
- f: corresponds to the insertion of an information that defines the transition from a *game* phase to a *hidden game* phase;

- g: corresponds to the insertion of an information during the *hidden game* phase.

The three classes of participants to the Virtual Community are prefixes of the alphabet in the input data stream, and are indicated by:

- c: coach;
- r: referee;
- p: player.

Given the defined grammar, the finite state model representing the Virtual Community is shown in Figure 1.

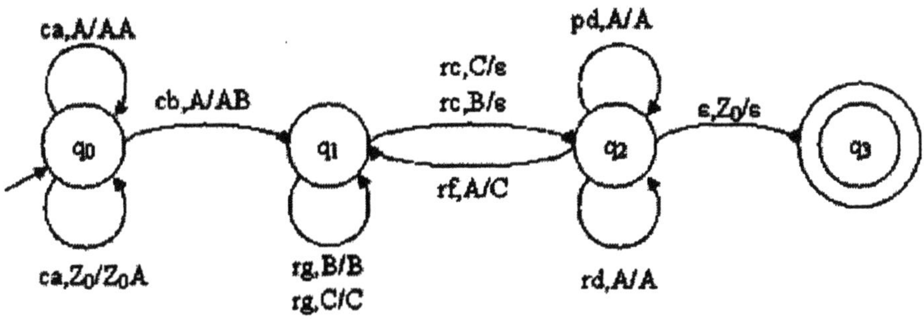

Figure 1. The finite state automaton representing the Virtual Community

3. THE DEVELOPMENT TOOLS

From a technological perspective, the VC is based on three-tier architecture that has been implemented by an Intranet web-based system.

The system development phase has been focused on the three logical parts typical of three-tier architectures: the user interface (clients), the business logic (web server) and the data manager (DBMS).

The critical factors that have driven the technological choices for the implementation were the possibility of a fast deployment to experiment, an inexpensive implementation and the use of user friendly interfaces.

Each of these modules is characterized by some critical factors which have driven the resulting technology choices. As a consequence, HTML has been chosen to build the presentation layer, which is, in turn, dynamically generated by a server side script. Consequently, actors can simply use a browser to operate the virtual community without the need of setting up any other software.

The business logic module and the data manager modules have been implemented using Microsoft Windows 2000 server and Microsoft SQL Server and no other solution has been explored.

The combined use of the Microsoft web server family (IIS, Internet Information Server) and of ActiveX components has been useful to build a simple architecture which allows management of files, scripts and the access to a database. In particular, IIS supports the ASP (Active Server Pages) environment which interprets and executes the server side scripts needed to implement the business logic described in the theoretical model, to generate the specific user interfaces for each game phase and, finally, to interface the application with the DBMS.

4. AN EXPERIENCE OF VIRTUAL COMMUNITY

After some years of experimentation of the VC in short courses, the validity of the teaching assumptions of the model has been recently more significantly tested during a seminar "Cases of Business Information Systems", held at University Cattaneo – LIUC and attended by 50 students. During the 15 hours of the seminar the students were introduced to the problem of business information flow analysis through two case studies, presented in electronic format (an e-book) and structured accordingly, so that each couple of students, thanks to the support of a VC, could experiment with a problem-solving approach. The constant interactivity which derived from this, together with the quality of the proposed cases with respect to both realism and complexity, made it possible to build a situation where the students progressively played the part intended for them by the VC, simulating the role of analysts/business consultants. Though with the limits of an estimation which is only quantitative, the number of proposals submitted by the different groups in each phase seems to confirm that the VC can be an effective tool to develop a modality of interaction among workgroups which is based on the maximum cooperation and productivity, more than what happens when a face to face interaction is requested.

This successful experience can be replicated on different subjects. In particular, we decided to verify its applicability in the modeling phase of digital systems, i.e. the most complex competence to grasp for undergraduate students in engineering courses.

In this example of Virtual Community, different players have to face the problem of partitioning a RSA public-private key generation algorithm into sub-functionalities, suitable for a subsequent hardware implementation. The players, that can be either individual students or small group, can access the specification of the system to be specified, written in natural language. As starting point, the algorithm for the pair generation is analyzed by the players. As an additional input, a library of general purpose functional components is given.

In the first phase, players propose a partitioning of the algorithm into interacting sub-functionalities, by compiling the row heading of a table, whose columns represent the following information:

- *provided interface*: set of services that the sub-functionality must offer, described with the corresponding input data types;
- *required interface*: set of services that the sub-functionality requires to be offered by other sub-functionalities, in terms of data types employed;
- *type*: classification of the functionality among the following classes: data intensive, control intensive, storage;
- *library IP*: setting the value of this field (that can be either *yes* or *no*), the student gives his opinion on the possibility to implement the functionality with a particular component of a library. The considered library is given as an input of the game;
- *target component*: if the value of the *library IP* field is *yes*, in this field the library component on which the functionality can be mapped must be pointed out; otherwise, another resource (processor, custom logic, etc.) must be indicated.
- *decomposable*: the value of this field records the opinion of the player on the opportunity of further decomposing the functionality into simpler tasks.

The first two columns contain information that in most design languages such as VHDL can be directly exploited to characterize modules boundaries. The other columns contain information that summarize some significant design choices.

Table 3 shows the table with the identification of the sub-functionalities that must be ratified during the hidden game by the referee. The column headings are preset by the coach during the system configuration, while the row headings result from the ratification and aggregation of the proposals of the two players. After the ratification, the players will have the same row headings, i.e. the same functionalities decomposition, and will be required to complete the columns. All tables are then analyzed by the referee who will ratify each single cell, identifying the correct answers and providing to both players a single view, which may be a mix of both tables or may be a modified version by the referee.

Table 3. Output for the ratification of sub functionalities phase

functionality	provided interface	required interface	type	library IP	target component	decomposable
random number generation						
primality testing						
prime numbers caching						
prime numbers multiplication						
exponentiation						
small random numbers generation						

Table 4 shows an output example for the "hidden game" phase of ratification of the functionalities proposed in phase 1.

Table 4. Output for the phase of ratification of the proposals made by the two players (decomp.: decomposable)

functionality	provided interface	required interface	type	library IP	target component	decomp.	player
random number generation	seed: bit[512]	rnd: bit[512]	Data intensive	no	processor	yes	A
primality testing	number: bit[512]	isprime: bit	Data intensive	no	custom logic	no	B
prime numbers caching	store: bit prime: bit[512]	p: bit[512] q: bit[512]	Storage	yes	bank register	no	A A
prime numbers multiplication	p: bit[512] q: bit[512]	n: bit[1024]	Data intensive	yes	multiplier	no	A A
exponentiation	p: bit[512] q: bit[512] e: bit[512]	d: bit[512]	Data intensive	no	custom logic	no	B B B
small random numbers generation	seed: bit[512]	e: bit[512]	Data intensive	no	processor	no	A

Next phase of the game foresees a synchronous discussion between players working on the same specification. This is implemented in the Virtual Community through a chat, to keep track of the discussion among the "competing" players about the table ratified by the referee in the previous phase. As an output a finale table, agreed upon by the group is obtained as output. In the hidden game phase, the referee reviews the output of the discussion and approves (or modifies) the table.

Next step of the game may be to restart the process with those modules that could be further decomposed, always considering two competing players.

Furthermore, different uses of the Virtual Community can be considered. For instance a competition among players in the code writing phase (either SystemC or VHDL or Verilog or any other language for which a simulator is available) could be setup. The goal is to teach students to write correct and efficient hardware specifications, by stimulating both competition and cooperation. The same could be said considering also the results of the synthesis, by making them discuss both the constraints and parameters set to the synthesis tool, and the results obtained, starting from a synthesizable version of the code.

5. CONCLUDING REMARKS

Aim of this paper was to present the model of a Virtual Community and its supporting framework. The results are encouraging and have shown that such a virtual community is very flexible and allows the creation of different learning situations that stimulate the students' interactivity. The experiences made so far have shown that, thanks to the confrontation and the direct cooperation required to the students, they become active elements in the class instead of passive listeners.

An interesting feature of the proposed model of Virtual Community is that it allows the possibility to create and alternate both competitive and cooperative situations during the same game. This aspect has been perceived as fundamental by the students that attended the Information Systems seminar. They have valued the experience as extremely positive. In particular, the students have pointed out the psychological effect which, thanks to the minor exposition filtered through computer mediated communication, helps to reduce the communicative and exposure difficulties which are typical of direct interpersonal relationships.

The results of this didactic experience have shown how the synergic employment of different hypermedial tools is useful to improve learning. In the classroom, the chat has enabled a quick and efficient communication, thanks to its synchronicity and focalization on problem solving. Moreover, the input of information in a highly structured context has made it possible to focus on the operative scope, with the benefit of the conciseness of the contents (for both students and teacher). Finally, the autonomous employment of the forum has allowed reaching a higher quality of the answers, significantly higher than the ones that what would be obtained through traditional tools.

REFERENCES

Girod, M., and Cavanaugh, S., 2001, Technology as an Agent of Change in Teacher Practice, *T.H.E. Online* Journal, http://www.thejournal.com/magazine/vault/A3429.cfm

Guttormsen Schär, and S., Krueger, H., 2000, Using New Learning Technologies with Multimedia, *IEEE Multimedia* 7(3):40-51, http://computer.org/multimedia/mu2000/u3040abs.htm

Kaplan, S., 2002, Building Communities – Strategies for Collaborative Learning, Learning Circuits, August 2002, http://www.learningcircuits.org/2002/aug2002/kaplan.html

Levine, L.E., 2002, Using Technology to Enhance the Classroom Environment, *T.H.*E. Online Journal, http://www.thejournal.com/magazine/vault/A3819.cfm

Marold K.A., Larsen G., and Moreno A., 2000, Web-based Learning: Is It Working? A Comparison of Student Performance and Achievement in Web-based Courses and their In-classroom Counterparts, in: *Challenges of Information Technology Management in the 21st Century*, M. Khosrowpour, ed., Idea Group Publishing, Hershey, USA, pp. 350-353.

Mitchell G., and Hope B., 2000, Educational Technology and Emergent Forms of Education, *Challenges of Information Technology Management in the 21st Century*, M. Khosrowpour, ed., Idea Group Publishing, Hershey, USA, pp. 833-834.

Mitchell, S., and Bacic, M., 2000, Using Real-Time Chat to Increase Student Interaction, *Learning Technology*, IEEE Computer Society, http://lttf.ieee.org/learn_tech/issues/july2000/index.html#mitchell

Piccoli, G., Ahmad, R., and Ives, B., 2001, Web-Based Virtual Learning Environments: A Research Framework and a Preliminary Assessment of Effectiveness in Basic IT Skills Training, *MIS Quarterly* **25**(4):401-426.

Saunders P., and Werner K., 2000, Finding the right blend for effective learning, Center for Teaching and Learning, Western Michigan University, http://www.wmich.edu/teachlearn/new/blended.htm

Simpson, W., 2002, Online learning: a Project to Develop an Innovative Approach to Control, *Learning Technology*, IEEE Computer Society, http://lttf.ieee.org/learn_tech/issues/july2002/index.html#8

Smith, G.G., Ferguson, D., and Caris, M., 2001, Teaching College Courses Online vs Face-to-Face, T.H.E. Online Journal, http://www.thejournal.com/magazine/vault/A3407.cfm

Syed, M. R., 2001, Diminishing the Distance in Distance Education, IEEE Multimedia 8(3):18-20, http://computer.org/multimedia/mu2001/u3018abs.htm

Tsinakos, A., and Margaritis, G., 2001, Employing Case Based Reasoning in Asynchronous Distance Education, *Learning Technology*, IEEE Computer Society, http://lttf.ieee.org/learn_tech/issues/july2001/index.html#3

THE E-LEARNING GRID: PEER-TO-PEER APPROACH

Vassil Alexandrov,[1] Nia Alexandrov,[1] Ismail Bhana,[1] David Johnson[1]

[1] *Center for Advanced Computing and Emergent Technologies, University of Reading, Whiteknights, P.O. Box 225, Reading, UK, RG6 6AY*

{v.n.,n.s,i.bhana,d.johnson }@reading.ac.uk

Abstract In this paper we present some of the approaches taken by the European E-Learning Grid consortium in building learning Grids. Some of the initial research has been done within the EC GENIUS project, which is a partnership between industry and academia. In this particular paper we focus on how in combining the collaborative and peer-to-peer approach with the relevant pedagogical paradigms we can arrive at the E-Learning Grid.

Keywords: e-Learning, peer-to-peer, Grid

1. Introduction

According to Equity Research (March 2000), the e-Learning market is one of the fastest growing markets worldwide. The key trends outlined are:

- Customer priorities shift away from stand-alone training, industry and customers demand a comprehensive approach to meet their needs. For example, such services as assessment and custom curriculum design, online mentoring and support reporting and tracking are in increasing demand.

- Increasing consolidation is required, since the market is very fragmented and we observe long development cycles inconsistent with the ageing of knowledge.

- Currently the global e-learning industry consists of approximately 5,000 participants offering every imaginable method of e-learning.

- Consolidation of Content, Technology and Services, in order to secure a sizable market share a complete e-learning solution has to be delivered. This can be done only in partnership.

- Within the current E-Learning landscape there are a series of players who have developed both processes and materials to make in-roads into this potential market place. To date much of the work has been in isolation with elements of competition involved.

Against this backdrop the overarching aim of our Grid approach is "to create an ubiquitous pervasive open collaborative e-learning environment focusing on and enhancing the dialogue phases of the learning process and based on the metacognition principles. This means a learner can take a course of their choice from a common distributed virtual content repository and have it delivered to them at a time/place/format of their choice in a personalized fashion, with support available as and when they need it, from anywhere within the EU and the world respectively".

Our solution to achieve this ambitious goal is to use Grid technology to create infrastructure and collaboratory to enable different players to work together. Thus the E-Learning Grid consortium was created, which currently consists of 22 members: University of Reading, UK, University of York, UK, Trinity College, Ireland, Aristotle University of Thessaloniki, Greece, University Carlos III Madrid, Spain, INESC Porto, Portugal, INSA, Lyon, France, University of Portsmouth, UK, Emory University, USA, University of Westminster, UK, University of Salford, Johannes Kepler University, Linz, Austria, several EC Centres of Excellence and major EC research centers (Bulgarian EC Centre of Exccelence, SZTAKI, Budapest, Hungary, Cyfronet, Krakow, Poland) several major IT companies (Intel, Portugal Telecom, Support IT, Giunti Interactive Labs), Ward Education Services and ICEL Ltd, Belgium.

2. The Approach

We apply multifaceted approach based on the integration of novel e-pedagogy, new technologies and organizational components (see Figure 1)

Most of the partners and especially all of the partners working in the Infrastructure working group are partners of current EC funded Grid projects such as CROSSGRID and Gridlab as well as national Grid and e-Science projects.

Most of the partners are also involved in EC GENIUS project [5]. The major results from GENIUS project have shown that:

- "Delivery (which may be as technologically enhanced as we wish) is not learning nor can it imply that learning is taking place." Hence the need of new pedagogy going hand in hand with the technology and organizational components.

- Our approach is based on *metacognition,* e.g. the awareness of and control over one's cognitive processes. Effective thinking and learning requires

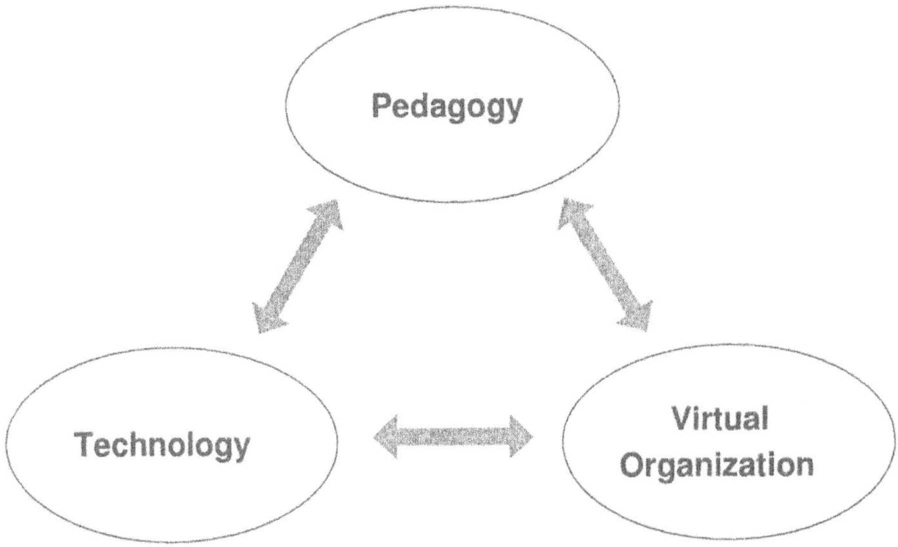

Figure 1. Our Approach.

frequent checking, goal setting, reassessing, and evaluation. We aim to improve further the quality of learning

- GENIUS also outlined the need of Organizational change and management of this change, so that we can improve quality of learning and minimize the costs.

- We should facilitate *blended learning,* due to the need of socialization [9] as an important element in the learning process. It should be noted that more than 70% of knowledge is not explicit, hence we need a system where socialization (exchanging knowledge in groups by social contacts) is a fundamental part of the system.

- The *collaboration* and *collaborative environments* facilitating collaborative learning and socialization are very important. Using the collaboration we can integrate workshops and independent learner groups.

- The learning should be *personalized and demand driven* thus being learner oriented and able to satisfy the demand for life long learning and minimize the costs through sharing of resources.

- Our experience outlined the importance of *sharing of educational materials,* which allows the teachers to concentrate in depth while preparing joint courses and at the same time minimizes the cost to the individual institutions of preparing these courses.

To translate this into practice we have to transform the conventional process of learning from constructing knowledge and acquiring skill in a traditional way to constructing knowledge using digital resources through utilizing tools and using digital communication in a virtual community (Peter Revill [4]). The management of this process and organizational clarity are also critical to this process.

In the next three sections we will give an overview of our peer-to-peer solution and finally will make some concluding remarks.

3. Pedagogy

Our pedagogical approach, following the achievements in [4, 7], is based on the educational model which assumes that the learning process is an interactive process of seeking understanding, consisting of three fundamental components: Conceptualization, Construction and Dialogue [10]. We are focusing on Construction and Dialogue phases of the learning process, since it is known [5, 10] that most of the learning is happening in these phases, and on the metacognition, which plays a significant role in developing person's learning capability. Thus we are investigating how to translate learning from theory into practice and especially in the case of e-learning, using digital tools, digital resources and digital communications [4, 5]. Collaborative learning can facilitate the Construction and Dialogue phases of the learning process and especially: team work and a combination of individual activities, with discussion all along the learning process involving lecturers and instructors from different institutions.

On the other hand, collaborative and Grid approach allows us:

- to efficiently share resources, e.g. learning material, computing resources, lecturers and instructors.
- to efficiently reuse the learning materials based on common standard.
- to collaboratively prepare learning materials and deliver them.

All this leads to the idea of the E-Learning Grid and defining such Grid infrastructure and collaborative environment based on this infrastructure which will allow multiple Virtual Organizations (VO) to co-exist.

4. The E-Learning GRID

As pointed out, our recent work has identified the need for an E-Learning Grid, allowing sharing of learning materials, collaborative preparation of such materials, collaborative learning, demand driven education based on Grid E-Learning services etc. It is apparent that other enabling technologies for content publishing, learning objects tagging to create metadata, Learning Management Systems etc are also part of the picture and essential components of the E-Learning Grid.

Indeed the overview of the E-Learning Grid layered architecture is presented in Figure 2.

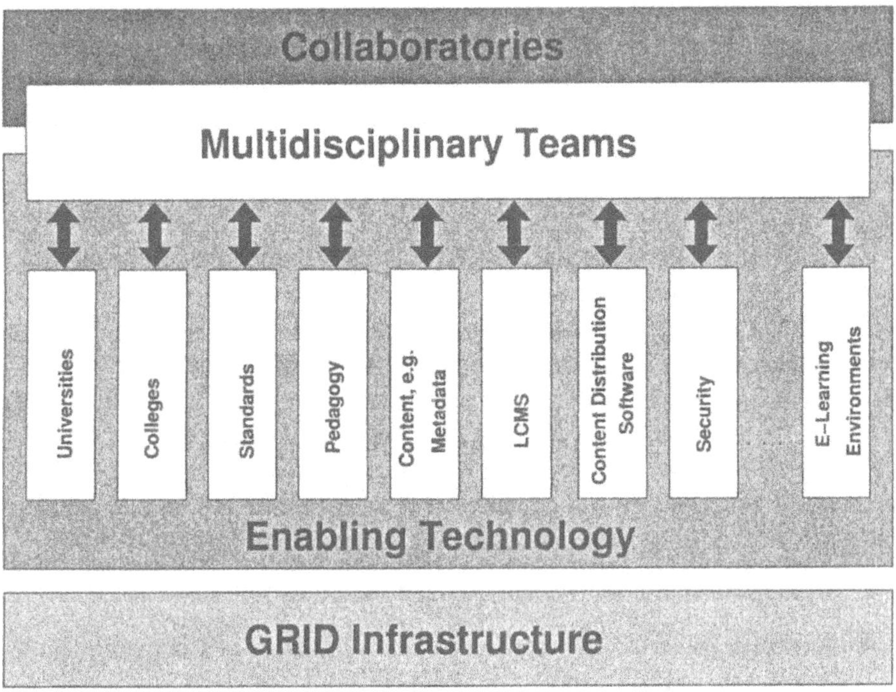

Figure 2. E-Learning Grid Architecture.

From our current experiments it is emerging that one approach ensuring scalability should be based on peer-to-peer technologies. Lets consider for example in more detail several layers of Figure 2.

Collaboratories for the E-Learning Grid

This involves sites in different Universities, Companies, and professional bodies, some developing content, and others developing Grid middleware, e-Learning software and interfaces. We need a common framework in which to interact. Hence we need a collaborative environment in which to work and place the existing components. Our approach here is based on the Collaborative Computing Platform *(Coco)*. Thus we will follow how the general description of the architecture presented in Figure 3 changes in this case.

The computing landscape is shifting rapidly. Computer networks are increasingly characterised by heterogeneity and diversity as computing begins to pervade every aspect of our daily lives; new mobile technologies are juxtaposing with traditionally network technologies to become mainstream tools for communication at home and in the workplace; network connectivity is increasingly transient and dynamic. Due to the proliferation of small mobile and wireless devices and the development of a range of network protocols and middleware to support device connectivity, it is likely that in the future network heterogeneity will be the order of the day. Work groups spanning physically distant locations will increasingly rely on a whole range of tools, including personal computers, PDAs, mobile phones etc. to cooperate and coordinate their activities and to bring a sense of cohesion and proximity to teams of collaborators on a global scale.

Traditionally, applications and tools supporting collaborative computing have been designed only with personal computers in mind and support only a limited range of computing and network platforms, such as TCP/IP or UDP. These applications are not well equipped to deal with network heterogeneity and do not cope well with dynamic network topologies. The goal of this project is to develop a framework and environment that supports the creation of multi-user collaborative sessions, allowing users to self-organise and communicate, share tasks, workloads, and content, and interact across multiple different computing platforms, network platforms and operating systems when they wish to:

- Form groups with shared interests and secure domains of trust.
- Form spontaneous collaborative sessions interacting over or manipulating shared data or documents.
- Interact with others synchronously or asynchronously.
- Be aware of other users and have access to user credentials for authentication.
- Share arbitrary content using metadata representations.

We are aiming for *heterogeneity* in terms of both network and operating system platforms centred on two fundamental technologies: JXTA and Java.

JXTA (a project initiated by Sun Microsystems, Inc.) is a set of open network protocols that enable communication, interaction, and the sharing of resources in peer-to-peer (P2P) networks. JXTA consists of a set of network protocols that standardize the ways in which network nodes (or *peers*) discover other peers, resources and services, organise into groups, communicate, and monitor each other. JXTA is designed to facilitate homogenous peer connectivity within heterogeneous network environments. JXTA makes few assumptions about the network environment. JXTA specifies *mechanisms* not *policies* relating to the way in which peers interact in the network [6]. As a result JXTA peers are able deal with highly partitioned networks, capable of traversing firewalls and NAT, and to exist in highly volatile network environments where devices may disappear from the network with high probability. The capabilities of other peers in the network may also range greatly, from simple resource-limited devices to network servers and supercomputers. JXTA therefore provides us with interoperability at the protocol level, the kind of interoperability that is well suited to collaborative architectures designed to support a range of network platforms and operating systems.

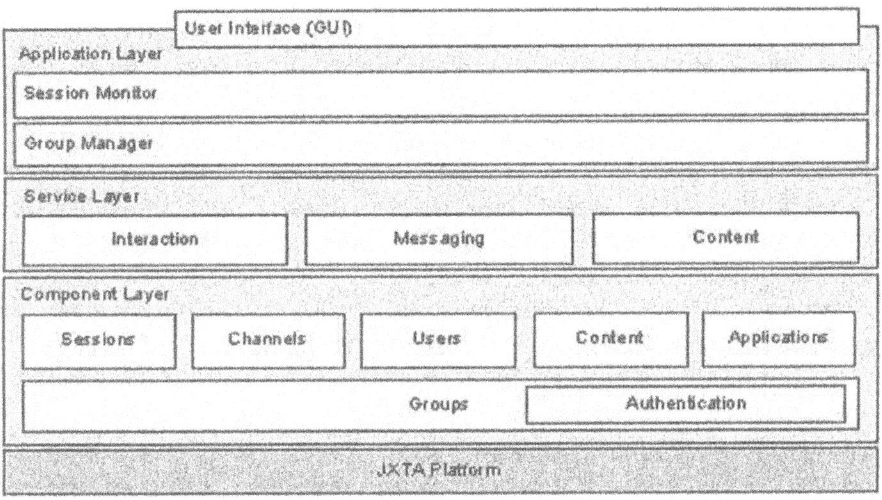

Figure 3. Coco Architecture.

Consider now the *Coco* architecture. *Coco* has been developed as both a programming environment, through a set of objects and a service APIs, and a runtime environment that allows users to create and announce collaborative sessions. The design of *Coco* platform is based on a layered architecture, illustrated by Figure 3.

The design focuses on three fundamental aspects that can be summarised as follows:

Components - the component layer contains a set of components that are integral to the platform. Components can be seen as manifestations of concepts and abstractions that were derived from an analysis of the system requirements. All components have an XML-based representation on the network that allows the *Coco* service layer to build on JXTA core services, providing the underlying propagation mechanism for the dissemination of messages between peers.

Current components include *sessions, channels, users, groups, content, and applications.*

Services - services encapsulate the network service functionality of the system. The architecture is designed to provide a number of services (exposed through a set of service APIs) that enable peers to access the resources of remote peers and groups, thus forming an interface that can be built on by applications. The design consists of three core services: the *interaction service*, the *messaging service*, and the *content service*. The services are fundamental to the system design as they completely specify the network behaviour of peers, allowing peers to discover resources, propagate messages, and communicate in the context of a heterogeneous network environment.

Applications - the application layer provides two platform applications that allow users to create groups and to create, discover, and join collaborative sessions within the context of groups.

Layering at the architectural level encourages the encapsulation of components into modules with well-defined interfaces, enabling higher-level services to be built using the facilities of lower ones. Layering also ensures that services and applications are separated (or *decoupled*) and reduces dependencies within the system. The combined elements of the architecture are designed to provide an interoperable substrate that can be built on by applications via the *Coco* service interfaces.

Coco is currently in an early stage of development and has therefore undergone little formal or rigorous testing. However, we have been developing demonstration applications concurrently to the development of the platform, including an instant messenger with file sharing capabilities, a shared whiteboard, a shared web browser, as well as progressively developing other components.

Peer-to-peer Technologies for Content Distribution

Here we would like to give an example of an enabling technology for content distribution. Note that peer-to-peer technologies [1, 2] for content distribution e.g. pull and push, such as the embedded version of Intel's ® Content Distribution System (*Intel ® CDS*). Intel ® CDS can be efficiently used to distribute content. These techniques have shown to eliminate the bandwidth bottleneck for cutting edge multimedia and e-Learning. Today e-Learning content developers are constrained in their design as they need to design for the narrowest pipe which transports an e-Learning module to a user. The use of client caching and peer-to-peer protocols dramatically improves file download times while reducing infrastructure costs [2]. This technology has been tested in an intranet environment with great results and in a wide area networks, where through GENIUS we have focused on the internet use of this technology and we expect it's broad deployment to enable a high performing cost effective e-Learning Grid.

5. Building Virtual Organizations

In the previous sections we have considered the pedagogical and technological components, Here we will very briefly focus on the organizational aspects. The above infrastructure allows us high degree of flexibility:

- It offers scalable solution, partners can join and various components such as modules etc being placed in the environment.
- Offers possibility to form groups with shared interests.
- Offers possibility to form collaborative sessions interacting over or manipulating shared data or documents.
- Interact with others synchronously or asynchronously.

Based on the above we can form different Virtual Organizations which can co-exist for delivering specific modules, courses etc. The collaborative capabilities allow facilitation of collaborative learning, collaborative preparation of materials etc.

6. Conclusion

In this paper we have presented a peer-to-peer approach to the E-Learning Grid. We have outlined a layered collaborative computing platform facilitating most of the functionality required for collaborative learning on the Grid.

Acknowledgments

The authors wish to thank Martin Curley, Intel Ireland Ltd, Leixlip, Co. Kildare Republic of Ireland, for his contribution to the paper with the material on Intel's® peer-to-peer content distribution system (Intel ® CDS). The authors also wish to thank, DG Education and Culture of the EC for their partial support for the work through the EC GENIUS project: 2001-3450/001-001 EDU-ELEARN.

References

[1] A. Oram, *Peer-to-Peer: Harnessing the Power of Disruptive Technologies*, O'Reilly, March, 2001.

[2] Martin G. Curley, "Peer-to-Peer Computing Enabled Collaboration", Proc. of ICCS2002, LNCS 2330, Springer-Verlag, 646–654.

[3] Nia Alexandrov, J.S.Pascoe, and, Vassil Alexandrov "Collaborative Computing and E-Learning". Proc of ICCS2002, LNCS2330, Springer-Verlag, 688–694.

[4] Peter Revill, "GENIUS project Pedagogical Report", 2003, www.genius.reading.ac.uk

[5] GENIUS - Generic E-Learning Environments and Paradigms for the New Pan European Information and Communication Technologies Curricula, EC project, 2001 - 2003, www.genius.reading.ac.uk

[6] A.B. Gong, L (2002): Project JXTA: A Technology Overview, Palo Alto, CA, USA: Sun Microsystems, Inc.,2002.http://www.jxta.org/project/www/docs/jxtaview_01nov02.pdf.

[7] Ian Foster, Carl Kesselman, Steven Tuecke, "The Anatomy of the Grid", http://www.globus.org/research/papers/anatomy.pdf

[8] Ian Foster, Carl Kesselman, Jeffrey M. Nick, Steven Tuecke, "The Physiology of the Grid", http://www.globus.org/research/papers/ogsa.pdf

[9] Nonaka, *The Knowledge Creating Company*, Harvard Business Review No. 91608, 1991

[10] Mayes, T., "Pedagogy, Lifelong Learning and ICT", A discussion paper for IBM Chair presentation, Glasgow 18 May, 2000.

AN INTELLIGENT VIRTUAL ENVIRONMENT FOR DISTANCE LEARNING

Cássia Trojahn dos Santos and Fernando Santos Osório
Unisinos University, Brazil

Abstract: This paper presents an intelligent, adaptive, three-dimensional and virtual environment for distance learning. The environment, used to make educational content available, has its structure and presentation customized according to users' interests and preferences (represented in user models) and in accordance with insertion or removal of contents. An automatic categorization process is applied in the creation of content models, used in the spatial organization of the contents in the environment. Moreover, the environment is populated by an intelligent agent, who assists users during the navigation and retrieval of relevant information.

Key words: intelligent virtual environments; virtual reality; distance learning.

1. INTRODUCTION

Virtual Reality (VR) became an attractive alternative for the development of more realistic and interesting three-dimensional visual interfaces for the user [Teichrieb, 1999]. The environments that make use of VR techniques are referred as Virtual Environments (VEs). In VEs, according to Avradinis et al. (2000), the user is a part of the system, an autonomous presence in the environment. He is able to navigate, to interact with objects and to examine the environment from different viewpoints. According to Frery et al. (2002), the 3D paradigm is useful mainly because it offers the possibility of representing information in a realistic way, while it organizes the contents in a spatial manner. In this way, a larger intuition in the visualization of the information is obtained, allowing the user to explore it in an interactive way, more natural to humans. Moreover, a more effective interaction can be obtained from the adaptation of interface, according to the characteristics of individual users or groups of users. According to Chittaro and Ranon (2002), the capability of (semi)automatically adapting the content, structure, and/or presentation of environment, to address the users' interests and preferences, is considered as a key factor to increase user satisfaction.

Moreover, nowadays, the focus of attention has been the integration of Artificial Intelligence (AI) and VEs. The objective is to obtain larger usability and realism from the interfaces, exploring the combination of 3D objects and intelligent entities. According to Aylett and Luck (2000), the environments that explore such integration are called Intelligent Virtual Environments (IVEs). An IVE is a virtual environment resembling the real world, populated by autonomous intelligent entities capable of a variety of behaviors. These entities may be simple, static or dynamic objects, virtual representations of life forms (virtual animals and humans), avatars of real world users entering the system, and others [Anastassakis et al. 2001]. According to Rickel et al. (2002), the potential applications for these environments are substantial, since they could be applied in a variety of areas, mainly related to simulation, entertainment and education.

In this paper, an intelligent and adaptive virtual environment for distance learning is presented. The paper is organized as follows. In section 2, the proposed environment is presented. Section 3 comments on the prototype developed to validate the environment. In section 4, the final considerations are presented.

2. THE INTELLIGENT VIRTUAL ENVIRONMENT

The proposed environment consists of the representation of a 3D world, accessible through the Web, used to make educational content available. In this environment, there is support for two types of users: information *consumer* (e.g., student) and information *provider* (e.g., teacher). The *consumer*, represented by avatars, explores the environment searching relevant contents and can be aided by the virtual agent, in the navigation and location of information. A *consumer model* is maintained, so that the environment can be adapted according to this model. The *providers*, responsible for made available contents, can explore the environment. A *provider model* also is kept. The consumer and provider models are managed by the *user model manager* module. The contents added, removed or updated by the provider are managed by the *content manager module* and stored in a *content database*. Each content contains an associated model (*content model*). The *provider*, aided by the automatic content categorization process, acts in the definition of this model. From the *content model*, the spatial position that the content will occupy in the environment is defined. Content, consumer and provider models are used in the environment adaptation. The representation of the contents in the environment is made by 3D objects and links to the data (e.g., text document, web page). The *environment generator module* is responsible for the generation of different 3D structures that form the environment and to arrange the information in the environment, according to user and content models. The environment adaptation involves its reorganization, in relation to the arrangement of the contents and aspects of its layout (e.g., use of different textures and colors, according to user's preferences). Besides, this module transmits to the *agent* the applicable information about the user interacting with the environment, and information about the contents and their locations, so that it holds enough information in order to assist the users. In the following sections are detailed the main components of the environment.

2.1 USER MODEL MANAGER

This module is responsible for initialization and updating of user models. The user model contains information about the users' interests, preferences and behaviors. In order to collect the data used in the composition of the models, the explicit and implicit approaches are used. The explicit approach is adopted to acquire the user's preferences compounding an initial user model and the implicit one is applied to update this model. In the explicit approach, a form is used, to collect the following data: name, e-mail, gender, areas of interest and preferences for colors. The three last data are used in the initial environment adaptation. In the implicit approach, the monitoring of user navigation in the environment and his interactions with the agent are made. Through this approach, the environment places visited by the user and the requested (through the search mechanism) and accessed (clicked) contents are monitored. These data are used to update the initial user model. The process of updating the user model is based on certainty factors (CF) ([Nikolopoulos, 1997]; [Giarratano and Riley, 1998]), which associate measures of belief (MB) and disbelief (MD) in a hypothesis (H), given an evidence (E). A CF=1 indicates total belief in a hypothesis, while a CF=-1 correspond the total disbelief. The calculation of the CF is accomplished by the following formulas:

$$MB\begin{cases} 1 \quad if\ P(H)=1 \\ \dfrac{\max[P(H \mid E), P(H)] - P(H)}{1-P(H)} \quad otherwise \end{cases}$$

$$CF = \frac{MB - MD}{1 - \min(MB, MD)}$$

$$MD\begin{cases} 1 \quad if\ P(H)=0 \\ \dfrac{\min[P(H \mid E), P(H)] - P(H)}{0-P(H)} \quad otherwise \end{cases}$$

The evidences are related to the environment areas visited and to the requested and accessed contents by the user. They are used to infer the hypothesis of the user's interest in each area of knowledge, from the CF. The user's initial interest in a given area (initial value of P(H)) is determined by the explicit data collection and it may vary during the process of updating the model (based on threshold of increasing and decreasing belief). Each n sessions (adjustable time window), for each area, the evidences (navigation, request and access) are verified and the CFs corresponding to the hypothesis of interest are updated. By sorting the resulting CFs, it is possible to establish a ranking of the user's interest area. Therefore it is possible to verify the alterations in the initial model (obtained from the explicit collection) and, thus, to update the user model. From this update, the reorganization of the environment is made - contents that correspond to the areas of major user's interest are placed, in a visualization order, before the contents which are less interesting (easier access). It must be addressed that each modification in the environment is always suggested to user and made only under user's acceptance.

2.2 CONTENT MANAGER

This module is responsible for insertion and removal of contents, and management of its models. The provider is responsible for defining the content model, being able to be assisted by an automatic content categorization process. In the insertion of content, the provider must inform the following data, used in the composition of the content model: category (among a pre-defined set), title, description, keywords, type of media and corresponding file. For textual contents, an automatic text categorization process is available, thus the category and the keywords of the content are obtained. For non textual contents (for instance, images and videos), textual descriptions of contents can be used in the automatic categorization process.

The categorization process proposed in this work is based on the use of machine learning techniques (see [Sebastiani, 2002]), such as Decision Trees [Quinlan, 1993] and Artificial Neural Networks [Haykin, 2001]. This process is formed by a sequence of stages: (a) document base collection; (b) pre-processing; and (c) categorization. The document base collection consists of obtaining the examples to be used for the training and the test of the learning algorithm. The pre-processing involves, for each example, the elimination of irrelevant words (e.g., articles, prepositions and pronouns), the removal of affix of the words and the selection of the most important words, used to characterize the document. In the categorization stage, the learning technique is then determined, the examples are coded and the classifier learning is accomplished. After these stages, the classifier can be used in the categorization of new documents. In a set of preliminary experiments (details in [Santos and Osorio, 2003]), the decision trees showed to be more robust and were selected for use in the categorization process proposed. In these experiments, the pre-processing stage was supported by an application5, extended from a *framelet*, whose kernel contemplates the basic flow of data among the activities of removal of irrelevant words and affixes, selection of important words and generation of scripts submitted to the learning algorithms. After applying the learning algorithm, the "learned model" – rules extracted from the decision tree – is connected to the module content manager, in order to use it in the categorization of new documents. Thus, when a new document is inserted in the environment, it is pre-processed, has its keywords extracted and is categorized automatically. Based on the content model, the spatial position where the content must be placed is determined.

2.3 INTELLIGENT VIRTUAL AGENT

In the environment, a virtual agent assists users during navigation and retrieval of relevant information. It has the following characteristics: perception of the environment, ability to interact, user/content knowledge, certain degree of reasoning and autonomy and graphic representation. The agent's architecture reflects the following modules: knowledge base, perception, decision and action. The agent's knowledge base stores the information that it holds about the user and the environment. This knowledge is built from two sources of information: external source and

[5] Framelet available in: http://www.inf.unisinos.br/~cassiats/dissertacao

perception of the interaction with the user. The external source is the information about the environment and the user, and they are originated from the environment generator module. A perception module observes the interaction with the user, and the information obtained from this observation is used to update the agent's knowledge. It is through the perception module that the agent detects the requests from user and observes the user's actions in the environment. Based on its perception and in the knowledge that it holds, the agent decides how to act in the environment. A decision module is responsible for this activity. The decisions are passed to an action module, responsible to execute the actions (e.g., animation of graphic representation and speech synthesis).

The communication between the agent and the users is made in a verbal way, through a pseudo-natural language and speech synthesis, and non verbal way, by the agent's actions in the environment. The dialogue in pseudo-natural language consists of a certain group of questions and answers and short sentences, formed by a verb that corresponds to the type of user request and a complement, regarding the object of user interest. During the request for helping to locate information, for instance, the user can indicate (in textual interface) Locate <content>. The agent's answers are suggested by its own movement through the environment (moving towards the information requested by the user), by indications through short sentences, and by text-to-speech synthesis. In the interaction with provider, during the insertion of content, he can indicate Insert <content>, and the agent presents the data entry interface for the specification, identification and automatic categorization of the content. Moreover, a topological map of the environment is kept in the agent's knowledge base. In this map, a set of routes for key-positions of the environment is stored. In accordance with the information that the agent has about the environment and with the topological map, it defines a set of routes that must be used in the localization of determined content or used to navigate until determined environment area. Considering that the agent updates its knowledge for each modification in the environment, it is always able to verify the set of routes that leads to a new position of a specific content.

3. PROTOTYPE

In the prototype, a division of the virtual environment is adopted according to the areas of the knowledge of the contents. In each area a set of sub-areas can be associated. The sub-areas are represented as subdivisions of the environment. In the prototype, the following areas and sub-areas were selected: Artificial Intelligence (AI) – Artificial Neural Networks, Genetic

Algorithms and Multi Agents Systems; Computer Graphics (CG) – Modeling, Animation and Visualization; Computer Networks (CN) – Security, Management and Protocols; Software Engineering (SE) – Analysis, Patterns and Software Quality. A room is associated to each area in the environment and the sub-areas are represented as subdivisions of rooms. Figures 1 (a) and 1 (b) show screen-shots of the prototype that illustrate the division of the environment in rooms and sub-rooms. In screen-shots, a system version in Portuguese is presented, where the description "Inteligência Artificial" corresponds to "Artificial Intelligence".

According to the user model, the reorganization of this environment is made: the rooms that correspond to the areas of major user's interest are placed, in a visualization order, before the rooms which contents are less interesting. The initial user model, based on explicit data collection, is used to initial organization of the environment. Figures 2 (a) and 2 (b) represent examples of the initial environment adaptations. In the environment of Figure 2 (a), the user (female gender) has interest by AI and use of clean color; in the environment of Figure 2 (b), the user (male gender) has interest by CG and use of dark color. As the user interacts with the environment, his model is updated

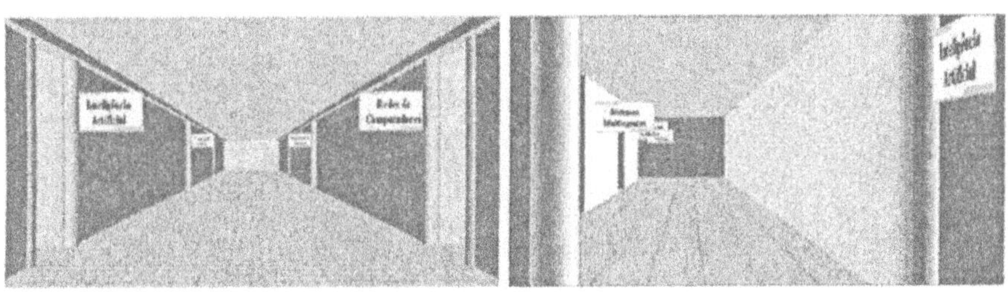

(a) (b)

Figure 1. (a) Rooms and (b) sub-rooms of the environment

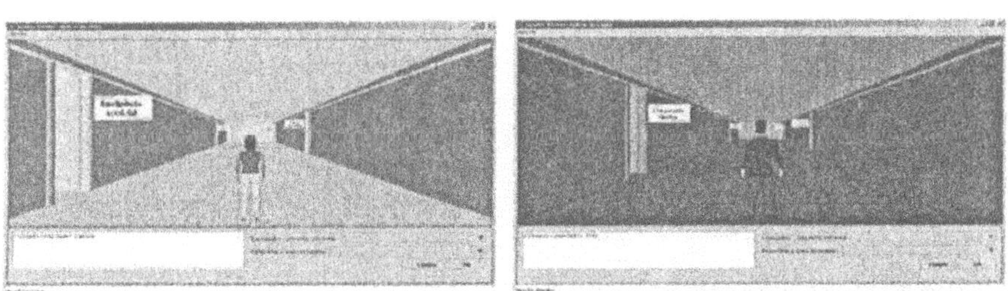

(a) (b)

Figure 2. (a) User with interest in AI; (b) user with interest in CG

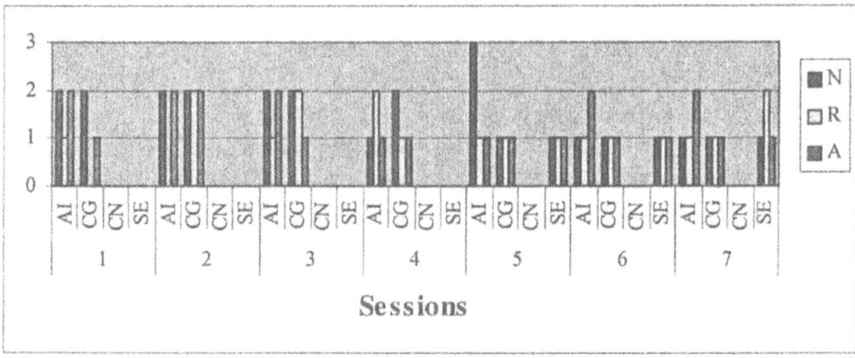

Figure 3. Navigations (N), requests(R) and access (A) for session

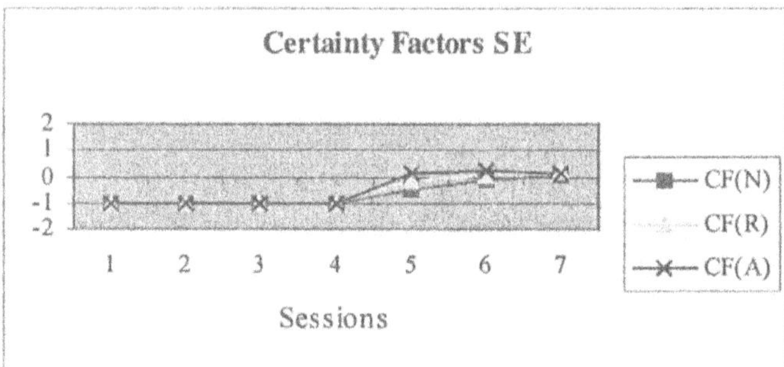

Figure 4. Certainty factors corresponding to evidences of the SE area

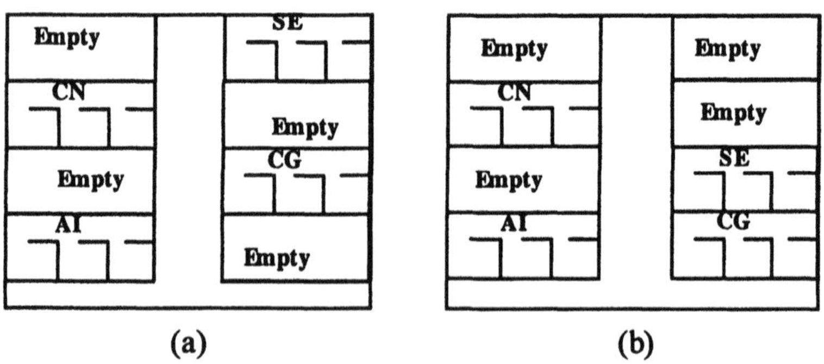

Figure 5. (a) Organization of the environment according initial user model; (b) organization after the user model changes

After n sessions, for each area, the evidences of interest are verified, in order to update the user model. For instance, with a user, who is interested about AI, is indifferent to contents related to the areas of CN and CG, and does not show initial interest about SE, the initial values of the CFs, at the beginning of the first session of interaction (without evidences), would be respectively 1, 0, 0 e –1. After doing some navigations (N), requests (R) and access (A), presented in the graph of Figure 3, the CFs can be reevaluated. According to Figure 3, it is verified that the CN area was not navigated, requested and accessed, and on the other side, the user started to navigate, to request, and to access contents in SE area. As presented in the graph of Figure 4, an increasing of the CFs had been identified as related to the SE area. In that way, at end of the seventh session, the resulting CFs would be 1, -1, 0.4 and 0.2 (AI, CN, CG, SE, respectively). By sorting the resulting CFs, it would be possible to detect an alteration in the user model, whose new ranking of the interest areas would be AI, CG, SE and CN. Figures 5 (a) and 5 (b) represent an example of the organization of the environment before and after a modification in the user model, as showed in the example above.

On the other side, in relation to manipulation of contents in the environment, the provider model is used to indicate the area (e.g., Artificial Intelligence) that belongs the content being inserted, and the automatic categorization process indicates the corresponding sub-area (e.g., Artificial Neural Nets), or either, the sub-room where the content should be inserted. In this way, the spatial disposal of the content is made automatically by the environment generator, on the basis of its category. In the prototype, thirty examples of scientific papers, for each sub-area, had been collected from the Web, and used for learning and validation of the categorization algorithm. In the stage of learning, experiments with binary and multiple categorizations had been carried through. In the binary categorization, a tree is used to indicate if a document belongs or not to the definitive category. In the multiple categorization, a tree is used to indicate the most likely category of one document, amongst a possible set. In these experiments, the binary categorization presents better results (less error and, consequently, greater recall and precision), being adopted in the prototype. In this way, for each sub-area, the rules obtained from decision tree (C4.5) were converted to rules of type IF – THEN and associated to content manager module.

In relation to communication process between the agent and the users, they interact by a dialog in pseudo-natural language (section 2.3). As a way to simplify the communication model, the user selects one request to the agent in an options list. The agent's answers are showed in the corresponding interface text window and synthesized to speech. Figures 6(a), (b), (c) and (d) illustrate, respectively: a request of the user for the localization of determined area and the movement of agent; the localization of an area by the agent; the user visualization of a content; and the visualization of details of a content, after selection and click in a specific content description.

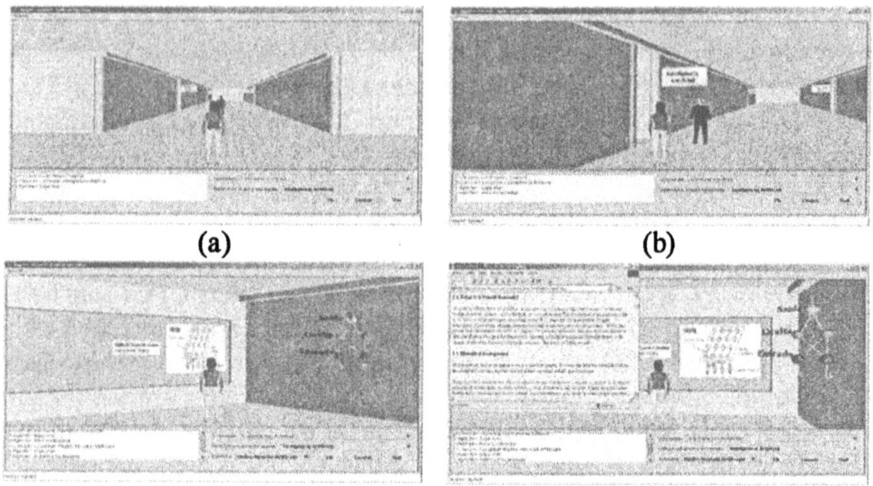

(a) (b) (c) (d)

Figure 6. (a) Request of the user; (b) localization of an area by the agent; (c) visualization of contents; (d) details of a content

4. FINAL REMARKS

A large number of distance learning environments make content available through 2D environments, offering poor interaction with the user. This paper presented an intelligent and adaptive virtual environment that explores the resources of VR, seeking to increase the interactivity degree between the users and the environment. The spatial reorganization possibilities and the environment customization, according to the modifications (addition, removal and updating) in the contents available and the user models were presented. Besides, an automatic categorization process that aims to help the specialist of the domain (provider) in the information organization in this environment was shown. Finally, an intelligent agent that knows the environment and the user and acts assisting him in the navigation and location of information in this environment was commented. An important aspect considered in this work deals with the acquisition of users' characteristics in a 3D environment. Most of the works related to user models acquisition and environment adaptation are accomplished using 2D interfaces. Moreover, a great portion of efforts in the construction of Intelligent Virtual Environments don't provide the combination of user models, assisted navigation and retrieval of information, and, mainly, don't have the capability to reorganize the environment, and display the contents in a 3D. Usually, only a sub-group of these problems is considered.

REFERENCES

Anastassakis, G.; Ritching, T.; Panayiotopoulos, T. 2001. Multi-agent Systems as Intelligent Virtual Environments. LNAI 2174, pp. 381-395.

Avradinis, N.; Vosinakis, S.; Panayiotopoulos, T. 2000. Using Virtual Reality Techniques for the Simulation of Physics Experiments. 4th Systemic, Cybernetic and Informatics International Conference, USA, July.

Aylett, R. and Luck, M. 2000. Applying Artificial Intelligence to Virtual Reality: Intelligent Virtual Environments. Applied Artificial Intelligence, 14(1), pp. 3-32.

Chittaro, L. and Ranon, R. 2002. New Directions for the Design of Virtual Reality Interfaces to E-Commerce Sites. 5th International Conference on Advanced Visual Interface, Italy, May.

Frery, A.; Kelner, J.; Moreira, J., Teichrieb, V. 2002. Satisfaction through Empathy and Orientation in 3D Worlds. CyberPsychology and Behavior, 5(5), pp. 451-459.

Giarratano, J. and Riley, G. 1998. Expert Systems: Principles and Programming. 3 ed., PWS, Boston.

Haykin, S. 2001. Redes Neurais: Princípios e Prática, 2 ed. Bookman.

Nikolopoulos, C. 1997. Expert Systems – Introduction to First and Second Generation and Hybrid Knowledge Based Systems. Eds.: Marcel Dekker, New York.

Quinlan, R. 1993. C4.5: Programs for Machine Learning. Mogan Kaufmann, California.

Rickel, J.; Marsella, S.; Gratch, J.; Hill, R.; Traum, D.; Swartout W. 2002. Toward a New Generation of Virtual Humans for Interactive Experiences. IEEE Intelligent Systems, 17(4).

Santos, C. and Osorio, F. 2003. Uso de Técnicas de Aprendizado de Máquina no Processo de Categorização de Textos. Research Report (http://www.inf.unisinos.br/~cassiats/mestrado).

Sebastiani, F. 2002. Machine learning in automated text categorization. Computing Surveys, 34(1), pp.1-47.

Teichrieb, V. 1999. Avatares como Guias Interativos para Auxílio na Navegação em Ambientes Virtuais Tridimensionais. Universidade de Pernambuco, Recife, Brazil (Master dissertation).

DEVELOPMENT AND IMPLEMENTATION OF A BIOMETRIC VERIFICATION SYSTEM FOR E-LEARNING PLATFORMS

Elisardo González-Agulla, Enrique Argones-Rúa, Carmen García-Mateo and Óscar W. Márquez-Flórez
Signal Processing Group, Signal Theory & Communications Dept, University of Vigo, Spain

Abstract: We describe a biometric verification system to improve the security and reliability in services offered by e-learning platforms. We developed a prototype in the platform ILIAS to improve its online identification service. We use our extension of VoiceXML called BioVXML [1]. BioVXML is focused on user biometric verification. It is able to handle heterogeneous biometric samples, such as voice samples or frontal face images and takes them into account in order to do a multimodal biometric verification. This prototype is used to acquire a biometric database, the BioDB. This database will serve us as a test environment for the different biometric verification methods.

Key words: VoiceXML Biometric Verification; Biometric Algorithms; Internet identification.

1. INTRODUCTION

E-learning has emerged in the recent times as an alternate solution to the traditional education. One of the main drawbacks of the e-learning is the difficulty to do an online user verification. The current e-learning platforms that provide online user identification implement methods that are not secure in order to prevent an impostor to supplant a user [2-5].

Our objective is to build an independent verification system based on processing biometric features such as voice or frontal face images. This system can be embedded in web applications and is intended to improve security and reliability in the access to some web services. In particular we want to improve the e-learning platform ILIAS [5] developing a biometric verification module to avoid user supplantation.

The verification tasks are modeled as human-machine dialogues. The main contribution of this work is the way these dialogues can be specified. They are defined in an extension of the markup language VoiceXML. This extension provides multimodal verification support to the system, and we decided to name it as **BioVXML**. BioVXML enables us to use different types of biometric features, such as voice or frontal face images, and an easy way to incorporate new biometric algorithms and modalities. BioVXML separates the application development from biometric algorithmic development, so the application developers do not need a background on biometrics to incorporate them to its client/server application.

The behaviour of the system is specified in the dialogues stored in the BioVXML files associated to the enrollment task and the verification task. Each BioVXML file defines an interaction between the user and the client of the verification system. This interaction is implemented by a graphical interface. The user collaborates in the biometric features acquisition process following the instructions of the application.

The verification system reports the e-learning platform on the verification process result. The e-learning platform calls the verification system for user authentication, and it must handle the results from the verification process.

2. DESCRIPTION OF THE BIOMETRIC VERIFICATION SYSTEM

Below we describe the environment where the verification system must be integrated, how the human-machine dialogues are built, the structure of the system, its architecture and its implementation.

2.1 The environment

The environment we use to test the feasibility of BioVXML is the e-learning platform ILIAS. This e-learning platform uses the traditional login and password in order to gain access to its different tools. Our goal is to improve these techniques using biometric procedures to tighten the e-learning platform security up. This improvement is achieved by using different authentication algorithms based on face and speech. User-tracking must be carried out by the system in order to avoid dynamic supplantations.

Also, a report file must be stored to deal with possible problems detected during the session.

2.2 Design of the verification dialogue system

In the early design phase of the verification system some alternatives were analyzed in order to get an appropriate model for the verification process. Standards such as BioAPI, VoiceXML and X+V [6-9] have been studied, but we have finally opted for making an extension of VoiceXML 1.0 due to this markup language provides flexibility and an adequate client/server approach.

VoiceXML was originally intended for applications where the access is usually done by telephone and it just manages audio data. Our application is over an IP network and must manage multiple types of multimedia data. In order to take these aspects into account the VoiceXML must be extended appropriately.

2.3 BioVXML specification

We need a simple way to define human-computer dialogues, but these dialogues must be able to make all the biometric identity verification tasks, so we must extend VoiceXML to get our objective. BioVXML [1] must be able to handle the different kinds of biometric data, such as voice and face images. Therefore we added the new tags **enroll** and **verify** to the *VoiceXML.dtd*, and we modified the tag **record**. We named the DTD obtained so as *BioVXML.dtd*. Below we detail the functionality and syntax of the new or modified tags.

- Tag **<record>**: this tag is used for recording audio in VoiceXML. We added the new attribute **src** to it. It indicates the kind of biometric data to be recorded. Our parser BioVXML allows *src* to have two different values, *voice* and *face*, corresponding to audio samples or frontal face images. The parser could implement in a future any biometric value, just adding the associated functionality to the parser. If the attribute *src* is omitted, we will regard it as an audio source, keeping compatibility with VoiceXML.
- Tag **<enroll>**: this new tag is used to make the enrollment task. Its attributes are **name**, name of the variable associated with the result of the enrollment; and **type**, this is used to distinguish the different enrollment algorithms. The biometric data and configurable parameters for the methods are added like BioVXML parameters.
- Tag **<verify>**: this new tag is used to make the biometric identity verification. It has the same attributes than the tag enroll (**name** and

type), with the same meaning. The biometric data and configurable parameters for the methods are also added like BioVXML parameters.

A parser BioVXML was developed to interpret the BioVXML documents. These documents must abide by the BioVXML.dtd specified.

3. ARCHITECTURE AND STRUCTURE OF THE SYSTEM

The biometric verification system is a web application with client/server architecture. It provides identity verification services through man-machine dialogues defined through BioVXML documents. This verification system can be used by E-learning platforms to increase security in user accesses. Figure 1 shows the modular architecture of the verification system. Three main parts can be distinguished: The client application, the server application and the biometric application. Next, we describe the functionality of each of these parts:

The client application must handle the multimedia devices, such as the microphone and the webcam, to acquire biometric data, and send these features to the server. The application must show an appropriate graphical user interface, monitor the users, it sends reports and, eventually, a video/audio flow to the server.

Inside the server, we can distinguish several independent modules. One of them, the so-called Biometric Application embeds different multimodal algorithms for biometric user authentication. This module has an own database where templates, logs, scores and enrolment data (wav and jpeg files) are stored. The module constitutes an independent part of the system, offering a HTTPS access interface, so that different applications can access it. The other main module inside the server, the Server Application, constitutes the kernel of the system, and it offers two access interfaces, one of them towards the web platform in which it is embedded. This way, the web platform is able to:

- Setup the verification system.
- Choose the authentication mode.
- Request a report of the user behaviour during the session, etc.

The other interface is used for communication with the different users, who must be verified by the system.

The kernel of this application manages the Web Platform requests, the client incidences detected and the user verification process. Events happened during this process are annotated in a BioVXML document. So, this file shows a human-machine dialogue, which can be divided into three main parts:

- Capturing samples.
- Invoking authentication algorithm.
- Reporting results.

The BioVXML Interpreter runs the file containing the appropriate authentication algorithm and it must deal with the following tasks:

- Request the necessary samples to the client application.
- Invoke the verification method specified in the BioVXML file (this file is owned by the Biometric Application).
- Report the result of the verification process to the client and to the web platform.

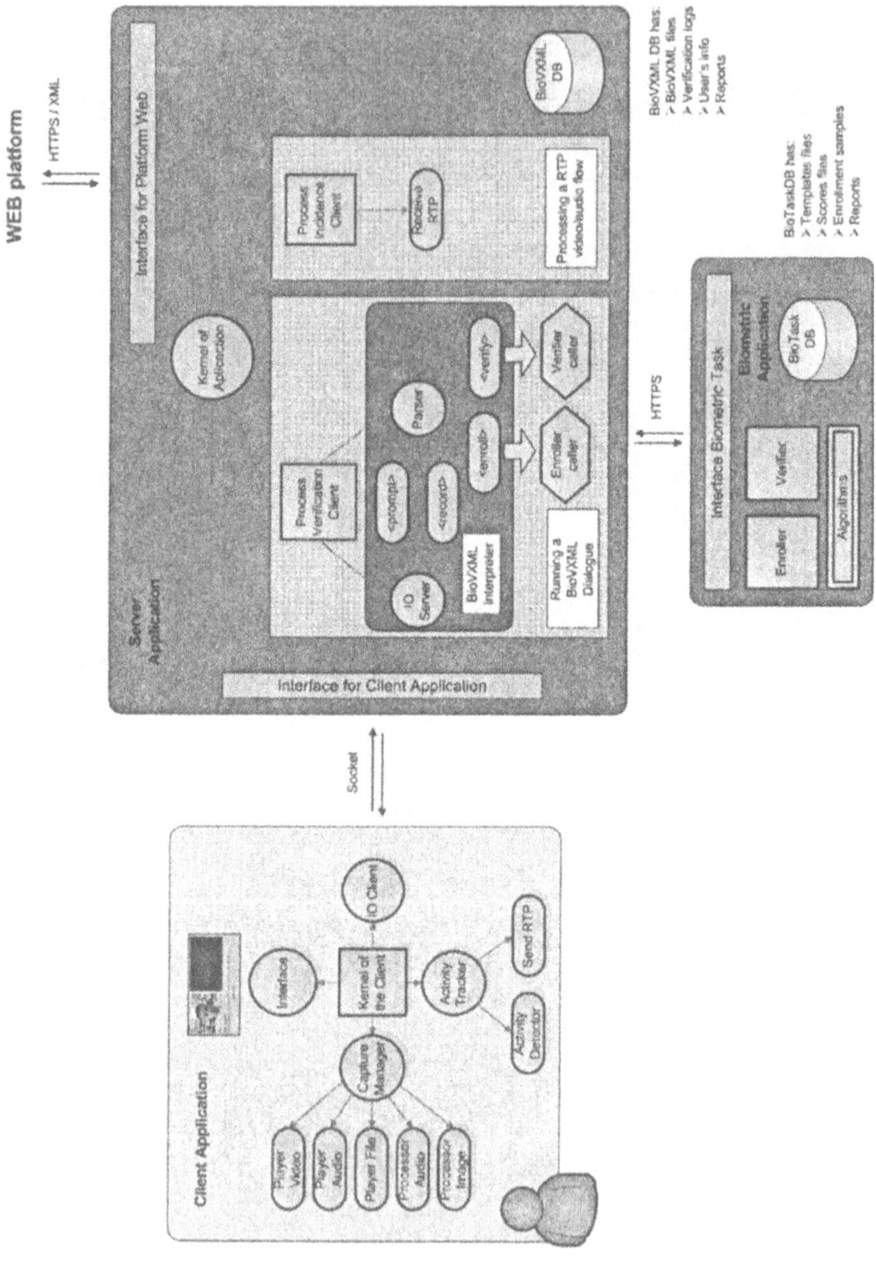

Figure 1. Architecture of the Biometric Verification System

4. IMPLEMENTATION OF THE VERIFICATION SYSTEM

In Figure 1 we show a structural scheme of the prototype we developed. Below we describe the implementation of its components:

4.1 Client description

We have considered the following requirements during the design of the client: Modularity; Multiplatform; Integration in the Web platform; Handling of multimedia devices and multimedia data; and easily to update.

These requirements made a **Java WebStart Application** [10] an appropriate solution because the users run always the last version of our client application. We must use the Java package **JMF** [11] in order to handle multimedia devices and multimedia data and its RTP features; and we use **Swing** in order to provide an adequate graphical user interface in multiplatform environment.

Our application consists of the packages **Client** and **Capture**. It is packed in the file **ClientApplication.jar** to minimize the number of connections to the HTTP server. The graphical interface, as example, is showed in Figure 2.

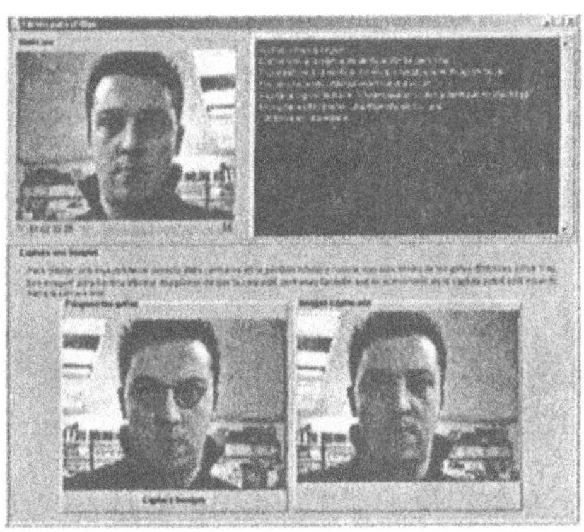

Figure 2. Frontal face image acquisition interface

4.2 Server Application description

Our server manages the user verification queries from the Platform Web in an independent way. It makes the verification or enrollment task depending on what the Web Platform is asking for. It manages the possible events sent from the clients, reports them to the administrator and stores the associated video flow sent from the client.

We implemented a BioVXML **parser** in Java. Our **BioVXML Interpreter** uses this parser to work with BioVXML documents. This interpreter uses the different methods provided by the **Implementation Platform** in order to communicate with the clients, access to the BioVXML documents and communicate with the MySQL database.

The server is packed in the JAR file **ApplicationServer.jar** and the **class *ServerApplication*** is the kernel of the server. It manages the client requests and processes them in independent threads. When a verification user request is received from the Web Platform, the server application runs the corresponding BioVXML dialogue, and it sends the instructions to the client by a TCP/IP socket channel. When the application server receives the different biometric samples, it calls to the biometric application by a HTTPS channel to run the verification algorithms.

4.3 Biometric Application description

The biometric application is a servlet java. This servlet processes the verification queries. It must build the call to the different biometric verification, taking into account the claimed identity, the identification of the algorithm to be used and the biometric data needed. Once the algorithm returns the verification result, the servlet returns this result back to the server application.

This servlet uses a database to store data related to every verification session, the biometric enrollment data, the result files, the log files, etc.

5. INTEGRATION OF THE VERIFICATION SYSTEM IN ILIAS

The integration of the verification system in the web platform must be done in the user access control module. More precisely, after a user has been identified by the usual methods. ILIAS was designed according to the layer-based architecture shown in Figure *3* [12]. The verification module that was developed must be inserted in the **ILIAS Core** layer, so that the authentication process of the system is strengthened.

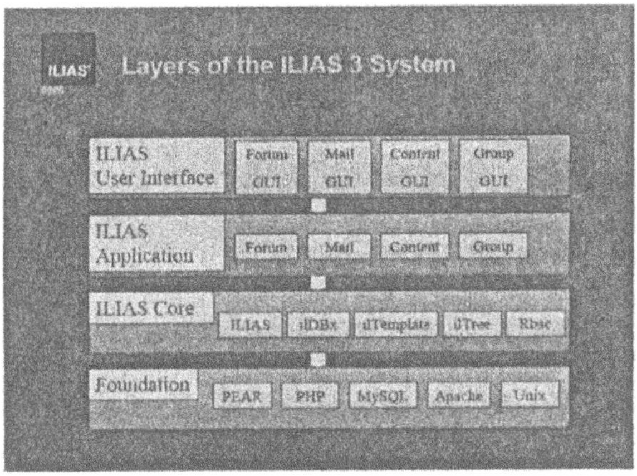

Figure 3. Layers of ILIAS

ILIAS was developed using PHP, it uses a MySQL database. The interface of the server application of the Web Platform offers us functions to do differents tasks such as user verification, functionality configuration of the verification system, selection of the different dialogues BioVXML to run, etc. With this interface the Web Platform invokes in a configurable way the user verification application, and then, this platform must interpret the verification result.

6. CONCLUSIONS AND FURTHER WORK

The verification system developed can be embedded inside any elearning platform due to the independence of its components. Every BioVXML document defines itself a biometric verification dialogue. The BioVXML specification enables us to separate the definition of the different biometric dialogues from the way these are implemented algorithmically. So we can modify the dialogue definition changing the number of biometric data to be recorded, the sentences to be read by the user and the instructions to show him without any change in the structure of the verification system, due to the flexibility provided by BioVXML. BioVXML facilitates the development of multiple verification applications over the same architecture.

Currently this system is still under development. It has just been installed in a web server and it works with a reduced number of users. However it is soon to evaluate any quantitative results. In order to test different biometric algorithms we are constructing the biometric database BioDB. We use an enrollment BioVXML document to construct this database. With this database we plan to test multimodal biometric algorithms based on face recognition and speaker recognition in future works. Once we do this we will have quantitative real world performance results on biometric identity verification of our system.

On the other hand, the modular design of our verification system allow us to integrate it easily inside any Web Platform independently of its language of development (php, asp, jsp, etc).

ACKNOWLEDGEMENTS

This project has been partially supported by Spanish MCyT and Xunta de Galicia under the projects TIC2002-02208 and PGIDT02TIC32201PR respectively.

We would like to thank Daniel González Jiménez for his collaboration developing the BGM image verifier.

REFERENCES

1. Enrique Argones-Rúa, Elisardo González-Agulla, Carmen García-Mateo, Óscar W. Márquez-Flórez, User verification in a Bio-VXML framework. Odyssey 2004.
2. E-learning Platform WebCT <http://www.webct.com/>
3. E-learning Platform LearningSpace <http://www.lotus.com/products/learnspace.nsf/wdocs/homepage?opendocument>
4. E-learning Platform BlackBoard http://www.blackboard.com/
5. ILIAS open source <http://www.homer.ILIAS.uni-koeln.de/ILIASdoc/doc/html/1.html>2003.15 September.
6. BioAPI Consortium, BioAPI Specification Version 1.1 <http://www.bioapi.org>2003.15 September.
7. VoiceXML 1.0 <http://www.w3.org/TR/voicexml/> 2003.22 September.
8. VoiceXML Forum <http://www.voicexml.org>2003.24 September.
9. X+V 1.1 --- XHTML + Voice Profile <http://www.voicexml.org/specs/multimodal/x+v/11/> 2003.2 October.
10. Java Sun <http://java.sun.com/> 2003.10 October.
11. Java Media Framework API (JMF) <http://java.sun.com/products/java-media/jmf/> 2003.10 October.
12. "The ILIAS Architecture", <http://www.ilias.uni-koeln.de/conference/2003/pdf/WS1-ARCHITECTURE.pdf>

A TESTING METHODOLOGY FOR AN OPEN SOFTWARE E-LEARNING PLATFORM

Ana Cavalli, Stéphane Maag, Sofia Papagiannaki and Georgios Verigakis
GET / Institut National des Télécommunications
Laboratoire SAMOVAR / UMR CNRS 5157
9 rue Charles Fourier
F-91011 Evry Cedex, France
e-mails : {Ana.Cavalli, Stephane.Maag, Sofia.Papagiannaki, Georgios.Verigakis}@int-evry.fr

Fatiha Zaïdi
University of Paris Sud 11,
Laboratoire de Recherche en Informatique,
UMR CNRS 8623
Bat. 490 University of Paris Sud
91405 Orsay Cedex, France
e-mail : Fatiha.Zaidi@lri.fr

Abstract This paper presents an outline of a methodology for the test of an open software e-learning platform. The methodology includes a test generation method from UML descriptions, in particular Sequence, Activity, Class diagrams and Navigation maps. The studied open software e-learning platform is dotLRN, an open source enterprise-class suite of web applications and portal framework for supporting course management, online communities and collaborations. The work presented in this paper is being developed in the framework of the E-LANE[1] project, an European and Latin American collaboration for the creation of an open software integrated platform for e-learning.

Keywords: UML, dotLRN, XMI, OCL, testing methodology, test generation methods

1. Introduction

In the last few years major progress has been achieved in the design of e-learning methodologies and platforms, particularly developing tools and methods to facilitate to users the access to these technologies. More recently, this evolution has strengthened the idea to develop open software platforms by

[1] http://www.e-lane.org/

integrating existing applications already used for e-learning. In this context, educational organizations can organize the teaching of a collection of courses using e-learning technologies, overcoming the geographical barriers, addressing to a larger audience and last but not least, by reducing the costs. To reduce the costs, organizations only need to deploy a powerful web server with the goal that the users may access these services using an open software platform connected to internet. Moreover, these platforms are designed to stimulate users to use and integrate new services.

This paper presents the work being developed in the framework of the European-Latin American New Education (E-LANE) project, an European and Latin American collaboration for the creation of an open software integrated platform for e-learning in which GET/INT is a partner. This project is part of the European Commission program @LIS Demonstration Projects. The base platform for the development of E-LANE is dotLRN, which is an open software platform composed by a suite of web applications and a portal framework of an e-learning system.

These open software e-learning platforms integrating existing applications developed by different teams need to be tested to insure that these applications are integrated together smoothly and correctly. The integration of new services by users also needs to be checked to guarantee the systems functionalities are preserved. In particular, these systems are exposed to many threats: a web server has to respond to requests from each node in the network. For instance, testing should guarantee that a user cannot gain permissions over the system he is not supposed to have. In addition to this, modern web applications are becoming increasingly complex and mission critical. This situation becomes even worse because of the lack of standardization in the web clients (browsers). Testing has to assert the system usability. For instance, an user is unable to complete a process because the content of the web page does not appear correctly or, due to a slow network connection, he may be unable to login because of an unrealistic timeout value. Our approach takes into account how these functional aspects have been implemented, checking that they conform to the specification.

In this paper, we propose a testing methodology for the dotLRN platform based on a test generation method and present some ideas of how to test new services integrated by the users. We also give a short presentation of a new approach for testing e-learning services, which is complementary of the test generation method. In this new approach, we propose to describe in OCL [9] the expected properties of the web service and to check these properties on the service execution traces.

The methodology presented in this paper is inspired by the work presented in [1, 3], which describes how UML diagrams developed in the Analysis phase are analyzed in an automated way to produce test cases. In relation to this work the paper presents several new contributions. First at all, none of these work is well adapted to the test of a web application tool. In our work, we need to check the graphical user interfaces but also the content of the generated pages. There is an extension of UML for Web Applications but it is more focused on the Design View. One of the contributions of this paper is to provide an answer to these issues. Therefore, in order to produce diagrams which convey the information needed to feed our tests we considered the work presented in [7] and [6].

Other contributions given by this paper are the following: to present the techniques and tools which are used for the conformance testing of the platform. The methodology we propose includes the following steps: description of the web services in UML, in particular use cases using Activity diagrams, Sequence diagram, Class diagram and Navigation map; export of diagrams into XMI format [10]; parsing of the XMI in order to generate test scripts; generation of tests scripts (using the different languages for scripts). This paper also presents a data modelling approach using UML profiles.

In the following sections the article first describes the dotLRN platform (section 2). Section 3 presents how to specify dotLRN using UML models for testing. In section 4, we describe the tools to automate the test generation from these models. Section 5 introduces an approach for the data modelling and section 6 presents the perspectives for this work. Finally, section 7 gives the conclusion.

2. The dotLRN e-learning platform

dotLRN [2] is an open source web based e-learning platform and portal framework, designed to support course management, online communities and collaboration.

In dotLRN there are three main portal types: *user*, *class* and *community* portals. The user portal is the private space that each user owns, while the class and community portals contain all the pages related to a specific class or community. Each of these three portal types is divided into four sections: the main space, the calendar, the files and the control panel. The pages in dotLRN are composed of *portlets*. Portlets are small portals that have some specific functionalities, like the forums, the news or the calendar.

A user portal is created automatically whenever a new user is registered in dotLRN, but the class and community portals are created by the *site-wide administrator* according to the needs of the users. When a new class or community portal is created, the site-wide administrator assigns one or more users as administrators of this portal. For example, for computer science class portal, the administrators can be the professor and his teaching assistants, while for a photography group community portal, the administrator will be one or

[2] http://www.dotlrn.org

more students. The responsibilities of a portal administrator are to add content, customize the layout and decide the policy of the portal.

When a class or community has an *open* policy, any user can join, while when the policy is *closed* only the administrator can add users. A third policy exists, the *wait* policy, where any user can ask to join and then the administrator will decide to accept or deny this user.

3. UML models for testing

In order to derive our test cases, we need to grasp and describe the functionality of the system in a formal way. A model-based approach development of Web applications can be performed using UML notation. We use a design methodology which is based on a UML extension for hypermedia [8]. It consists of three main steps that constitute the conceptual model, the navigation map, and the presentation model.

The conceptual model is built taking into account the functional requirements captured with use cases. We discover the use cases of the system under consideration and document them in a *Requirements Document* which contains the scope of the system, the main actors, the use case diagram and textual description of each use case [5].

>From this conceptual model, the navigation space model, also represented as a static class model, is constructed. It defines a view on the conceptual model showing which classes of this latter may be visited through navigation in the Web application. Finally, a dynamic presentation model is represented by UML sequence diagrams describing the collaborations and behaviors of the navigational objects and access primitives. In order to specify our model, the following diagrams are involved:

- Class Diagram to introduce the main classes of the system.
- Activity Diagram for each actor to display dependencies among the use cases.
- Navigation Map to provide information about the dynamic content of the web pages.
- Sequence Diagram for each use case describing the main and the alternative scenarios of the use case to represent the dynamic presentation model.

In our lab we develop a tool that implements our methodology and its components are shown in Figure 1. Initially it analyzes the dependencies found in the activity diagrams and combined with the data input generates test sequences. These test sequences are then used in the test execution component, along with the information in the Use Cases and the Navigation Map in order to

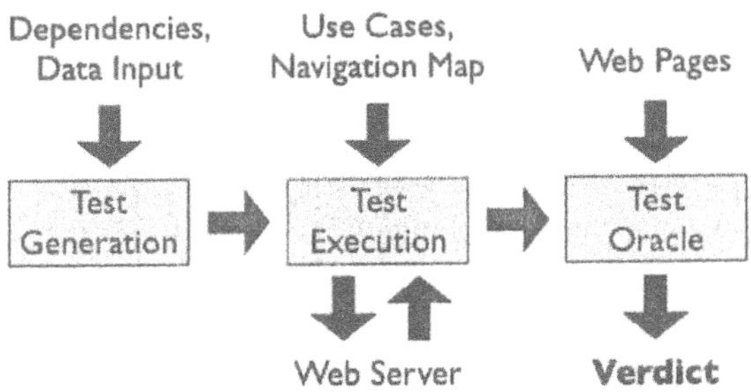

Figure 1. Outline of our methodology

perform the actual requests to the dotLRN server. The last component, parses the response of the server and compares it with the UML specification of the expected web page. Finally, it gives the verdict to show that either the test has executed succesfully, or that it has failed.

3.1 From Conceptual Model to Navigation Map

In order to specify the dotLRN platform we first need to build a conceptual model of the application domain taking into account the functional requirements captured with use cases. Techniques such as finding classes and associations, and defining inheritance structures are used.

Then, the Navigation Map of a web application introduced in [7] is used because it provides information about the dynamic content of each web page which is part of the system as well as the links between the different web pages. This information is essential during the parsing of the HTML pages (section 4.3). The Navigation Map is a Class diagram where each web page is a class and a link between two pages is an association between the two respective classes.

3.2 Modelling Use Case Dependencies

The use cases of a system are not independent. In order one use case to be executed, another should have taken place before. For instance, in dotLRN the user should login before being able to do anything else. Since the automation of the testing procedure is also of concern, we have to describe somehow these dependencies.

We achieve this by introducing an activity diagram where the vertices represent use cases and edges are sequential dependencies between the use cases. An edge in such a diagram denotes that the use case in the tail has to be executed before the use case in the head.

In the testing phase, before simulating the scenarios in the Sequence diagrams these activity diagrams should be scanned to obtain the sequence by which the use cases will be tested.

3.3 Sequence Diagram

In UML, a Sequence diagram realizes the interaction of objects via the interchange of messages in time. Similarly, as in activity diagrams the objects are instances of a class described in the Class diagram. Usually the sequence diagrams describe a single scenario.

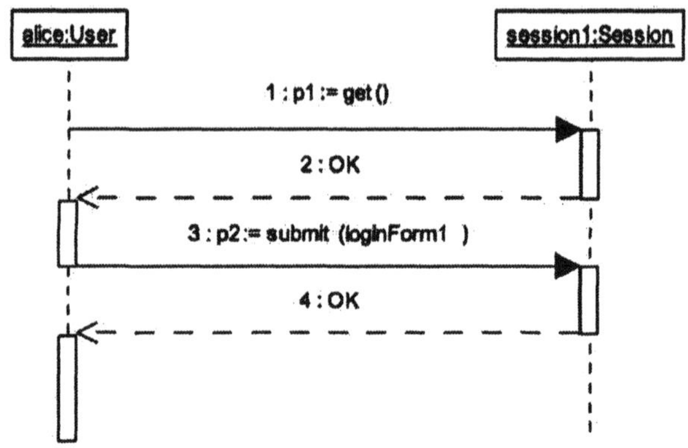

Figure 2. Sequence diagram for "Login" use case

We enumerate the messages as described in [3] so we can illustrate a number of alternative scenarios in the same diagram. According to this convention, capital letters denote alternatives (error messages). By adopting this tactic we can derive easily the different *Message_Sequences* [1] related to the same use case. Figure 2 shows the respective sequence diagram for the "Login" use case.

Our Sequence diagrams are also parameterized since input parameters can influence the execution and constitute separate *Choices* [1]. Such a parameter can be the email of an expected User. If this is the case, the dotLRN page is displayed, otherwise a warning appears in the Log In page.

4. Automating the test generation

To automate the test generation, our goal is first to parse the UML diagrams obtained from the previous steps. Therefore, based on these diagrams, we generate the necessary requests to the dotLRN server and then check if the server's replies are as expected by the previous models.

Based on these requirements, we had to choose the components that were required to build our test suite.

4.1 The programming language

Since we are dealing with UML, it would be more efficient to choose an object-oriented language. We also wanted this language to provide easy string handling and a high level of abstraction for network communications. The programming language that we found as the most suitable was Python [4]. Python is a modern object-oriented language which combines remarkable power with very clear syntax. Its built-in modules provide numerous functions that facilitate string handling and networking.

4.2 Parsing and executing the UML

Although we could use any XML parser to parse the XMI, due to the high complexity of the standard we decided to use a specialized XMI parser. The one we used was the parser included in the System Modelling Workbench tool [3]. It is free, open-source and also is written in Python, making it easier to integrate with our code. Being open-source it also enabled us to fix some incompatibility issues that appeared when used with XMI produced by the Poseidon tool.

4.3 Parsing the HTML pages

Since HTML mixes presentation and content data, the HTML output of dotLRN does not allow us to extract the information we want without first looking the implementation details. To avoid this we need to change the page templates of dotLRN in order to provide the data in a more formal way. We achieve this by adding *id* attributes to the tags we want to query. For example, to the td tag that contains the user's name in the user pages will have an attribute *id="username"*. That way we can query any page independently of the implementation of the layout of the page.

5. Inserting Test Data into the Model

In order to execute our tests and observe the behavior of the system it is necessary to substitute the formal parameters by the actual values. For instance in case we want to test whether a user with a valid email and password can log in successfully in the system, we have to provide to the test a valid pair of email and password. In related literature the tester provides this input through the user interface of the test suite before the execution of each test. In our case since we are interested in automatically creating some scripts which will be immediately executed we would like to integrate somehow this information in our model.

[3] http://www.abo.fi/~iporres/html/smw.html

An approach to the problem of representing data values in UML is the use of a UML Profile. UML Profiles are an extension mechanism provided by UML that enables us to add specific features. UML profiles are implemented using *stereotypes* and *tagged values*.

Different solutions could be proposed for the design of a suitable UML Profile, but our solution will focus on simplicity and ease of implementation. When we want to represent an instance **I** of a class **C**, we can define **I** as a new class having the same attributes and operations with **C**. Each attribute of **I** will have a tagged value containing the actual value of the respective attribute of **C**.

This method requires some extra development effort in order to check the correctness of the given values. However, it can be used with older versions of UML that are supported better from most of the currently available open source CASE tools.

6. Perspectives

The software tool presented in the previous sessions perform the parsing of the UML specification, the generation and translation of the tests to the XMI form and their execution on the dotLRN platform. The approach that we introduced automatically parses and executes the UML diagrams. However it could be equally possible instead to generate the code that will do the specified test. The generated code could be written in any language and will have the benefit that it can be used to run the tests from any computer, since it will run without the need of our software.

Concerning the test, in a first step, we started with the test of communication interfaces and user requirements. Next steps will be the test of authentication mechanisms and application contents (for instance, to check the content of the required web page). For that purpose, we need to treat data at the specification level. Indeed, to test if a user is permitted to access to the system, we need to check if it enters his proper login and password.

Another issue that we still investigate is related to a new test method. Indeed, we decide to propose another step-wise approach to automate the test generation and execution. This approach has no interaction with the system under test as the test generation method presented in this paper. This new approach is well fitted for service developers that do not intend to spend time at the analysis phase. The approach is based on the verification of service properties directly on the service trace execution. For that purpose, we install a *sniffer* between the client and the server to obtain dynamically all the *html* pages of each request on the service. At the specification level, we associate to each class and each operation, properties that have to be verified once the execution of the service is performed. These properties are written using the OCL language and represent the requirements of the web service that we want to test. This language is not usable straightforward. We need to transform it in order to check it on the traces. Thus, we translate the OCL described properties in regular expressions. Afterwards, these regular expressions are those that we will check on the real traces execution. At GET/INT, we have developed a tool to perform this verification [2].

This approach using OCL constraints allows to define formally functionalities that services are intended to supply. Furthermore, this solution can also be used for the test of new services. Using this approach, we are able to check if the new added service (i.e. new functionality) works properly according to the OCL defined constraint. Moreover, we are able to test that existing services are preserved, performing regression tests by reusing OCL constraints already checked.

7. Conclusion

We have presented in this paper a new approach to test the functionality of an e-learning, web based system, the dotLRN platform. This platform presents the advantage to be an open source toolkit for building scalable, community-oriented web applications.

The method and the software tool we propose has been applied to dotLRN platform but they are generic enough and can be applied to other e-learning and web based systems.

The test method is based on the test of objectives, which are selected taking into account the experts and designers advice. These tests are based on use cases and cover all relevant aspects of the system behavior. Even if we cannot guarantee a total error coverage, it can be guaranteed for the selected tests. We propose a UML models technique for testing, that relies on a design methodology divided in three main steps, i.e. the conceptual model, the navigation model and the presentation model.

References

[1] F. Basanieri, A. Bertolino, and E. Marchetti. The Cow_suit Approach to Planning and Deriving Test Suites in UML Projects. *Proc. Fifth International Conference on the Unified Modeling Language - the Language and its applications UML 2002, LNCS 2460, Dresden, Germany*, pages 383–397, September 2002.

[2] Emmanuel Bayse, Ana Cavalli, Manuel Nunez, and Fatiha Zaidi. A passive Testing Approach based on Invariants: Application to the WAP. *Computer Networks journal*, 2004.

[3] L. C. Briand and Y. Labiche. A UML-Based Approach to System Testing. *Software and Systems Modeling*, 1(1):10–42, 2002.

[4] Jr. Drake Christopher A. Jones, Fred L. *Python & XML*. O'Reilly & Associates, 1st edition, 2001.

[5] A. Cockburn. *Writing Effective Use Cases*. Addison-Wesley, 1st edition, 2000.

[6] J. Conallen. Modelling Web Application Architectures with UML. *Communications of the ACM*, 42(10):63–70, 1999.

[7] J. Conallen. *Building Web Applications With UML*. Addison-Wesley, 2nd edition, 2002.

[8] N. Koch, H. Baumeister, R. Hennicker, and L. Mandel. Extending UML to Model Navigation and Presentation in Web applications. *Proc. of Modeling Web applications in the UML Workshop, UML2000*, 2000.

[9] UML Object Constraint Language (2.0 submission). http://www.omg.org/cgi-bin/apps/doc?ad/03-01-07.pdf.

[10] XML Metadata Interchange. http://www.omg.org/cgi-bin/apps/doc?formal/03-05-02.pdf.

PART SEVEN

E-LEARNING EXPERIENCE

LEARNING OBJECTS DEFINITION AND USE IN <E-AULA>

Towards a Personalized Learning Experience

Pilar Sancho, Borja Manero and Baltasar Fernández-Manjón

Facultad de Informática. Universidad Complutense de Madrid, c /Juan del Rosal, 8 28040 Madrid, SPAIN. E-mail: {pilar, borja, balta}@sip.ucm.es

Abstract: This paper describes how learning objects are defined and treated in <e-aula>, a pilot e-learning system that aims to offer a personalized learning experience geared to individual student's needs. The term learning object (LO) has been on the educational agenda for several years now and has become the Holly Grail of content creation and aggregation in e-learning, promising smart learning environments, fantastic economies of scale and exciting learning experiences tailored to individual needs. Nevertheless, there are a number of aspects where more research is needed. First, there is a lack of conceptual clarity in the definition, standardization and use of LOs. Also, there has been limited emphasis on the need for introducing adaptable learning features within the LO construct. The objective of this paper is to contribute to the practical application of these concepts by presenting the <e-aula> learning objects and how the system handles personalization features to create an infrastructure for performing an individualized learning.

Key words: e-learning; learning objects; Adaptive systems; educational standards; markup languages.

1. INTRODUCTION.

The combination of Internet technologies, new learning design models and usage of markup technologies have largely enhanced the possibilities offered by traditional computer assisted instruction (Fernandez-Manjon, 1997). We are getting close to constructing learning applications that could make real the promises offered by "student centred" learning paradigm. This means a customized education capable of accommodating the different learning styles, strategies, and preferences of diverse learners (Manouselis, 2002).

In this context, the concept of Learning Object (LO) plays a basic role. The term was first popularised by Wayne Hodgins in 1994, and the idea behind the LO concept is that educational materials are no longer structured in a monolithic way, but instead, are disaggregated into pieces of reusable learning chunks.

The LO approach for course development promises more efficiency in content management not only by preventing multiple development of the same content, but also because it facilitates content update and modification. In addition, the LO approach could enhance the possibilities of personalizing the learning environments: LOs could be dynamically assembled to create courses that meet individual needs.

For this vision to be achieved, instructional content must be developed as reusable, stand-alone objects, properly annotated with metadata so that they can be located and retrieved. Moreover, the learning objects, their associated metadata and the e-learning courses should be developed in a uniform manner according to standard guidelines.

In the past five years considerable efforts in the e-learning field towards the standardization have been made. As a result of these efforts several agreements have been reached among a number of organizations involved in the standardization process, leading to increasing the accessibility of the learning content that can be shared (e.g. Learning Object Metadata standard). These organizations include the IEEE Learning Technology Standards Committee (LTSC), the IMS Global Learning Consortium and the Advanced Distributed Learning initiative.

We have found two different problems in standardization proposals hindering the final LO objective model. First, there is a lack of conceptual clarity of what a LO should be: LOs are different things to different e-learning professionals (ASTD, 2002). Many inconsistencies in what is stored under the name of learning object, have been detected in the available LO repositories (e.g. see Educational Object Economy http://ww.eoe.org, or ARIADNE http://www.ariadne-eu.org/).

The second problem arises when trying to implement personalization features according to the existing standard specifications: the main focus of the standardization initiatives is LO interoperability. There has been limited emphasis on the need for introducing adaptive learning features within the LO construct. Under the current version of these standards, LO are treated as opaque entities that cannot yet be adapted to student's needs. Therefore, to obtain all the potential benefits offered by the LO approach more research has to be done within the frame of adaptive applications implemented according to e-learnng standards and used in real educational contexts.

This paper aims to offer an experimental response to these problems based on the experiences obtained in the <e-aula> project. First we provide several guidelines for creating LOs, and then we address the shortcomings in the content of learning objects to suit the level of learners, accommodating the learning experience his/her profile and needs, and enabling a dynamic generation of personal learning.

2. LEARNING OBJECTS DEFINITION IN <E-AULA>.

<e-aula> is a pilot e-learning system conceived as a research platform to study the possibilities facilitated by educational standards and new learning design methodologies under two main features: content reuse of previously existing educational material, and content adaptation to meet individual needs (basically students' previous knowledge and his / her knowledge objectives).

Our objectives are to develop reusable, flexible, and scalable methodologies, contents and environments by using design specifications (educational standards), markup languages and web technologies.

Some requirements for achieving these objectives are:

- To design a content oriented methodology to create the system. This allows the environment to be quite independent of the contents. Adding new contents to the system should be easy, so <e-aula> becomes easily scalable (See Figure 1).
- To develop the necessary system architecture to create and deliver courses based on user profiles. By using e-learning standards as a reference, we will do research on user centred learning.
- To develop several courses with real contents and test them in a university-learning context.
- To implement different prototypes taking into account different standarization proposals and evaluate their possibilities in a real environment.

Even though <e-aula> is conceived as an e-learning infrastructure aimed at testing e-learning standards at all the levels in the course creation process, this paper is mainly focused on the LO aspects. In this section we first analyze the existing confusion when trying to determine what a LO is (Sosteric, 2002; Polsani, 2003), then we provide several guidelines collected from the LO literature to create LOs as consensuated as possible, and finally we offer the <e-aula> vision for constructing LOs.

2.1 But, what is a learning object?

There is a broad understanding among the members of the LO community about the functional requirements a LO should have (Polsani, 2003):

- Accessibility: the LO should be tagged with metadata so that it can be stored and referenced in a data base.
- Reusability: once treated, a LO might be used in different instructional contexts.
- Interoperability: the LO should be independent of both the delivery media and learning management systems.

But this is very much all the consensus reached up to date about the concept of LOs. There is still a great vacuum in descriptive, analytical and critical examinations of LO technologies.

Derived from the impractical overarching definition offered by the Learning Object Metadata v6.1 standard, which describes a Learning Object as "any entity, digital or non digital, that may be used for learning, education or training", many authors and institutions have given their own vision of what a learning object should be in practice. See for example (Wiley, 2002; Wisconsin Online Resource Center http://www.wisc-online.com; L'Allier, 1997).

Like in other research works (Friesen, 2001; Polsani, 2003; Sosteric, 2002), we think that there is an important predicate in the LO concept that cannot be left out: learning and context. Contrarily, other authors depict LOs as instructionally neutral (Downes, 2001).

For a digital object to acquire the status of a LO, it should be wrapped in a learning intention. For example an image of a picture can be used during technology-supported learning, and even reused in different educational contexts. But, just looking at the picture teaches nothing. It needs to be wrapped with contextual information. In a traditional educational setting, the instructor would provide this information, would interpret the object and would reorganize the context creatively, which requires a vast amount of background information.

Let's now state what are the necessary requisites to design a course that fulfils the LO philosophy. Firsly content creators have to construct the LOs, attaining a high level of abstraction, in order to enable reusability, and wrap them with enough contextual information for them to be instructionally useful. Second, instructors and course designers have to decide according to their learning objectives, the pedagogical methodology and instructional design theories how LOs have to be related in a certain course. Finally, the design has to be flexible enough to suit individual students, permitting, for instance, those concepts that don't fit their knowledge needs to be skipped and the learning experience to be adapted to their own preferences.

If this is not enough, LOs have to be properly marked with standard metadata in order to enable interoperability, accessibility and reusability: the construction of recovery mechanisms according to different criteria for LOs is needed to enable LO reuse.

No wonder why the LO economy objectives are still elusive.

2.2 LO definition in <e-aula>

<e-aula> LOs are self-contained units designed to be instructionally independent. When designing <e-aula> LOs we try to keep in mind the concepts stated in section 2.1: abstract enough to be reusable (that means, they must be as independent of use as possible) and wrapped with contextual information to meet the "learning" principle (aimed to teach a particular concept or ability).

Another feature we have taken into account is granularity: having small units of LOs increases the annotation effort, but implies better reusability.

Our own demands in personalization and reutilization together with the basic principles outlined in point 2.1, have led us to create learning objects for <e-aula> as an aggregation of digital resources consisting of: core material (typically <e-aula> files encoded in XML) containing mainly textual and graphical explanations with the scope of a learning topic, a set of examples, notes and a set of assesments.

In <e-aula> all the basic course contents are also represented directly in XML and not in HTML as is done in most e-learning systems. When a specific content is accessed in the web server an XSL transformation is applied to the content obtaining the HTML that is delivered to the web client (see figure 1). This approach is similar to the one used in other projects such as ARIADNE (ARIADNE, 2003). XML contents also simplify the automatic processing of LOs for coping with the frequent evolution and changes in e-learning standards and specifications. In many cases these changes can be automatically done by means of a XSL transformation.

3. <E-AULA>: TOWARDS PERSONALIZED LEARNING.

We believe that the learning object approach is the first step towards achieving personalized content which addresses the learning needs of each and every student. The idea is to segment existing course material (and annotate it properly using IMS LOM metadata schema) to dynamically compose courses "on-demand" adapted to individual learning needs. Well-structured metadata can facilitate the search, retrieval and manipulation of LOs without compromising their integrity.

Many research works have been carried out to develop a system capable of adapting its learning strategies in agreement to the learning profile(Brusilovsky 1996a, Brusilovsky 1996b). Our approach is closer to (Atif, 2003) in which most of the intelligence is embedded in the learning objects themselves.

In our system, we have used LO personalization properties in two different ways: different organizations of the LOs into the course and LO content marked up according to different knowledge level of each user. These aspects are discussed in the next sections.

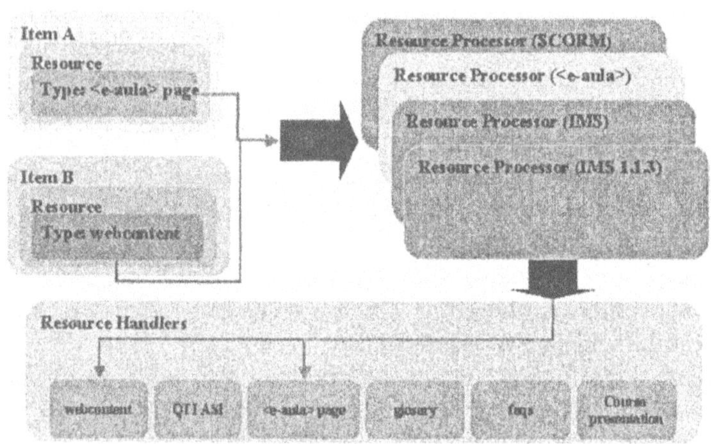

Figure 1. <e-aula> Delivery System Architecture that is able to deal with different LO formats

3.1 Learning Objects Metadata

Our objective is to facilitate an efficient pre-selection of the learning objects suitable for different learning needs. LOM metadata schema permits us to have a very rich and flexible file about LOs classified in 9 categories. However, this flexibility comes with a price due to its extension and the annotation effort it involves.

In our current implementation we consider that the following elements and sub elements are essential for our reutilization and personalization purposes:

- <general>
  - <identifier>
  - <title>
  - <language>
  - <description>
- <lifecycle>
  - <contribute>
- <educational>
  - <interactitytype>
  - <description>
- <classification>

As the LOM specification explicitly states, its scope does not include "how a learning technology system represents or uses a metadata instance for a learning object". It turned out that these elements are enough to annotate and query our resources, and represent a compromise between more abstract and more detailed annotation sets.

The main problem we have faced when trying to implement our system adaptation properties is that under the current version of the standard, learning objects are treated as opaque entities (Rodriguez 2003). The description of the LOs is intended to advance the goals of interoperability, but does not address the need for accessibility to the internal composition of the LOs which is essential for the goal of adaptation.

The intelligent discovery and assembly of learning objects require information not supported by the current set of elements of the LOM standard. A learning object has a context that is specific for its use. It is necessary for each learning object to specify exactly how that learning object is related to concepts in a particular domain within its context, i.e., an ontology of concepts in a particular domain.

We think a LO created using this annotation principle gets new dimensions of reusability and adaptivity. This way created LOs are more suitable for retrieving since their content can be inspected using ontology-based conceptualization. With this kind of knowledge, an agent can compare the course structure developed for a specific learner profile with the learning object, based on a common understanding of how they relate to each other.

LOM Metadata records can be effectively linked to ontologies. We are using Meta-Metadata elements to declare dependencies of the metadata record with ontologies, and links to ontology terms in the Classification element as proposed in (Sicilia 2002). This permits data in learner profiles to be linked to ontology terms, which not only should enhance system adaptation features, but should also make personalization easier.

3.2 Learning Objects and XML

We have added a supplementary granularity level: the object content itself is marked using XML, which provides deeper and more detailed information that can be used for more extended adaptation mechanisms. The system is able to display the information contained in a learning object according to the student's level of knowledge (<e-aula> the system has three possible levels: low, medium and high) (see figure 2). As previously stated, XML contents also preserve content from external changes, even changes in standards specifications. XML contents provide our contents with structure instead relying on IMS recomentations (i.e. contents in HTML format).

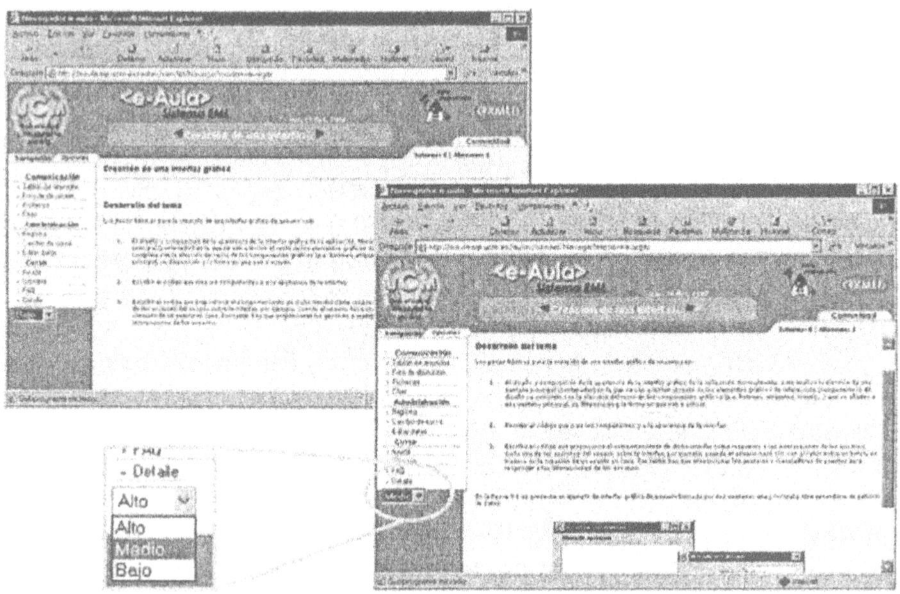

Figure 2. Different educational contents displayed for medium and low knowledge levels

4. CONCLUSIONS AND FUTURE WORK

<e-aula> is a pilot e-learning system conceived as a research platform to test and evaluate new learning technologies (learning standards, new learning design models (LO approach), markup and web technologies) in order to reach a personalized learning experience adapted to student's needs.

Based on our experiences working with these technologies we have reached the following conclusions:

- The first difficulty to be faced when trying to implement a LO approach, is the vacuum of conceptual clarity in LOs themselves. In our opinion, more work has to be done in order to reach a standard and within the LO community. Real interoperability can only be achieved if all the parties involved agree on what is behind the word LO.
- A learning object has a context that is specific to its use. An understanding of the many contexts in which an object is used, would result in the increase of its reusability. To make this possible, it would be necessary to articulate the relationship between the metadata associated with the object and the surrounding objects, and report that relationship to the repository. To compose a course from a set of learning objects, an appropriate modeling of conceptual dependencies between fragments is needed. We are developing a concept taxonomy to describe the structure of the concepts and to specify the conceptual relations between fragments and concepts.
- The information about content itself offered by IMS metadata is not enough in terms of defining adaptation methods based on students' knowledge level, knowledge objectives and learning method preferred. We consider that better results would be obtained reaching a deeper granularity level. We have obtained promising results marking up our LO's themselves using XML.

The next steps in the <e-aula> project are to fully implement the IMS Simple Sequencing specification and to study how the new functionality recently added to IMS LIP, called IMS Accessibility for LIP, could be used to customize and personalize the system for each student.

ACKNOWLEDGEMENT

The Spanish Committee of Science and Technology (TIC 2001-1462) and the Universidad Complutense de Madrid (PIE 2002/15) have supported this work.

REFERENCES

ARIADNE, "The Alliance of Remote Instructional Authoring and Distribution Networks for Europe," 2003. http://www.ariadne-eu.org/

ASTD & Smart Force (2002). A field guide to Learning Objects. Learning Circuits.

Atif, Y., Benlamri, R., Berry, J. (2003) Learning objects based framework for self-adaptive learning. Education and Information Technologies 8:4, 345-368.

Brusilovsky, P., Schwarz, E., Weber, G. (1996a) ELM-ART: An intelligent tutoring system on World Wide Web. In: C. Frasson, G. Gauthier and A. Iesgold (eds.) Intelligent

Tutoring Systems. Lecture Notes on Computer Science, Vol. 1086, (Proceedings of Third International Conference on Intelligent Tutoring Systems, ITS-96, Montreal, June 12-14, 1996) Berlin: Springer Verlag, pp. 261-269.

Brusilovsky, P., Schwarz, E., Weber, G. (1996b). A tool for developing adaptive electronic textbooks on WWW. In: H. Maurer (ed.) Proceedings of WebNet'96, World Conference of the Web Society, San Francisco, CA, October 15-19, 1996, AACE, pp. 64-69.

De Bra, P. M. E. (1996) Teaching hypertext and hypermedia through the Web. Journal of Universal Computer Science 2 (12), 797-804.

Downes, S. (2001). Learning Objects: resources for distance education world wide. International Review of Research in Open Distance Learning 2:1. http://www.irrodl.org/content/v2.1/downes.html.

Fernandez-Manjon, B., Fernandez-Valmayor, A., 1997. "Improving World Wide Web educational uses promoting hypertext and standard general markup language content-based features". Education and Information Technologies, vol 2, no 3, pp. 193-206.

Friesen, N. (2001). What are Educational Objects? Interactive Learning Environments, 9 (3) 219-230. http://www.careo.org/documents/objects.html.

IEEE Learning Technology Standards Committee, 1998. Learning Object Medatada (LOM): Draft Document v2.1.

L'Allier, J. J. (1997). Frame of reference: NETg's map to the products, their structure and core beliefs. NetG. http://www.netg.com/research/whitepapers/frameref.asp. Retrieved 02/02/2004.

Manouselis, N. and Samson, D. (2002). Dynamic knowledge route selection for personalized learning environments using multiple criteria. In Proceedings of IASTED International Conference on Applied Informatics, February, pp. 351-605.

Nakabayshi, K., Koike, Y., Maruyama, M., Touhei, H., Ishiuchi, S, And Fukuhara, Y. (1995) An intelligent tutoring system on World Wide Web: Towards an integrated learning environment on a distributed hypermedia. In: H. Maurer (ed.) Proceedings of ED-MEDIA'95-World Conference on educational multimedia and hypermedia, Graz, Austria, June 17-21, 1995, AACE, pp. 488-493.

Okazaki, Y., Watanabe, K. and Kondo, H. (1996). An implementation of an intelligent tutoring system (ITS) on the World Wide Web (WWW). Educational Technology Research 19(1), 35-44.

Polsani, P. R. (2003). Use and Abuse of Reusable Learning Objects. Journal of Digital Information, Article No. 164, 2003-02-19.

Rodriguez O. et al, 2003. Open Learning Objects: the case for inner metadata. The Journal of Computing in Small Colleges. Volume, 18. Issue 4. 56-64. April 2003.

Sicilia M. A. et al, 2002. Learning Links: reusable assets with support for vagueness and ontology-based typing. Workshop on Concepts and Ontologies in Web-based Educational Systems, ICCE, December 3-6.

Sosteric, M., Hesemeier, S. When a learning object is not an object: a first step towards. International Review of Research in Open and Distance Learning. October, 2002.

Wiley, D. A. (2002). Connecting Learning Objects to instructional design theory: a definition, a metaphor, and a taxonomy. The Instructional Use of Learning Objects. Bloomington, IN: Agency for Instructional Technology.

E-LEARNING ENGINEERING: RECOMMENDATIONS FOR CONSUMER-DRIVEN BLENDED LEARNING

Experiences in an Electronic Marketing Course

Roland Gabriel[1], Martin Gersch[2] and Peter Weber[1]

[1]*Business Informatics, Ruhr-University of Bochum;* [2]*Competence Center E-Commerce at the Institute of Management, Ruhr-University of Bochum*

Abstract: "Blended Learning" is seen as a means of enhancing learning and promoting reasonable input of E-Learning elements in university education. In this context evaluation results offer interesting suggestions for advanced learning-arrangements and point out the didactical concept to be the decisive factor for the success of these arrangements. Therefore this paper describes lessons learned and offers recommendations for future Blended Learning concepts, based on concrete E-Learning experiences and evaluations.

Key words: Blended Learning; Didactical Concept; Electronic Marketing; Evaluation Results; Managerial Economics; Three-divided Learning-arrangement; Web-Based Training; Recommendations for E-Learning-Engineering.

1. INTRODUCTION

This submission describes lessons learned by blending classical university-education with modern E-Learning elements. It draws conclusions of the gathered and evaluated experiences and points out resulting possibilities of sensible improvement of future lectures.

"Blended Learning" is understood as the combination of face-to-face teaching, online-support of the learning process and knowledge brokerage through web-based-trainings (WBTs). It is seen as a means of enhancing learning and promoting reasonable input of E-Learning elements in university education. (Littlejohn, A.; Higgison, C., 2003, p. 6) This understanding corresponds with common definitions of Blended Learning, e.g., given by Annette / Werner Sauter (Sauter, A. M.; Sauter, W., 2002, p. 246) and Andrea Back (Back, A.; Bendel, O.; Stoller-Schai, D., 2001, p. 288).

The recommendations for an advanced Blended Learning concept are based on three steps. First, the submission will open with a description of the "Electronic Marketing" lecture and the underlying didactical concept. Next, the submission will explain examples of evaluation results that show possibilities for advancement of learning. Finally, the submission will draw conclusions from these results and outline a suggested learning arrangement.

2. "ELECTRONIC MARKETING" AND THE UNDERLYING DIDACTICAL CONCEPT

2.1 Electronic Marketing

In summary, the subject matter of the lecture can be described as the presentation of changes in managerial-economics, caused by advancing digitization and networking – in short, the "New Economy" from an economic perspective. It deals with implications of new information technology for market-driven management, e.g., with a detailed analysis of changing technological and economical frameworks, new business models and modern forms of coordination. More than 50 participants took part (in average) at each of the 15 sessions in summer 2003 (April – July 2003) - all the students were stage II students in economics with marketing and / or business informatics emphasis and distinct previous knowledge. The lecture was enriched with E-Learning elements in several ways:

First, the complete learning process was supported by the E-Learning platform Blackboard. (Blackboard, 2004) Blackboard was mainly used for resource allocation, online-discussions (with lecturer, participants and / or external experts), WBT-distribution and for securance of a contemporaneous flow of information.

Second, web-based-trainings (WBTs) were engaged for content placing. To be more exact, the WBTs were used either for assimilation of basic-knowledge levels, for repetition and preparation for the exam and as an optional means of deepening knowledge.

The individual WBTs as well as the whole lecture were evaluated in order to gather information about contentment of students.

2.2 Media-didactical analysis

An important step on the way to a successful learning arrangement is undoubtedly an accurate analysis of objectives, the target group and other essential conditions. All organizational decisions, in particular those concerning the "Blending-Strategy", have to be seen in the context of these conditions. This task has been carried out with the help of the so-called "mediendidaktische Analyse" ('media-didactical analysis') of Michael Kerres. The following table shows the translated scheme of analysis recommended by Kerres (Kerres, M., 2001, p. 15) and syllabi of concrete answers in matters of the E-Marketing lecture.

Table 1. Media-didactical analysis

Scheme of analysis for planning hybrid learning arrangements		
1. Project objectives	What does the project intend to accomplish?	– Enhancement of the effectiveness of the E-Marketing lecture. – Rise in motivation of students. – Gathering of expert knowledge concerning Blended Learning. – Exploiting E-Learning advantages while avoiding its disadvantages[6].
2. Target group	Who is the learning arrangement designed to benefit?	– Students: – of stage II studies in economics, – with marketing and / or business informatics emphasis, – accessible to technological development.
3. Educational content and objectives	What content shall be transported and what are the objectives behind it?	– Management knowledge in conjunction with economical consequences of the progressing digitization and networking. – Keeping students up-to-date with regard to technologically-driven economical changes.
4. Didactical structure and method	How is the content supposed to be edited didactically?	– Within the lecture, content was provided in a consecutive way. – The WBTs offer random access to each topic. – An active knowledge construction is intended by the use of case studies[7].

[6] Examples for possible advantages in: Bayne (2000), p. 5

[7] Unlike the rather cognitive character of traditional WBTs the case-studies tend to constructivism as a modern learning paradigm which points out the confrontation of

Scheme of analysis for planning hybrid learning arrangements		
5. Learning organization	What organizational layout is intended?	– Content was distributed subject to the lectural progress. – Individual learning in conjunction with collaborative learning (case studies). – Online-tutoring, based on the E-Learning platform Blackboard. – Integration of external experts.

After this presentation of the lecture and the underlying didactical concept, we now turn to the evaluation. All recommendations will be derived from the results of this evaluation.

2.3 Evaluation Results

The evaluation process was carried out in order to get a survey about quality, functionality, impact and benefit (Niegemann, H. N. et al., 2004, p. 291) of both the lectural Blended Learning concept and the WBTs. With the brevity of the submission in mind, a presentation of the evaluation-process has been omitted. It goes without saying though, that the evaluation process was carried out anonymously and voluntarily. Yet it should be mentioned that the evaluation-scheme for the WBTs was basically developed within an interuniversial research project named “New Economy” (Research Project "New Economy"), which is supported by the German Federal Ministry for Education and Research. The project was also the basis for the development of the engaged WBTs. Complete details of the research project are accessible at http://www.internet-oekonomie.org, where WBT-examples and media-examples can be seen. The lecture was evaluated with the present evaluation-scheme of the Ruhr-University of Bochum, complemented with special E-Learning elements. The following figure shows selected E-Learning-focused results of the lectural evaluation.

(A small selection of other than E-Learning-results is included because of eventual influence on other aspects).

learners with complex and realistic problems and their active and intensive work on these problems to be the decisive factor for successful learning.

Statement	Average Approval*	
There was a clearly seen conception which was kept up throughout the lecture.	1.76	Lecture
The lecture was well-structured.	1.59	
Requirements were too high.	3.06	
[...]		
I enjoyed the inclusion of external experts.	1.18	External lecturers
There was an interesting set of topics.	1.56	
[...]		
Blackboard (E-Learning platform) eased the learning process.	2.00	E-Learning Elements
The offered learning material (excl. the WBTs) was comprehensible and reasonable.	2.12	
I would use Blackboard again.	1.79	
Supporting the lecture with WBTs was helpful.	1.91	
The WBTs were not helpful in deepening knowledge.	3.38	
Independent learning with WBTs was a good experience.	2.13	
The amount and relevance of WBTs within the lecture should be raised.	2.97	
All lectures should be supported with WBTs.	2.67	
Overall Grade for Lecture**	1.82	
Content was presented in a comprehensible fashion.	1.36	Lecturer
The lecturer appeared well-prepared.	1.18	
The lecturer appeared scientifically capable.	1.26	
[...]		
Overall Grade for Lecturer**	1.35	
I'm interested in the subject of the lecture.	1.36	Participants
Age:	25.33	
Terms studied so far:	8.06	
[...]		

* Approval to the given statements on a scale from 1 to 4 (1 = absolutely yes. ....4 = absolutely no)
** Overall grades on the basis of the german grading-system (1 = very good, 2 = good, ..., 5 = inadequate)

Figure1. Evaluation results

Since the WBTs were an important element of the learning arrangement, they will now be looked at a little more closely. What were students' impressions? What problems do they experience and what preferences do they have?

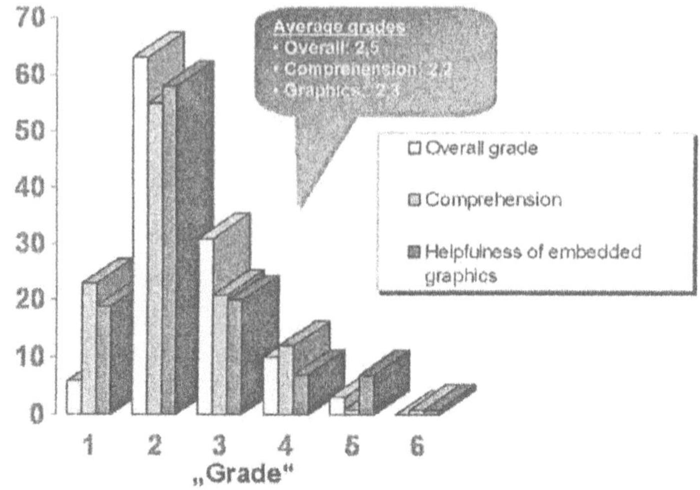

Figure 2. Average grades for WBTs (overall)

Figure 2 gives an impression of the WBT-evaluation. It shows the average overall grade, the average grade for comprehension and the average rating for the helpfulness of the embedded graphics, interactive animations and / or video sequences. Six WBTs were judged based on a total of 113 evaluations. The grades of each WBT were weighted by the number of evaluations referring to it. (grades: 1 = very good, 2 = good,..., 6 = inadequate)

In addition some student comments are presented in order to point out problems and preferences from a learner's perspective (comments in brackets identify contradictory statements):

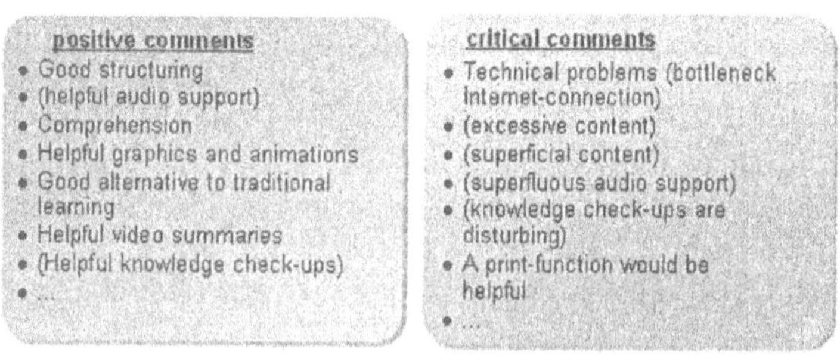

Figure3. Comments

Most of the problems pointed out by the critical comments have been solved in the course of the lecture. The solutions discovered are part of the recommendations given in this paper, which are also based on the evaluation results set forth above.

2.4 Recommendations

The following statements represent recommendations for future E-Learning concepts, which can be drawn out of the evaluation results and the critical comments concerning the WBTs. It is understood that the infinitesimal empirical basis is not sufficient groundwork for hard decisions, but it nevertheless offers interesting suggestions that should not be ignored.

a) **High relative importance of the lecturer.** Despite good results of embedded E-Learning elements, a high relevance and reputation of face-to-face interaction was ascertained.
b) **Economic practice wanted.** The positive evaluation of external lecturers and practical examples points out students' wish for dealing with practical knowledge and therefore promotes case studies as an important element of Blended Learning.
c) **E-Learning is not always the best solution.** E-Learning should only be used when there are reasonable possibilities. Besides, quality criteria should be defined for the WBTs at the outset. (Referring to this see: Schanda, F., 1995, p. 171pp; Schulmeister, R., 2002, p. 387pp).
d) **Technological alternatives must be guaranteed.** Computer rooms should be kept free in order to guarantee learning possibilities for insufficiently equipped students.
e) **E-Learning platforms are an instrument-of-consequence.** Since there is great acceptance of E-Learning platforms such as Blackboard, these platforms are a possible basis for intensification of E-Learning activities.[8]
f) **Web-based-training acceptance: A question of dosage, quality and support.** There are split opinions on WBTs. Successful intensification not least takes profound support of the learning process.
g) **Individual interest and learning habits should be respected as much as possible.** There should be enough content for interest-driven students, but also enough structure for exam-driven students.[9]

[8] This result can be confirmed by the *Blackboard user-statistic*, which points out an intense use of the platform in the course of the lecture (4024 Course-Hits).

[9] Referring to this the so-called "core-statement-approach" ("Kernaussagenansatz" = a special approach for didactical design of WBTs) was developed in: Gersch, M.; Malinowski, T., 2003, p. 36-44.

h) **High relevance of the didactical concept.** The didactical concept is the decisive factor for the success of the whole learning-arrangement. In comparison, technological innovations are clearly secondary.[10]
i) **Except for main functions all components of the WBTs (like video-sequences, animations, audio-support, knowledge check-ups, etc.) should be kept optional.** The different learning habits should be considered in preparing of adaptable WBTs. Besides, these differences underlie the idea of a preferably flexible learning-arrangement.
j) **A learning-arrangement with regard to the different learning phases should be designed.** The different learning phases should be considered in form of adequate learning-scenarios.

3. CONCLUSION

This paper will close with a proposal for learning-arrangement that is divided into three parts. Especially case studies offer opportunities for innovative Blended Learning and therefore will be focused on in future concepts!

Individual studying with WBTs is recommended for the assimilation of basic-knowledge. Preparation for important exams needs to be accompanied by tutors, e.g., with the help of online discussion-boards, in order to guarantee appropriate support of the learning process. A qualified way for including practical knowledge is seen in interactive multimedia case studies. Case studies allow the combination of realistic and practical tasks (including professional presentations of work results in front of groups!)[11] with the negotiation of theoretical knowledge, and at the same time they offer chances for sensible integration of external experts. Therefore, they are considered to be an interesting vehicle for Blended Learning concepts that should definitely be paid attention to.

[10] This statement confirms Hankel, O. et. al, 2003, who point out, that information and communication technology driven learning environments "bear the danger of being didactically set on traditional, unilateral scenarios putting students in a passive position as recipients of fixed-content."

[11] According to this high relevance, a special schooling was integrated in the concept.

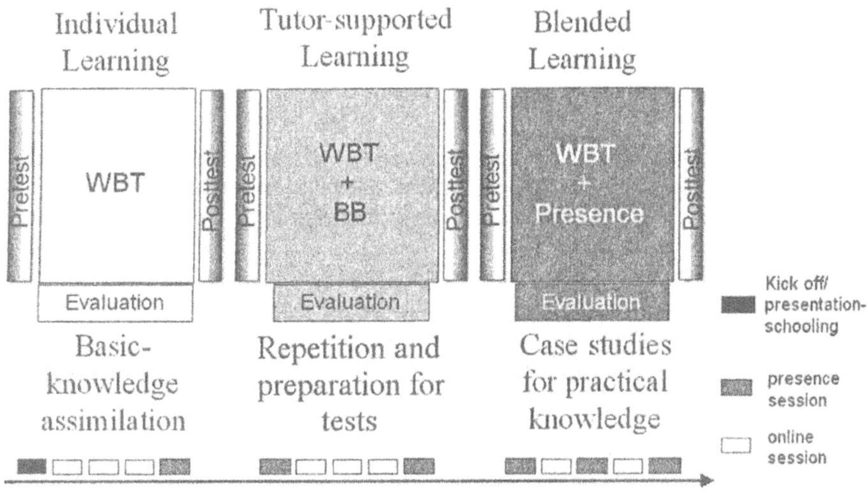

Figure4. **Three-divided learning-arrangement**

In addition to this "3 scenarios-model", evaluations and pre-/post-tests are recommended. This way an ongoing critical analysis and advancement of learning can be guaranteed. This brief draft represents the basic structure of new seminars and lectures at the Ruhr-University of Bochum in 2004. The initial evaluation results in January 2004 (currently incomplete) underlie the estimated positive effect of the advanced Blended Learning approach.

REFERENCES

Back, A.; Bendel, O.; Stoller-Schai, D., 2001: E-Learning im Unternehmen: Grundlagen – Strategien – Methoden – Technologien, Zürich 2001.

Bayne, S., 2000: An introduction to learning technology, Learning Technology Support Service, Bristol, http://www.ltss.bris.ac.uk./pdfs/LTintro.pdf, (called-up on January 12, 2004).

Blackboard, 2004: E-Learning platform at the Ruhr-University of Bochum, http://e-learning.ruhr-uni-bochum.de.

Gersch, M.; Malinowski, T., 2003: Didaktische Aufbereitung zur Gestaltung von Lernsoftware – Dargestellt an einem konkreten WBT-Entwicklungsbeispiel, Arbeitsbericht des Lehrstuhls für Wirtschaftsinformatik, Nr. 03-46, Ruhr-Universität Bochum 2003.

Hankel, O. et al., 2003: Technical and Didactical Scenarios of Student-centered Teaching and Learning, in: Kerres, M.; Voß, B. (ed.): Digitaler Campus – Vom Medienprojekt zum nachhaltigen Medieneinsatz in der Hochschule, Münster 2003, p. 411-419.

Niegemann, H. N. et al., 2004: Kompendium E-Learning, Berlin [et. al.] 2004.

Kerres, M., 2001: Online- und Präsenzelemente in Lernarrangements kombinieren, in: Hohenstein, A.; Wilbers, K. (ed.): Handbuch E-Learning: Expertenwissen aus Wissenschaft und Praxis, Neuwied, Köln, München 2001, chapter 4.5, p. 1-20.

Littlejohn, A.; Higgison, C., 2003: A guide for teachers, e-Learning Series, No. 3, LTSN Generic Center 2003.

Research Project "New Economy", sponsored by the German Federal Ministry for Education and Research, Projectno.: 08NM106E, http://www.internet-oekonomie.org.

Sauter, A. M.; Sauter, W., 2002: Blended Learning: Effiziente Integration von E-Learning und Präsenztraining, Neuwied, Kriftel 2002.

Schanda, F., 1995: Computer-Lernprogramme: Wie damit gelernt wird. Wie sie entwickelt werden. Was sie im Unternehmen leisten., Weinheim, Basel 1995.

Schulmeister, R., 2002: Grundlagen hypermedialer Lernsysteme: Theorie – Didaktik – Design, 3. Edition, München 2002.

PART EIGHT

IMPACT OF TECHNOLOGY ON E-LEARNING

IMPACT OF TECHNOLOGY ON LEARNING PARADIGMS AND TEACHING PRACTICES

Fulvio Corno[1], Tina Ebey[2], Anna Grabowska[3], Iliana Nikolova[4], and Evgenia Sendova[5]
[1]Politecnico di Torino, Italy; [2]Pacific Research Center, USA; [3]Gdansk University of Technology, Poland; [4]Sofia University, Bulgaria; [5]Bulgarian Academy of Sciences

Abstract: The panel will seek answers to various questions related to the impact of technology on learning by presenting examples of particular experiences and then extrapolating in order to arrive to common conclusions or identify and reason controversial opinions.

Key words: e-learning; ethical education; web-based communities; distance education; course management systems; telework.

1. INTRODUCTION

Will media and technology influence learning? There has been an on-going debate in the educational community and views ranging between the two extremes of the continuum have been expresses. The globalization of the society and the remarkable developments in the ICT and global networking have given birth to the e-learning phenomena, which broadens the horizons of the traditional learning and creates opportunities, but also challenges, for all stakeholders in the teaching and learning process. Researchers and practitioners argue about pro's and con's of e-learning, but most are convinced that in order to ensure good quality of learning a whole range of issues have to be carefully considered with the learner in mind and a delicate balance of traditional and e-learning approaches has to be achieved.

The discussion about the impact of technology on learning paradigms and teaching practices raises a number of questions, among which: What is good learning? What should the role of the teacher in e-learning be? What makes a good e-teacher? What are the difficulties in e-learning —for the teacher, for the students? What kinds of methods should be used and which are most effective? How to create a student driven environment? How does the technical learning environment increase student's capability? Can the student in a "happy" learning environment do more in e-learning framework than in a traditional classroom? How does the teacher avoid media hype?

This panel will seek answers to such questions by presenting examples of particular experiences and then extrapolating in order to arrive to common conclusions or identify and reason controversial opinions.

Following are four contributions, highlighting panelists' views and concrete experiences. The first one discusses e-learning issues for advanced technical topics. The second focuses on e-learning tools —it describes TeleCAD, an Internet based course management system, and comments on its usability and evaluation. The third entry presents a technology enhanced learning experience in which researchers, teachers and young students collaborate and learn together. Reflections about the impact on learning and teaching practices in such technology rich environment are made. The fourth entry provides a more general stand of e-learning, addressing its human and ethical dimension.

The four contributions focus on different aspects of e-learning and illustrate various approaches to utilize technology in order to enhance and support learning. We believe, though, that each of them illustrates the idea that the key to producing good quality of learning is in the right mix of traditional and innovative pedagogical approaches, from the one hand, and, supporting technology and learning services, from another, both centered on the needs and specifics of the learner. Though the role of technology is supportive and not central in learning, the appropriate choice of technology *can* facilitate learning and enrich learners' experiences.

Designing an effective technology enhanced learning environment is a difficult task, which could be eased by employing modern e-learning standards and by using relevant support tools, including course and content management systems.

E-LEARNING ISSUES FOR ADVANCED TECHNICAL TOPICS

The case of Electronic Design Automation training

Fulvio Corno
Politecnico di Torino, Italy

Abstract: This paper describes the problems found in applying e-learning methodologies and tools to an advanced technical topic: training in Electronic Design Automation at the University level. Several problems are identified, that lie in the critical path to successful implementation of learning programs for future electrical and computer engineers.

Key words: Electronic Design Automation; E-learning.

1. INTRODUCTION

The social and economical impacts of e-learning suggest its application to several learning ages and knowledge fields. In this section, we will concentrate on teaching technical topics to higher-education students.

At Politecnico di Torino, several degrees in Engineering are being taught with distance learning technologies (computer engineering, electronic eng., telecommunications eng., logistics and management eng., mechanical eng. and electrical eng.), using three different methodologies:

- Completely on-line courses, where students receive lectures recorded on VHS tapes or Video CDs, and find additional study material and practical assignment texts and solutions on a web site. Students are followed by a tutor, who is available over the phone or by e-mail, and can participate in a mailing list with other students enrolled in the same course. The tutor also organizes in-presence sessions, where students may travel to the University and review some theoretical concepts, solve some exercises proposed by the tutor, or ask for clarifications on any issues. You may find further information at the URL http://corsiadistanza.polito.it.

- Blended approach, that we apply on a remote site located in a rural area of Sardinia: students have great incentives to get a technical degree in order to find work, but bad logistics and transportation costs prevent many of them from attending university. Therefore, Politecnico di Torino opened a Learning Center (Centro Multimediale Montiferro) where students must be physically present every afternoon, and they are assisted by local tutors (not university professors, but technical workers, high-school teachers, etc). The learning sessions may be of 4 types: (a) videoconference with a University teacher from Politecnico di Torino, for dealing with some theoretical topic, (b) vision of recorded video lectures, re-using the same material available for completely on-line courses, but with the assistance of the local tutor that may answer questions in real time or clarify specific points, (c) solving exercises and assignments with the help of the local tutors, (d) videoconference with a University teacher from Politecnico di Torino, for a question-and-answer session. You may find further information at the URL http://www.montiferru.it.
- Supporting traditional courses through on-line material. In this case, traditional university courses are supplemented my additional study material, lecture notes, exercises, past exams, etc, available over the Internet. There is a strong effort from the Faculties to keep the study program as much aligned as possible (compatibly with the freedom of individual teachers) in order to be able to reuse materials produced for on-line courses as support material for traditional courses, and vice-versa. You may find further information at the URL http://didattica.polito.it.

Experience over several years suggest that the potentials for e-learning are great, but we must face several difficulties to make it effective. In the following, we will concentrate mainly on problems arising in advanced technical topics. As a case study, we will analyze training in **electronic design automation (EDA)** field.

2. CASE STUDY: CHARACTERISTICS OF EDA TRAINING

EDA is a very important topic for engineers in ICT (computer engineers, electrical engineers), as it is the basis for the design of all current electronic devices. The complexity of current electronic circuits, ranging in the orders of tens or hundreds of millions of transistors, completely prevents manual design: circuit designers must use advanced automatic tools to help them design, simulate, implement their chips. Such tools are constantly lagging behind the complexity of circuits, so using the tools is a challenge by itself, and involves combining design knowledge and tool experience.

These requirements imply that Electronic Design Automation students must become proficient in three main areas:

- Understanding and designing complex algorithms and data structures, coping with information size (e.g., graph structures with millions of nodes) and with the intractability of the problems (i.e., NP-complete algorithms for almost any problem of practical interest). Students are required to gain competence about algorithm design and complexity, the most used complex data structures, and to develop intuition about the trade-off between algorithm complexity (running time and required memory) and the quality of the result (circuit optimization).
- Understanding the design process of VLSI circuits. This is a complex flow, made of many steps, describing the circuit starting from a high level representation and progressively adding lower level detail, and ranging through: hardware-software partitioning, architectural design, interface and protocol definition, scheduling and allocation, register-transfer level design, logic synthesis, timing optimization, circuit layout, area optimization. Each step is followed by a verification or validation step, usually through simulation of the design. At each step the designer uses *different tools*, describes the circuit using *different languages* (graphical or textual), and simulates with *different models*. Student should gain experience about the problems of each phase, know what tools and languages are used, and understand the limitations of tools.
- Designing a circuit. This means being able to carry out the several phases of the design process, and understanding the design methodology at each of the description levels. Usually, students specialize on some level (high-level versus low-level areas of the design flow), but curricula tend to expose all students to all levels, at least on some small-scale circuit.

Teaching methodologies involve mixing three levels: theoretical information (algorithms, design flow, design methods), practical exercises (algorithm implementation, circuit designs), and usage of the tools in a laboratory setting.

3. E-LEARNING FOR EDA

How can this experience be transferred to e-learning? Can state-of-the art teaching methodologies and LMS implementations support the students in this hard, complex, yet essential discipline?

Current e-learning solutions appear insufficient for this knowledge domain. Generally speaking, the "theoretical" and the "methodological" parts of EDA can be easily transferred to an on-line learning solution. However, the practical parts, involving design exercises and tool usage, still pose incredible challenges. Some of the major issues are raised below.

Concerning *algorithm design and implementation*, how can we help the students developing their intuition and capability to evaluate trade-offs? In the context of EDA, programming skills are not enough, since due to the complexity of the problems much relies on experience, intuition, trial-and-error and experimentation, hardly supported by existing e-learning solutions.

On the other hand, developing *design experience* usually requires both acquiring methodological information, which can be easily included in LMS contents, and practical skill deriving from trying to design several circuits or circuit parts, of increasing complexity. The LMS may help in providing the necessary infrastructure for storing the design exercised and for delivering them in the right complexity progression, by supporting the personalized learning curve of the student. However, current automatic *evaluation* solutions are not enough. No single solution exists for a design exercise: each student may develop a different, yet completely correct, design solution. Manual correction of such exercises is still necessary, and this involves heavy burdens on the facilitators and tutors.

Finally, the third challenge is on gaining *experience and familiarity with the tools*. This involves letting the students to use a set of tools that should be comparable to the ones currently used in the EDA industry. There are three main problems to overcome. First, the cost of the tools: such software is priced towards the industry needs and financial capabilities. Universities can get limited educational versions, for use in university laboratories, but licenses usually prevent remote usage by on-line students. Second, minimum hardware requirements by EDA tools (operating system, available memory, and processor type) are usually much higher that common PCs owned by students. Licensing problems aside, it would be impossible to run these tools on students' machines. Third, tools are not integrated with the learning management system: the learner should switch between the LMS and the EDA tool while learning to use the tool, and later he or she would need to use the EDA tool to solve some exercises proposed by the LMS.

The whole situation is made more complex by the rapid evolution of involved technologies: both VLSI technology (and the associated design flows) and EDA technology (and the associated design tools) evolve rapidly, with new versions or new innovations every semester. This makes it difficult and more expensive to capitalize the production of learning material or the deployment of virtual laboratory settings.

On the positive side, there are several experiences of successful use of e-learning in limited EDA contexts. Most EDA tool vendors offer e-learning solutions to learn their tools: such courses replace or supplement training seminars needed when new tools are introduced in industry practice. Such solutions are cost-effective and appreciated in industrial contexts (on learning-on-the-job settings), since individual designers may study on their spare time and need not synchronize their agendas. Furthermore, most learners already have design experience or used similar tools in the past. The same courses are not directly suitable in university contexts, due both to the limited design knowledge of the students and the necessity of learning several tools from different vendors, whose learning management systems are not integrated.

Some universities have also taken the challenge, and are offering EDA courses on-line. Some are offering custom solution to be able to use EDA tools (either thanks to limited educational PC versions or through remote connectivity with university servers). Some rely on the collaboration capabilities of the LMS to help the student develop their designs in a joint fashion, under the supervision of a facilitator. In fact, it appears that the only viable solutions are the adoption of advanced collaboration frameworks, allowing application sharing, and collaborative problem solving, sketching capabilities, and working primarily in the synchronous mode.

4. CONCLUSIONS

The adoption of e-learning models, supported by effective learning management systems, is crucial to cover the demand for skilled engineers in circuits and systems design. However, the vastness of this knowledge domain, the requirement for strong practical experiences, and the complexity of the involved software tools are posing great challenges for the successful implementation of study programs. Universities, industry learning centers, and EDA tool vendors are all struggling with the development of learning models, and the associated learning tools, that may help engineering students and employed designers to gain sufficient skills in this crucial area for ICT development. Effective solutions for e-learning in advanced technical topics are still open problems. Instructors and LMS developers should join and try to solve the fundamental issues of teaching intuition, design mentality, and sophisticated tool usage.

REFERENCES

1. C.Anderson, M. Brennan, eLearning in Practice - Proprietary Knowledge and Instructional Design, IDC, 2001, http://www.e-learningsite.com/download/white/isd-idc.pdf
2. D. Jansen, The Electronic Design Automation Handbook, Kluwer Academic Publishers, 2003

TELECAD COURSE ONLINE AND EVALUATION PROCEDURE

Anna Grabowska, PhD
Gdansk University of Technology, G. Narutowicza 11/12, 80-952 Gdansk, Poland. E-mail: blanka@pg.gda.pl

Abstract: In the article the Learning Management System TeleCAD (Teleworkers Training for CAD Systems' Users, Leonardo da Vinci, 1998-2001) is presented. The system background is described. Usability of the system is presented within CURE project (Research Framework Programme 5, 2003-2005). Evaluation procedure for online courses is described on a basis of experiences in EMDEL project (European Model for Distance Education and Learning, Leonardo da Vinci, 2001-2004).

Key words: Learning Management System; AutoCAD; telework; evaluation.

1. TELECAD – WHAT IS ALL ABOUT

TeleCAD (Teleworkers Training for CAD Systems' Users) is a course of AutoCAD and teleworking basics. Actually the course is delivered in distance mode as an Internet based course.

The project TeleCAD was co-financed by European Union Leonardo da Vinci Programme (1998-2001). It was developed in a consortium of six foreign institutions from four countries: Greece, Finland, Italy and Poland.

The idea of the course evolved from the AutoCAD course delivered on Civil Engineering Department at Gdansk University of Technology. During the course students are expected to prepare a series of drawings, at different levels of complication. For the purpose of final assessment students had to prepare a drawing that used all introduced techniques.

In the past the AutoCAD course was delivered in a traditional mode – as lectures and activities in computer laboratory. In order to reduce the load in lecture rooms the idea to convert the course to the distance mode was born.

In 1998 a few students took part in an experimental distant course. They were given printed course materials and were supposed to contact the teacher using e-mail only. Both consultations and final assignment submission was done by e-mail. All students succeeded in finishing the course. After the course there was an extensive study of experimental course results. More than 60 students took part in the experimental AutoCAD courses delivered by Distance Education Centre at Gdansk University of Technology (DECTUG) together with Civil Engineering Department in ODL mode. Both students and the teacher were satisfied with the course and experiences gathered were used during the TeleCAD project application preparation.

As a result of Leonardo da Vinci project students have for their disposal course materials consisting of 10 modules covering basics of drawing in AutoCAD. Every module includes a set of tasks that should be performed by students, with description of appropriate solution. The course materials are prepared as HTML pages to be acquired by the WWW or from the CD-ROM. Polish version of the materials is also available in a printed form. The TeleCAD course incorporates a module about basics of teleworking. Current technology and methodology of teleworking is presented to the students, and an example of our system is used for exercise. Students are supposed to prepare a project in groups. They should prepare the project in co-operation between each other, using the Task Management Module of the system as a platform for project design. The final assignment of the course is a drawing prepared by a student and sent by mail to the tutor. To prove that the student actually was an author of the drawing, he may be asked to make some changes to the drawing in the presence of the tutor. The whole course is performed in a blended mode. There are two face to face meetings: 1st for teaching how to use TeleCAD and 2nd for examination purpose.

While the method of TeleCAD course delivery was discussed several WBT platforms were considered to be used. DECTUG was involved in DE Phare projects with different platforms e.g. WebCT, Learning Space, First Class. They differ in offered capabilities and price. Most of them are oriented towards course materials delivery. They provide user authentication, customisable start pages, user homepages preparation tools etc. For example First Class focuses only on student-tutor communication. Some of the platforms offer tools for organising chat rooms or computer conferences. The main drawback of available packages is lack of good monitoring system. What is also very important, there is very little support for manager of the distance teaching institution. In most platforms there is no support for the course evaluation or tutors' reports. All communication between the tutor and course manager must be performed outside the system.

The system should also organise the co-operation between course developers. This includes communication, file sharing and project management tools. The system will also play a role of the course delivery platform. It will provide students management, support for tutors, communication environment and assessment tools. The main stress should be put on the management of Internet based ODL solution. The course manager, who is usually responsible for many virtual classes, should have information about students' and tutors' activities. He (she) should know if a tutor's activities are relevant to students' needs. This includes answering students' questions fast and in satisfying degree, preparing FAQs (Frequently Asked Questions), preparing and marking Tutor Marked Assignments (TMA's) etc.

Students' progress is a very important issue in distance education. There are a few ways to monitor it with a web based environment. Students perform self-assessment tests and TMAs that give insight to their progress. System may monitor students' activity on discussion lists, access to course material web pages, FAQ lists etc. The last but not least is students' own opinion about their own progress reported by questionnaires.

It is not certain that all above techniques give satisfying information about students' and tutors' performance. However, they give some indication when somebody may have problems. In such situation the manager has opportunity to investigate the issue personally. Without any monitoring support, the manager is incapable of assisting many people simultaneously.

The system is divided into several independent parts and consists of course delivery subsystem, course management and monitoring subsystem and personal information database subsystem.

The subsystems share the tools, they have a common database of users and a common user interface. They may be however used separately — without the second one installed.

The system is designed in thin client-server architecture. The server is based on the SQL engine (currently MySQL) and a web server capable of running PHP3 scripts (apache server with mod_php3 extension). The whole system logic is contained in the PHP3 scripts. The hardware platform for the system is a PC computer with Linux operating system. The client is a graphical web browser with no additional software needed. This architecture was chosen to ensure ability to work from any place in the Internet. Taking into account the actual parameters of Internet connections, it was decided to reduce the amount of data at the cost of user interface of the system. TeleCAD system tools are shown in Table 1.

Table 1. The prototype TeleCAD course tools

Course Information:	Requirements Timetable Staff Information Students list Announcements FAQ
Course Materials	Guide for learner AutoCAD handbook online Teleworking survey online Library of drawings Library of links
Assignments	Requirements and forms and deadlines for assessments Class book The quiz
Communication	Bulletin Board Discussion list E-mail

2. TELECAD USABILITY AND EVALUATION

The proposed system TeleCAD covers educational needs of students and academic teachers in the field of AutoCAD and telework subject. In the Table 2 there is a list of TeleCAD environment usage (2000-2002).

Table 2. Usage of TeleCAD from 2000 to 2002

TeleCAD implementation	Number of users
Pilot international (2000/2001)	89
Pilot PL (2000/2001)	35
TeleCAD exam in (sem. 2, 2000/2001)	240
TeleCAD exam in (sem. 4, 2000/2001)	166
TeleCAD extra mural (sem. 4, 2000/2001)	62
TeleCAD extra mural (sem. 3, 2001/2002)	24
TeleCAD extra mural (sem. 4, 2001/2002)	40
TeleCAD exam in (sem. 2, 2001/2002)	259
TeleCAD in summer 2002	4

The most significant achievement seems to be offering the course for postgraduate MSc students from Civil Engineering Department in the academic year 2003/2004 in CURE project (Centre for Urban Construction and Rehabilitation: Technology Transfer, Research and Education, Research Framework Programme 5, 2002-2005).

There is another aspect of distance education which could not be neglected. It is quality of distance education courses. Quality issues are addresses in EMDEL project (http://www.emdel.org/).

The main goal of the project EMDEL is development of an European Teletraining System which, from what already has been produced, could immediately start a process of co-operation at the level of production and organisation of distance training services. This approach should bring to the reduction of costs, the harmonisation of local systems and the rapid increase of the offer of formative courses.

The main objectives of the project are following:

- Production of an on-line catalogue "Showcase of Distance Learning Modules".
- Production and share of a basic software programme for the assessment of customer satisfaction and quality of Distance Learning Modules.
- Exchange of the best Distance Learning Modules.
- Virtual mobility through on-line utilization of Distance Learning Modules installed on the servers of the partners' net. It should enable to utilize of distance training products in original language by a person living in a partner country without an action of postproduction. Local services of support should be assured in the original language).
- Dissemination, through the presentation of a model of realization, of a European Teletraining Network to demonstrate the concrete possibilities of construction, starting from an existent distance training system based locally but with transnational connections. The dissemination also aims at extending the number of agencies of distance training, which want to co-operate for the maintenance of the catalogue and for the increase of the exchange of products.

The project moves from the results achieved in previous projects by partner countries in the field of the European financing. The Regione Toscana, within the frame of activities provided by the Fondo Sociale Europeo, has given birth to a Regional System of Teletraining (Trio Project, http://www.progettotrio.it) and to the production of didactic contents for Distance Learning chiefly addressed to apprentices, drop out young people, workers, managers of small enterprises, besides old people. Also the partners' experience has lead to the creation of distance learning models and, particularly, to the production and evaluation of materials which can be used in High Training as well as in the trainers' training.

The project has started from collecting information about partners' institutions and their offer in the subject of Distance Learning Modules.

The evaluation procedure and the questionnaires were prepared by University of Liege from Belgium (Table 3).

Details of TeleCAD course evaluation will be presented during the panel discussion.

Table 3. Quality and Customer Satisfaction Table

1.	**Expert's assessment** I. Content II. Activities III. Evaluation IV. Technical aspects V. Aesthetics and multimedia VI. Mode of usings VII. Mode of using
2.	**Tutor's assessement** I. Content II. Activities III. Evaluation IV. Technical aspects V. Aesthetics VI. Mode of using
3.	**Customers' Satisfaction** I. Number of responses: ... II. Overall impression III. Contents IV. Activities V. Evaluation VI. Navigation, technical design and ergonomics VII. Tutoring *Customers' satisfaction rating is quantitative. For each of the six items a graph in the form of a line is drawn. One end of this line is labelled "Poor", the other, "Excellent". The rank is based on the average rating of each item.*
4.	**Impact on customers** Percentage of students who dropped the course *(if any)* Rate of successful outcome *(if any)*

REFERENCES

Grabowska Anna (2001). Model for Distance Eduaction System in LAN and WAN. 150 pp. PhD thesis /2001.11.20/. Gdansk University of Technology, Faculty of Electronics, Telecommunications and Informatics.

Grabowska Anna (2003). Web Based Training system TeleCAD (Teleworkers training for CAD system users). Global Engineer: Education and Training for Mobility. SEFI Conference 2003. Porto. Portugal, 7-10 September 2003. Ed: Alfredo Soeiro, Carlos Oliveira Universidade do Porto Faculdade de Engenharia, Porto 2003, s. 282-287.

Grabowska Anna (2003). Searching for evaluation procedures for Web based courses . cases from EU projects. 12th EDEN Annual Conference. The Quality Dialogue. Integrating Quality Cultures in Flexible, Distance and eLearning. Rhodos. Greece, 15-18 June 2003. Ed: dr Andras Szucs, dr Erwin Wagner, dr Costas Tsolakidis, Rhodos 2003, s. 226-231.

http://www.dec.pg.gda.pl/dec/index.php?id=telecad_en TeleCAD course online
http://www.emdel.odrg/ EMDEL project main page
http://www.pg.gda.pl/cure/ CURE project main page

WEBLABS: A VIRTUAL LABORATORY FOR COLLABORATIVE E-LEARNING

Evgenia Sendova, PhD[1], Iliana Nikolova ,PhD[2], George Gachev[2] and Liliana Moneva[1]
[1]*Bulgarian Academy of Science. E-mail: jenny@math.bas.bg, lylymo@yahoo.com;*
[2]*University of Sofia, Bulgaria. E-mail: {iliana, gachev}@fmi.uni-sofia.bg*

Abstract: The paper presents research carried out within *WebLabs*, a European project, where researchers, teachers and young students learn collaboratively in a technology enhanced environment. Experiences gained by the Bulgarian participants are discussed from an e-learning perspective.

Key words: visual programming; web-reports; collaborative e-learning; multiple representations.

1. THE *WEBLABS* PROJECT

Recent educational research emphasizes on "knowledge put into functional use in a multitude of different situations and contexts" [1]. Many educators are working in the filed of "new cultures of assignments", "project-oriented work" and are very interested in constructing environments in which the learners can actively work on a conceptual level [2]. This is especially true in the case of mathematics taught at junior high school level where the mathematical concepts are often "shadowed" by the necessities of calculating, symbol manipulating by hand, drawing, etc. Restricting the math education to these technical skills creates a very twisted image of mathematics and the young learners can hardly experience the real spirit of mathematics as a research field.

To cultivate abilities of young learners to generate, test, play with ideas and to build a culture of communicating them to their peers from different countries is one of the fundamental goals of the *WebLabs* project [3]. The project aims at creating a virtual laboratory and a community of young learners, teachers and researchers exploring collaboratively mathematical and science phenomena.

1.1 The focus of *WebLabs*

This is a 3 year EU-funded educational research project carried out by scientific and educational institutions of Bulgaria, Cyprus, Italy, Portugal, Sweden and UK. It creates a new representational infrastructure for e-learning. The focus is on collaborative construction, description and interpretation of important mathematical and science concepts by means of modern ICTs. A web-based environment, *wplone*, is used to mediate collaboration so that the participants can share ideas and constructively criticize each other's evolving knowledge and working models [4]. The project embraces exploratory activities in the following domains: *mathematics, kinematics and dynamics, complex biological and ecological systems, robotics.*

1.2 The computer environment *Toon Talk*

WebLabs uses an environment for visual programming called *Toon Talk* in which the source code is animated thus allowing for abstract computational concepts to be represented by concrete analogues, instantiated in cartoon-like characters [5]. *ToonTalk* has some unique features suitable for visualizing and exploring mathematics concepts and ideas when working with junior-high school students. The mathematical activities are integrated in a natural way with cultivating some programming skills. The programs in *ToonTalk* take the form of animated robots, which can be named, picked up and trained to perform a certain sequence of elementary steps. After the training, the robots run *forever* if the initial conditions are satisfied. Such type of programming is especially appealing to young programmers since it is amusing, requires creativity and stimulates the acquiring of new skills for solving problems.

1.3 Developing a collaborative community

The students in *WebLabs* have the chance of working together not only with their peers from other countries, but also with distinguished researchers. Rather than being just *reality check for researchers* they are real partners in a research process, in which new learning methods and computer technologies are used and experimented with. When using *ToonTalk* as a means for modeling the students learn how to work with contemporary computer environments in a natural way. In the context of carefully designed educational activities they gain knowledge about important processes and phenomena from mathematics, physics, biology, and compare their understanding with the rest of the participants. The communication is carried out by the so-called *Webreports* —a specially designed concept enabling the young learners to share and discuss the problems they have solved, and even more interesting— the problems they have formulated and implemented by means of *ToonTalk* robots.

1.4 *WebLabs* e-learning elements

The *WebLabs* project embraces various elements of e-learning. The specific means through which they are implemented are:

- *long distance birds:* a *ToonTalk* concept for information exchange among different computers;
- *Web-reports*: a mechanism for the participants to describe and share their ideas and programming constructs; a visual on-line editor is available to compose web-reports on individual or group work, to add comments and publish working *ToonTalk* models of students' ideas as they develop;
- *Plone*: a web-based environment used to mediate the collaborative learning activities over distance.

What follows, are excerpts from web-reports written by WebLabs students from Sofia and reflecting two class sessions on number sequences.

1.5 *Weblabetics* —a children's endeavor for a better communication in an international context

Excerpts from a group web-report [6]:

When browsing through plone in search for interesting sequences we had very unexpected experience. We moved step-by-step through the sequences suggested by Nikmous, Kiriakos, Irakli - all in Greek. The sequences are very clear but when the comments are in a language, which we don't understand, it is very annoying. So George, our teacher, asked us: Can you think of a way to express ToonTalk ideas so that anyone could understand them? Yana suggested to use pictures for representing the ToonTalk characters and drew some on the board (fig. 1):

	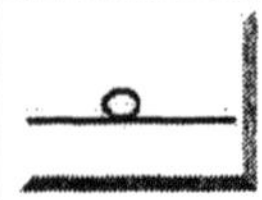	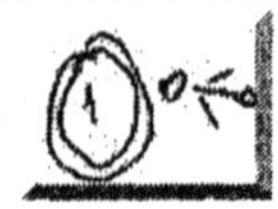			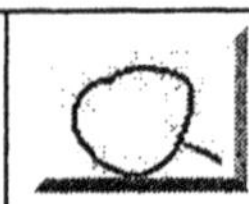
Robot	Magic wand	Nest and Bird	Hand	Box with no information	Thought bubble

Figure 1. Pictures representing ToonTalk tools

George challenged us to translate our Counting Robot in the new language. We all thought that this was easy but soon realized that we didn't have symbols for actions in our alphabet (or rather – weblabetics). So we added arrows for "puts" and "takes". Here is the Counting Robot in weblabetics (fig. 2):

Figure 2. Program code (Counting Robot) in *weblabetics*

Isn't this clear for everybody? Well, just in case you lack the experience:

A robot puts 1 in a box, then copies the content, gives it to a bird, which puts it in its nest. Afterwards everything is repeated. Do you see the ":||" sign at the end —this is the music symbol for a repetition –Peter thought of it! In short, this is our old friend— the Counting Robot (in new clothes...)

We hope that now it would be easier to talk about ToonTalk and our ideas to everyone in the WebLabs project.

George told us the story of the Babylonian tower —a common language for everyone is more effective than many languages for a few.

Reflection: Children were faced with a typical e-learning problem while trying to learn collaboratively over distance —the language problem. In an attempt to overcome it, they reached the idea of designing a graphical scripting language for visual programming.

1.6 When the math gauntlet is thrown from a distance

After hearing from Yishay Mor, a researcher from the UK WebLabs team, that there is a new challenging sequence on the "Guess my robot" page [7] published by a Portuguese girl (Rita), the Sofia teachers (George and Jenny) asked the students to solve it as a homework. Two students, Nasko and Ivan, took the challenge and reported to the class that they had guessed the rule and had even built robots generating it. The teachers decided to use this as a basis for the topic "Different representations of number sequences" [8].

Jenny: *Nasko, please try to translate your robot in algebraic language?*

Nasko: *Here is the relationship between the consecutive terms (fig. 3)*

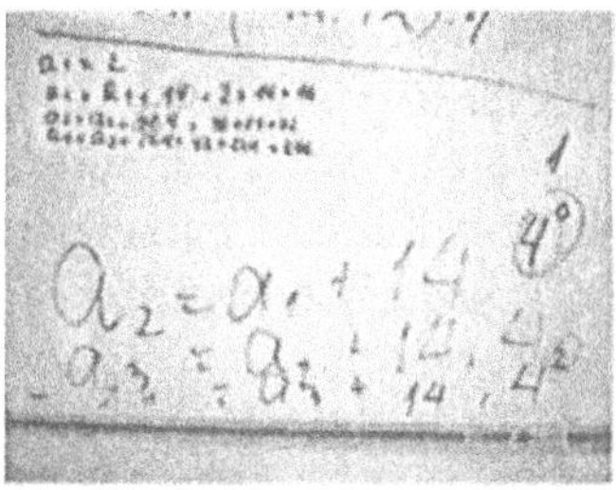

Figure 3. In algebraic language

Figure 4. In "Robot" language

Vessela: *Ah, it means we have to present 1 as* 4^0

Jenny: *Rita's robot in algebraic language looks like this:* $a_1=2$, $a_n= 4(a_{n-1} + 2)$. *Are these sequences the same?*

Teddy: *Ah, this looks much easier. Let me try to translate it in a "robot language"* (Fig. 4)

Jenny: *Do you think that your and Nasko's robot will produce the same sequence?*

Teddy: *Sure! Absolutely!*

Jenny: *How do you know? Take for example the sequence 3, 5, 7, ... Which is the next term?*

Teddy: *9, of course!*

Jenny: *Do you agree, George?*

George: *I am thinking of 11.*

Jenny: *Of course!* (Both of us are thinking of a subsequence of the prime numbers (of course!!!))

Teddy: *Oh, I see, so you could extend the sequence in more than one way... —adding twice 2, and then adding twice 4, etc. So, I could write it in algebraic way as follows:* $a_n = a_{n-1} + 2^n$

Vessela: *What about* $a_n = a_{n-1} + a_{n-2} - 1$?

Ivan: *My robot also uses 2 previous terms :*$a_{n+1} = a_n + (a_n - a_{n-1})*4$ *and its first numbers coincide with Rita's ones.*

Teddy: *Oh, how could we compare so many robots?*

Jenny: *I am not telling you! But I hope to hear your ideas next time. Please consider for the following questions from our English partners [9]:*

1. *How did you guess the rule of Rita's sequence?*
2. *Which is easier for you —to translate from the robot language into algebraic one, or vice versa?*
3. *How could we check if two robots produce the same sequence?*

Reflections: In a panel discussion on the educational value of computer programming diSessa [10] proposes the idea that *the intellectual power the programming representations can have for learning science is at least comparable to, if not greater than, algebra.* We can easily adopt it in the context of learning mathematics – gaining the flexibility of moving from a programming to algebraic representation of a sequence contributes to a deeper understanding of the mathematical ideas.

An important element for a good learning is the students' motivation – in our case the problem was formulated as a challenge by a peer of theirs. As for the teacher, s/he is seen as a facilitator, as a guide in a discovery process, providing new tools only when needed.

1.7 Conclusions

The effect of working with young students in the framework of *WebLabs* is not reduced to learning specific aspects of certain subject areas but has a much larger scope. On one hand, *the scientist in the learner is enhanced* – the students get used to pose questions, to look for answer no matter how sophisticated they might be. They develop an understanding of mathematics as a science in which formulating hypotheses, carrying out experiments, and attacking open problems plays a crucial part. The students are partners in a research process and can influence both the development of the computer environment and the design of the educational activities. They can communicate among themselves, with teachers and researchers locally and globally alike. During this communication they acquire specific social experience and are stimulated to build valuable personal skills and abilities, such as:

- to generate and verbalize ideas;
- to present their results according to a concrete standard;
- to share their experience by means of electronic communication;
- to discuss their work and to work in a team;
- to be (self-)critical to the work published in the virtual environment

ACKNOWLEDGEMENT

We acknowledge the support of the *WebLabs* project: "*WebLabs*: new representational infrastructures for e-learning"; contract number IST 2001-3220

REFERENCES

1. ICMI, Study 14, Application and Modeling in Mathematics Education, Discussion Document, 2003
2. Loethe, H. Concept Oriented Learning Environments: a Project Using Sequences in Scheme, in "Be Creative...re-inventing technology on education", Proceedings of Eurologo 2003, Portugal
3. WebLabs http://www.weblabs.eu.com
4. Mor, Y, Sendova, E. *ToonTalking about mathematics*, in Proceedings of the International Congress MASSEE 2003, p.36-43
5. Toon Talk http:// www.toontalk.com
6. http://www.weblabs.org.uk/wlplone/Members/Sofia/my_reports/Report.2004-04-13.0957
7. http://www.weblabs.org.uk/wlplone/Members/Rita/
8. http://www.weblabs.org.uk/wlplone/Members/Sofia/my_reports/Report.2004-02-26.2431
9. Mor et al, Thinking in Process, (to appear in MicroMath)
10. Klopfer, E. et al. Programming Revised – The Educational Value of Computer Programming, http://www.cs.berkeley.edu/~abegel/papers/icls04.pdf

BUILDING THE E-LEARNING ENVIRONMENT

Creating The Technical Side of Peace

Tina Ebey, M.A., M.F.A. PhD candidate[1], Olivier Urbain, PhD[2]
[1]*Pacific Research Center, Inc.;* [2]*Transcend Peace University and Soka University, Japan.*

Abstract: In addition to academic technical training, distance learning concepts must embody forefront global human issues influencing human security. The purpose in writing this paper is to continue to become more motivated by the potential for cultivating a culture of peace with the awareness of how much wisdom based technical knowledge is necessary to ensure humanity's safety. Coursework from Soka University in Japan and an online network of artists from the TAP network have been selected as case studies to illustrate applied uses of technical learning in the arts and sciences building a global dimension to peaceful dialog and student driven learning.

Key words: human security; applied technical knowledge; ethical education; web-based conferencing.

1. HUMAN SECURITY ISSUES DETERMINE FOREFRONT TRAINING

The purpose of this paper is to identify an educational perspective based on academic training using electronic media and distance education toward building a culture of peace. The goals include learning to teach in a student driven environment and inviting the learner to develop skill to teach the teacher by applying understanding to issues of human security in the global community.

We have singled out the 2004 Peace Proposal of Daisaku Ikeda as a resource to create perspective. Issues bring focus to learning by siting attainable goals as parameters for scientists during their years of professional training and skill building with problem solving. The internet was originally designed as an instrument of DARPA, the American Department of Defense. As an agency of the U.S. defense industry why not turn it from a sword into a plowshare? With this goal in mind creating motivation in e-learning to globally relevant peace education becomes a technical challenge.

Daisaku Ikeda, President of the Soka Gakkai International and author of twenty peace proposals over the last two decades to the United Nations writes that in the world today 860 million adults are said to be illiterate, and 121 million children have no access to school. The Education for All campaign, spearheaded by UNESCO, aims to realize universal basic education with concrete benchmarks for achievement. Last year was also the start of the United Nations Literacy Decade (2003-2012). Two thirds of the illiterate are women. Creating learning methodology that embraces the lives of these women represents a huge challenge affecting families and the community. This challenge is both technical and practical demanding that teaching methods in the e-learning environment apply to their lives and cultivate skills in a relevant and humanistic way.

2. ETHICAL TECHNICAL EDUCATION

Our purpose in bringing these issues forward is to serve as a catalyst for moral criteria. It is our premise that ethics represents a significant soft power force shaping the forefront of technology as sited above in the need for literacy for women and access to education for children. This example is a call to bridge the digital divide between rich and poor as noted in The Declaration of Principles adopted by the first UN-convened meeting of the World Summit on the Information Society (WSIS) in December 2003.

Dramatically in parallel is the verification regime developed under the Comprehensive Test Ban Treaty (CTBT) calling for an international monitoring system utilizing the finest technology known to man to ensure the safety of the planet. This is a technical and ethical challenge which must mobilize public opinion to ensure ratification. The United States is among the twelve remaining nations who have yet to sign the treaty and demonstrate integrity in the international community.

Rapidly evolving information technology inherits the values of modernization, which can result in a weakening of the frameworks of family, community, workplace, school and state. A positive aspect of diminishing the relevance of physical distance is that people who are geographically separate can now be part of global networks with access to many choices for positive expansion of freedom of action in involvement.

Influenced by the philosophy of Japanese educator Tsunesaburo Makiguchi and his American contemporary John Dewey, Dr. Ikeda reminds us that part of learning is sharing the life experience of peers while trying to grow as an individual oneself. The virtual environment can be speculative and detached from any quality inherent in effective learning and teaching. Computers and communications technology can never be a substitute for the actual human contact of dialog and face-to-face interaction of meetings and classroom instruction.

The challenge therefore is to cultivate ways of mentoring using information technology that embraces the lives and needs of the participants and their relative life condition. Creating an e-learning environment with effective curriculum tools that builds discipline necessary to apply those skills to the human condition is a major scientific and methodological challenge. This approach can be counterintuitive and should be one in which the learner is taught to know "the wound and shock of other's pain as our own" (John Dewey).

3. DEFINING A GOOD LEARNING ENVIRONMENT

One characteristic of good learning is a balance between critical and ethical education.

1. Critical: enhances the learner's critical thinking, enables the learning to think about his/her situation and face what is happening in the world. However, this can lead to discouragement, that is why some ethical guidelines are necessary.
2. Ethical: together with critical thinking and awareness, education needs to provide the learning with a sense of hope and courage, that there is something that can be done, based on the awareness one has gained.

In their dialogue in book form called "Choose Peace", Johan Galtung (the founder of modern peace studies) and Daisaku Ikeda (a renowned philosopher and Buddhist leader) agree that one needs a cool head and a warm heart in order to contribute to a better world.[12]

With only a cool head, the learner will not be able to have the inspiration necessary to contribute something new to society. With only a warm heart, the learner will try to find solutions without knowing what is really going on behind the scenes. Both are therefore needed, a cool head and a warm heart for critical ethical education.

[12] Critical = a cool head, Ethical = a warm heart

4. WHAT MAKES A GOOD TEACHER?

A good teacher or mentor cultivates rapport with the student building dialog that reinforces freedom in learning. Through discipline the student develops confidence in his or her grasp of methods and the relationship to technical thinking. In the e-learning environment this can be difficult since kinesthetic awareness is a component of learning integral to an engineer's working knowledge and grasp of dimension. Although one picture is worth a thousand words the appropriateness of knowledge based wisdom in education is always more effective when reinforced face-to-face through personal interaction with the teacher or mentor including the spatial component of guided discovery.

In building a mentoring model the internet makes it possible to communicate rapidly and in a group. Unfortunately it can also create myopic over engagement and egotism and an inability to think critically and creatively as an individual. The purpose of e-learning should not be to stimulate rote learning. For some students, the opportunity to work on their own time and according to their own hours of availability is very freeing with access to more than one instructor as a research guide and open hours of participation.

5. THE INGREDIENTS IN LEARNING METHODS

Evaluation of teaching methods cannot be isolated from the learning environment. Defining a context establishes parameters in which to include hands-on technical training and skill building with problem solving. We will site two examples, which illustrate a high degree of opportunity and success through e-learning. The first uses the internet as a conferencing tool and open forum for dialog and applied research. Founded by Dr. Olivier Urbain at Soka University in Japan this project is called the TAP network. Involvement includes continual online discourse, individual and collective applied projects, virtual art galleries and an online journal.

The TAP network is an ongoing conference of very active artists who participate in dialog sharing their passion and life work. The technical side of collaboration involves bulletin boards, and opportunities for posting papers to share ideas. (www.tapnet.info). The website is a free space and provides the opportunity to engage working concepts online which will contribute to the TAP community. Many wonderful and powerful projects have come from this innovative approach including art and spirituality and the refugee project (http://eartharc.com/invision/index.php?showforum=23) and (http://eartharc.com/invision/index.php?showforum=22).

The second example of a successful case study is one in which Ebey was invited to participate as an online mentor to both a course about cinema and a course on the global environmental for an experimental class Dr. Urbain created for Soka University. In each case there were special projects by the students and lively, engaged online conferencing served to strengthen the work of the learners through dialog and formal electronic presentation. Course curriculum was outlined at the beginning followed by a highly participatory forum. The students diligently created websites, demonstrating prolific technical and artistic skill in their individual approaches to problem solving and fulfilling curriculum requirements. Collectively they responded to timely and relevant topics reflecting an interdisciplinary ability to cognitively organize responses to contemporary issues.

6. CONCLUSION

There are many factors to creating an effective e-learning environment that is academically rigorous both in the sciences and the arts. The challenge of responding to building human security through education is overwhelming and could potentially involve millions of people who otherwise would not have the opportunity to participate in the global community. To create a culture of peace educators must be critically aware and respond to the responsibility of engaged technical skills with wisdom and compassion and an eye to future generations.

REFERENCES

Bethel, Dayle (1994), *Makiguchi*, The Value Creator, Weatherhill, NY
Galtung, Johan and Ikeda, Daisaku, (1995) *Choose Peace,* Pluto Press, London
Ikeda, Daisaku, Soka Education, Middleway Press, Santa Monica, US
Daisaku Ikeda's 2004 Peace Proposal :
http://sgi.org/english/President/peaceproposal/peace2004.htm
TAP network http://tapnet.info

GPSR Compliance
The European Union's (EU) General Product Safety Regulation (GPSR) is a set of rules that requires consumer products to be safe and our obligations to ensure this.

If you have any concerns about our products, you can contact us on

ProductSafety@springernature.com

In case Publisher is established outside the EU, the EU authorized representative is:

Springer Nature Customer Service Center GmbH
Europaplatz 3
69115 Heidelberg, Germany

www.ingramcontent.com/pod-product-compliance
Ingram Content Group UK Ltd.
Pitfield, Milton Keynes, MK11 3LW, UK
UKHW020139290926
15471UKWH00003B/590
* 9 7 8 1 4 7 5 7 7 9 7 6 9 *